Atheism and Theism

Great Debates in Philosophy
Series Editor: Ernest Sosa

Dialogue has always been a powerful means of philosophical exploration and exposition. By presenting important current issues in philosophy in the form of a debate, this series attempts to capture the flavour of philosophical argument and to convey the excitement generated by the exchange of ideas. Each author contributes a major, original essay. When these essays have been completed, the authors are each given the opportunity to respond to the opposing view.

Personal Identity
Sydney Shoemaker and Richard Swinburne

Consciousness and Causality
D.M. Armstrong and Norman Malcolm

Agency and Necessity
Antony Flew and Godfrey Vesey

Critical Theory
David Couzens Hoy and Thomas McCarthy

Moral Relativism and Moral Objectivity
Gilbert Harman and Judith Jarvis Thomson

Atheism and Theism
J.J.C. Smart and J.J. Haldane

Atheism and Theism

J.J.C. Smart
J.J. Haldane

First published 1996
Reprinted 1997

Blackwell Publishers Ltd
108 Cowley Road, Oxford OX4 1JF, UK

Blackwell Publishers Inc
350 Main Street, Malden, Massachusetts 02148, USA

British Library Cataloguing in Publication Data
A CIP catalogue record for this book is available from the British Library

Library of Congress Cataloging in Publication Data
Smart, J. J. C. (John Jamieson Carswell), 1920–
Atheism and theism / J. J. C. Smart and J. J. Haldane.
p. cm. — (Great debates in philosophy.)
Includes bibliographical references and index.
ISBN 0–631–19291–3 (alk. paper) — ISBN 0–631–19292–1 (pbk: alk. paper)
1. Atheism. 2. Theism—Controversial literature. 3. Atheism—
Controversial literature. 4. Theism. I. Haldane, John.
II. Title. II. Series.
IL2747.3S588 1996   96–1607
211—dc20   CIP

Typeset in 10 on 12.5pt Melior
by Graphicraft Typesetters Limited, Hong Kong
Printed and bound in Great Britain
by Hartnolls Ltd, Bodmin, Cornwall

This book is printed on acid-free paper

Contents

Introduction   1
J.J. Haldane and J.J.C. Smart

1 Atheism and Theism   6
J.J.C. Smart
  1   Introduction   6
  2   Theism, Spirituality and Science   8
  3   The New Teleology and the Old   13
  4   Pantheism   15
  5   Fine Tuning and the Anthropic Cosmological
      Principle   16
  6   The Argument from the Appearance of Design   23
  7   God as an Ethical Principle   28
  8   The Argument from Contingency   35
  9   The Argument from Religious Experience   48
 10   Pascal's Wager   52
 11   Miracles   56
 12   Higher Criticism of the New Testament   60
 13   The Problem of Evil   66
 14   Historical Theism and Metaphysical Theism   73

2 Atheism and Theism   84
J.J. Haldane
  1   Introduction   84
  2   Theism and Science   90
  3   Some Varieties of Explanation   95
  4   'Old' Teleology   98
  5   'New' Teleology   121
  6   The Cause of Things   129

7 God and the World 140
8 God, Good and Evil 152
9 Liberty and Providence 160
10 Theism – Philosophical and Religious 164

3 Reply to Haldane 168
J.J.C. Smart
1 Methodology 168
2 Representation and Intentionality 173
3 Consciousness 175
4 Chicken and Egg 176
5 Eternity and Sempiternity 178
6 Theism and the Problem of Evil 183

4 Reply to Smart 190
J.J. Haldane
1 Methodology 190
2 The Existence of God 195
3 Metaphysical Matters 199
4 Reason, Faith and Revelation 202
5 A Religious Conclusion 210

Afterword 215
J.J.C. Smart and J.J. Haldane

Bibliography 220

Index 225

Introduction

J.J. Haldane and J.J.C. Smart

Philosophy aims at clarification and understanding. It is one of the
wonders and delights of the subject that anything can be a starting
point for the sort of investigation it conducts. A leaf falls and the
speculative mind sets to work: what is the nature of the motion, is it
determined or random? why do leaves fall, is it a matter of contingency or one of necessity? does the event serve a purpose or is it both
blind and unguided? Initially, it may look as if these questions are
ones for science, but even though detailed scientific enquiries are
necessary in our efforts to understand the world, they operate against
a background (or backgrounds) of assumptions which may themselves
be questioned.

What marks out an investigation as philosophical is its concern to
provide ultimate explanations and understanding, or failing this to
find some other final or halting description, such as 'mystery' or 'brute
fact'. Sometimes this feature of speculative thought is characterized
in terms which are usually taken to originate with Kant (1724–1804)
but which are, in fact, much older. Thus is it often said that the form
of a philosophical question is 'How is it possible that _____?' where the
blank is filled by a description of the thing to be explained. Consider
again the case of the falling leaf. It spirals down in the breeze and
someone asks why this happened. In reply he or she is told that it
being autumn the trees are beginning to shed their leaves. If the enquirer
is at all curious and persistent he or she is not likely to be satisfied
with this explanation. First of all, it offers a very general description,
apparently of an activity engaged in by trees, whereas the questioner
may have been looking for an account of the 'whys' and 'hows' of the
particular occurrence. More obviously, however, it raises a whole series
of further questions. Do all trees shed leaves, and if some do not, why

not? Is shedding a purposeful activity, an automatic process or yet
something else? Even if the general claim about the seasonal behaviour of trees is true it is an incomplete explanation since it does not
address the issue of why leaves *fall* as contrasted with merely becoming detached: why don't they hover or float upwards? Imagine these
questions being posed and a competent scientist or team of scientists
offering one answer after another. The several botanical sciences are
invoked to explain aspects of plant morphology, physiology and genetics, and in conjunction with these are offered meteorological explanations including some drawn from atmospheric physics. Now suppose
that as the many 'whys?' and 'hows?' are answered the enquirer starts
to add the query 'And how is that possible?' There will come a point
where the sciences will have given the most fundamental and extensive explanations of which they are capable. What remains to be provided, if it can be, is the condition of the possibility of there being such
things as organisms or molecules or motion or space and time,
or whatever the last stage in the scientific explanation had posited.

'How is it possible that _____?' The question seems endlessly repeatable, and science proceeds by continuing to ask it. Yet at some
points the character of the search and the style of the answers change
as philosophers offer what purport to be ultimate explanations. For
example, some may reason as follows: if what is necessary cannot fail
to be, then if it could be shown that some fact is necessary, *a fortiori*
the condition of its possibility would also have been established: such
and such *is* the case because it *could not be otherwise*. Again, some
might argue that the ultimate condition of the possibility of the various things investigated by science is the existence of a Divine being
that wills energy, space and time into existence and fashions an order
out of them. Alternatively, some may argue that beyond the point
of scientific explanation no further questioning is intelligible; extra-
scientific explanation is neither necessary nor possible.

As was mentioned, the formula 'the condition of the possibility'
is associated with the rationalism of Immanuel Kant, but the earliest
philosophical fragments of Pre-Socratic texts, preserved in the writings of later philosophers, show that in the first phase of philosophy
(in the sixth and fifth centuries BC) thinkers were struggling to find
some intelligible foundation for reality, some answer to the question
'How is the natural order (constituted thus and so) possible?' Indeed,
what separates the earliest philosophers from the poetic mythologists
who preceded them is not an interest in the heavens and the cosmic
events that might occur there, for that was of as much concern to the

philosophical Ionians as to the poets of Mesopotamia; rather it is the concern for explanatory adequacy.

Whereas the epic myths sought to account for the sorts of features and deeds that give perennial cause for puzzlement by tracing them to archetypes in the heavens and in the behaviour of gods, the philosophical fragments show an awareness of the need to avoid regressive explanations. For example, an account of terrestrial seasons that explains them by reference to heavenly seasons may be interesting, but anyone struck by the question of what explains seasonal recurrence *as such* is not likely to feel that his or her puzzle has been resolved. Thus, when we read in the *Miscellanies* of Clement of Alexandria (150–215 AD) that according to Heraclitus (*fl. c.*500 BC) 'This world order [*kosmos*] did none of gods or men make, but it always was and is and shall be: an everlasting fire, kindling in measures and going out in measures',[1] we should recognize the mind of a philosopher at work in trying to fashion an ultimate answer to the question 'Why and how is it thus?'

The search for metaphysical ultimates or stopping places became more precisely defined in later antiquity and in the tradition of mediaeval scholasticism, which in turn shaped the concerns of modern rationalist enquiry up to and beyond Kant, and to a lesser extent influenced empiricism. In the chapters that follow we continue this tradition of enquiry not in the spirit of those who believe they have new answers, but rather of those who hope to establish the merits and defend the adequacy of answers long ago proposed but still disputed. It is difficult to know when the issues of atheism and theism were first debated. The problem is not simply the lack of ancient texts, serious though that deficiency is; for there is also an interpretative-cum-philosophical question: *what are atheism and theism?* Thales of Miletus (died *c.*546 BC), by tradition the first philosopher, was accused of atheism, yet it seems that what he was held guilty of was infidelity to a civic religion not disbelief in a single ultimate source of being. We simply have no evidence as to whether he had opinions concerning the latter.

The civic religions of antiquity were polytheistic, believing in many gods, one or more per city. Unsurprisingly, neither of us is a polytheist. Smart believes there are no gods and Haldane believes that there is precisely one. Our debate is defined by the core of monotheism supplemented to some extent by the historical and theological claims of Christianity. As we both understand it, theism involves belief in a single, self-existent, eternal, immutable, omnipotent, omniscient, omnipresent, omnibenevolent, immaterial creator and sustainer of the universe. As if that were not already enough to argue over, we also consider features unique to Christianity, and Haldane discusses aspects of Roman Catholic doctrine to which his belief in theism is connected.

Here it is worth mentioning that ours is an unevasive debate. We are both agreed that theism makes a number of ontological claims which admit of rational assessment. That alone serves to distinguish us from some philosophers and theologians who have a less metaphysical view of Christianity and other monotheistic faiths. While for them religion may proceed notwithstanding the metaphysical non-existence of God, were it so, for us religion without God is fantasy and delusion.

In fact, though this is not directly at issue in our exchange, Haldane is willing to go further and affirm the Catholic dogma that the existence of God *can* be known by the natural light of reason. The point of concern here is not an emphatic expression of theistic belief, or a statement of personal hope or conviction that an argument for God's existence may be developed. Rather, it is that fidelity to the major tradition of Western theism *requires* one to believe that God's existence can be known.[2] To put it otherwise, Haldane is committed to the proposition that if it were impossible, *in principle*, to prove the existence of God (allowing some breadth to the notion of proof), then what his religion teaches in this important respect is false. His philosophical position, therefore, is that any 'meta' argument intended to show the impossibility of establishing the existence of God is unsound; and at one point he considers and rejects such an argument deriving from the premise that we cannot reason from features of the empirical world to the conditions of a transcendent super-empirical reality. That said, he makes no claim to have provided, or to be able to provide on his own account, an irrefutable proof of God's existence. What he offers, largely *a priori*, are considerations in support of theism.

Matters of particular doctrines are only broached for purposes of example or where they bear upon the central argument about the existence of the God of theism. For the most part the debate revolves around a familiar set of questions: is there reason to believe in the existence of God? are there grounds to deny that such a thing exists? is theism coherent? Yet this is not written as an introduction to the philosophy of religion. For one thing it does not cover the range of topics one might expect to see dealt with in such a work, and for another it goes into such specific questions as the evidential value of Christian scripture. Additionally, it places an emphasis on philosophical methods and metaphysical theses which would be unusual in a general guide to issues in the philosophy of religion. This emphasis is explained by two facts about the authors. First, we are both meta-physical realists who hold, in opposition to current trends, that there is a world independent of human thought and language which may yet be known through observation, hypothesis and reflection. Second, and as previously mentioned, we believe that theism is ineliminably metaphysical.

Our contributions both turn on these claims: indeed one might say, somewhat over-simplifying, that for Haldane metaphysical realism leads to theism while for Smart it leads to atheism. The format of the exchange is straightforward. In chapter 1 Smart lays out his case for atheism; in chapter 2 Haldane develops his argument for theism; chapters 3 and 4 consist of replies. Neither of us changes his mind on the main issue but each makes some concession to the position of the other, and the volume ends with a brief afterword in which we re-affirm our commitment to metaphysical realism, be it that we have different views about what reality contains. Like God, in one of Browning's poems, some readers may choose to consider our work so as to 'estimate success'; our hope, however, is that you will be prompted to enter in and contribute to the continuing debate between atheism and theism.

Notes

1 See G.S. Kirk and J.E. Raven (eds), *The Presocratic Philosophers* (Cambridge: Cambridge University Press, 1975), Fragment 30, p. 199.
2 This teaching is long-standing but was defined as an essential dogma of the Catholic Faith by the First Vatican Council in the words: 'If anyone shall say, that the one and true God, our Creator and Lord, cannot be known for certain by the natural light of human reason; let him be anathema'. See H. Denzinger, *Encheiridion Symbolorum*, 29th edn (Freiburg: Herder, 1953), Canon 1806.

Atheism and Theism

J.J.C. Smart

1 Introduction

In this 'great debate' I shall be giving what I hope will be seen as a sympathetic critique of theism. I was once a theist and I would still like to be a theist if I could reconcile it with my philosophical and scientific views. So I shall not be too sorry if John Haldane wins the argument. I do not really expect that we will come to agreement, but at least we may achieve a better and perhaps more sympathetic understanding of one another's positions. I hold that there are never – or perhaps rarely – knock-down arguments in philosophy.[1] This is because a philosopher may claim to question anything, so that both the premises and the methodology are liable to challenge. This can happen in science too, and if the challenge is to central and unquestioned beliefs or methods the scientific debate will be seen as philosophical. One important methodological principle of mine is that an important guide to metaphysical truth is plausibility in the light of total science. Of course other philosophers may take another tack. Some may even hold that our best theories will come to be overturned and that there is no accumulation of sure scientific knowledge. Here I think that they would have taken to extremes Thomas Kuhn's theory of scientific revolutions.[2] Is it plausible that revolutionary new theories about the ultimate constituents of matter or about what happened in the first microseconds after the 'big bang' will affect our understanding

Acknowledgement: I am grateful to the following persons who kindly read a draft of this essay and have made valuable comments and given useful advice much of which I have tried to take: John Bigelow, John Bishop, Peter Forrest, James Franklin, John Leslie, Graham Oppy, Ian Ravenscroft, Ross Taylor.

of the physiology of respiration, or the fact of evolution of species, the distance from the sun of Alpha Centauri, or why gunpowder explodes? There is controversy about the interpretation of quantum mechanics, but the facts it tells us seem secure. Even when a theory is overturned it can usually be seen as an approximation to the truth.

My position here may be castigated as 'scientism'. It may be claimed that there are ways of knowing that are additional to (or alternative to) the scientific method: for example the inner deliverances of consciousness, religious experience, or even the assumptions of common sense. I of course would attempt to explain or explain away such putative non-scientific ways of knowing. I should make it clear that I am taking a broad view of science and scientific method, so as to include much historical, archaeological and philological investigation, as will be apparent in my brief glance later in this essay at the higher criticism of the New Testament.[3] Another problem is that even if there were agreement about the importance of plausibility in the light of total science there may well be disagreement in the assessment of plausibility. This question of assessment of plausibility is closely related to that of probabilistic inference to a hypothesis. The method depends on the theorem that the probability of a hypothesis h relative to evidence e is equal to the probability of e given h multiplied by the prior probability of h divided by the prior probability of e.[4] How do we assess the prior probabilities or estimate the relative probabilities? Furthermore, the more antecedently improbable e is, the greater is the probability of h, but how do we know whether to accept the evidence or to attempt to explain it away in some way, perhaps by distrusting our observation or bringing in other considerations that reduce our previous assessment of the high probability of e given h? Thus we may reject a report of a visitation by a flying saucer by considering how far apart inhabited planets are likely to be, and whether it would not be much more apparent that there are flying saucers if there really were such visitations. Why are they so often seen by remote farmers and why do they never land in the Great Court of Trinity College, Cambridge, or some other well-known place?

Though my approach will be largely based on the relations between science and religion it will inevitably involve us in many of the traditionally philosophical concerns, such as the main themes of, for example, J.L. Mackie's fine and formidably acute and scholarly book *The Miracle of Theism*.[5] I shall pay a good deal of attention to theological speculations arising from recent physics and cosmology, which to some writers, such as the physicist Paul Davies in his popular book

The Mind of God,[6] and the philosopher John Leslie in his *Universes,*[7] have been thought to support broadly theistic conclusions.

2   Theism, Spirituality and Science

Notice that I have said 'broadly theistic'. A distinction between theism and deism is commonly made. In this essay I shall regard deism as a form of theism. Theism is normally taken to be the view that there is one and only one God who is eternal, is creator of the universe, is omnipotent, omniscient, benevolent and loving, and who is personal and interacts with the universe, as in the religious experience and prayerful activities of humans. I shall treat the concept of theism as what Wittgenstein called a family resemblance concept:[8] theism does not have to have all of these characteristics, so that provided that a doctrine refers to a fair number of these properties I shall tend to count it as theism. Deism is the view that there is a God who created the universe but who avoids interacting with it. Allowing the slack associated with a family resemblance concept deism can count as a form of theism. Such slack is usual in science: for example when the atom was shown not to be an indivisible particle, physicists still continued using the word 'atom' much as before. Historically 'deism' has been used especially in connection with certain British writers in the seventeenth and eighteenth centuries, such as Lord Bolingbroke (Henry St John). Latterly I think that the difference between deism and theism has become blurred, especially since so many theologians have tended to play down the miraculous elements in Christianity.

Atheism I take to be the denial of theism and of deism. It also of course includes the denial of the existence of the ancient Roman and Greek gods and the like, but anyway I do not count such polytheisms as coming under the concept of theism as I understand it. To a large extent I shall be concerned with the theism of Christianity, though some of what I say will be applicable to the theologies of the other great monotheistic religions.

Spirituality

The orthodox conception of God is that of a spiritual being. Though the concept of the spiritual pre-dates Descartes, the usual notion of the spirit is close to that of a Cartesian soul: something immaterial, not even physical. There is, however, an emasculated notion of spirituality that can cloud the issue. One might talk of the spirituality of some of Haydn's music, meaning no more than that it was uplifting or that Haydn was influenced in his writing of it by adventitious connections with his religious beliefs. A materialist about the mind could consistently use the word 'spiritual' in this emasculated way. Again even a materialist and an atheist could agree in describing Mary who is happy in an enclosed convent as a 'spiritual' person, meaning simply that she is a person who has a strong urge to engage in prayer and worship, notwithstanding the fact that the atheist will disagree about whether there is such to and fro communication with a divine being.

Prayer, and other cognate activities, at least as they are understood by orthodox believers, as opposed to sophisticated theologians who themselves verge on deism or atheism, do not seem to be explicable on normal physical principles. We communicate with one another by sound-waves and light rays. Such communication fits in with neurophysiology, optics, theory of sound and so on. What about prayer? Are there spiritual photons that are exchanged between God and a soul? Perhaps the theist could say that God is able to influence the human brain directly by miraculous means and that he can know directly without physical intermediaries the worshipful thoughts in Mary's mind or brain. This story will just seem far-fetched to the deist or atheist.

Materialism and the 'New Physics'

Materialism has of course been thought to be inimical to theism and some theistic writers have incautiously rejoiced at the demise of nineteenth-century physics with its ontology of minute elastic particles, elastic jellies, and the like. That great man, Lord Kelvin, spent some of his exceptional talents and energies in trying to devise mechanical models to explain Maxwell's equations for electromagnetism. The idea is now bruited about that since modern physics rejects this sort of materialism the omens are better for a more spiritual account of the universe.

A good recent example of this can be found in the very title, *The Matter Myth*, of a popular book by Paul Davies and John Gribbin.[9] Matter is not mythical: a stone is a piece of matter and it is trivial that stones exist. Looked at quantum mechanically (e.g. in terms of an extraordinarily complex wave function whose description we could never hope to write down) the stone indeed has properties that may look queer to common sense. Thus its constituents would not have simultaneous definite position and velocity, there would be phenomena of non-locality and descriptions would be more holistic than their rough equivalents in classical physics. Indeed even the stone, supposing it to be on the top of a cairn, would be only approximately there and it would to a tiny extent be everywhere else, though the extent would be so small that we can totally ignore it. Not so with small constituents of the stone, such as electrons, which cannot even approximately be treated classically. Still, being constituents of the stone they surely deserve the appellation 'matter'. Even so the domain of the physical is wider than that of the material. Thus I am inclined to believe in absolute space–time (though not absolute space and time taken separately) and to believe that space–time is made up of sets of points. Points and sets of them are hardly 'material', but if physics needs to postulate them we must regard them as physical. Similarly Quine has held that we should believe in mathematical objects, for example, numbers and sets of them, because mathematics is part of physical theory as a whole, and the theories are tested holistically by observation and experiment. If Quine is right we must regard the mathematical objects as physical, and yet they are not material. Thus I prefer to describe myself as a physicalist rather than as a materialist, except in the context of the philosophy of mind where I hold that the distinction is not important. A neuron or even a protein molecule is a macroscopic object by quantum mechanical standards. The theory of electrochemical nerve conduction, the operation of neurons, nerve nets, and so on, is hardly likely to be affected by quantum field theory and the like.[10] I concede that quantum mechanical effects can occur in the neurophysiological domain: thus the retina is sensitive to the absorption of a single photon. This need not be of any significant importance for understanding the general working of the brain.

As a corrective to the presently canvassed idea that the so-called 'New Physics' is more compatible with religious views than was the deterministic nineteenth-century physics of Newtonian particles and gravitational attractions, together with some ideas about electromagnetism and thermodynamics, let us compare the present situation with that of the middle and late nineteenth century when William Thomson (Lord Kelvin) questioned the estimates that geologists had made of the antiquity of the earth. Kelvin had several arguments, of which the most persuasive were (1) the rate of cooling of the sun, assuming that the only source of its radiant energy was due to the loss of potential energy in its gravitational collapse, and (2) calculations based on the rate of cooling of the earth and plausible assumptions about the initial temperatures inside the earth. Geology and evolutionary biology seemed incompatible with physical laws, since Kelvin's calculations allowed only an age of 50 or 100 million years at most. The situation was saved in Kelvin's old age by the discovery of radioactivity. This suggested that there were other possible sources of energy, even though the theory of nuclear fusion and of the reactions that keep the sun going still lay in the future.[11] In any case Kelvin thought that it was unbelievable that the emergence of life could be accounted for on the basis of physical law. Though he was not a vitalist in the crude sense, since he denied the existence of a specific vital energy, he seems to have thought that though living beings obeyed the principle of conservation of energy, a vital principle enabled them to get round the second law of thermodynamics which had been propounded years before by Kelvin himself.[12]

Contrast modern biology, with its strong biophysical and biochemical core, its neo-Mendelian and neo-Darwinian theory of evolution, and molecular biology in genetics. It is true that it is not known how life arose naturally from inorganic matter, but there are hints that the problem at least is not as hopeless as Kelvin thought.[13]

Is there a Conflict between Science and Religion?

Why then is it commonly said that conflict between science and religion is a thing of the past? At least the outlook is bleak for those who see a 'God of the gaps'. Certainly the 'New Physics' makes us see the universe as very different from what untutored common sense tells us. Moreover the more physicists discover and the more they are able to unify their theories (e.g. of the four fundamental forces) the more wonderful the universe seems to be, and a religious type of emotion is liable to be aroused. On the other hand developments in biology can go the other way. As I suggested earlier, biology has become increasingly mechanistic. It is true that a sort of wonder is also appropriate, since it is hard imaginatively to grasp the amazing adaptations that have occurred by means of natural selection. Consider the complexity of the human immune system, or the extraordinarily subtle and complex sonar system of the bat. However I think that this wonder is different from that to which physics has led us. We have difficulty in grasping the biological complexity mainly because we fail imaginatively to grasp the vast periods of time in which this complexity developed as a result of mutation, recombination and natural selection. We can also forget the highly opportunistic ways[14] in which earlier structures have been adapted to different functions, as in the evolution of the mammalian eye and ear. Sometimes also the theory of evolution can explain mal-adaptation. Consider the human sinuses, in which the 'sump hole' is at the top, thus predisposing us to infections, inflammation, catarrh and pain. This is because we evolved from four-legged mammals, whose heads were held downwards, and in their case the 'sump holes' were well positioned. It should be observed that if we have a plausible general idea of how something could have occurred in accordance with known scientific principles, then it is reasonable to hold that it did occur in this natural way or in some other such way, and to reject supernatural explanations. It is interesting that (so my observation in talking to them goes) biologists are more frequently hard boiled in metaphysics. They are forced to look at human beings mechanistically and have it deeply impressed on their minds that we are mammals – 'poor forked creatures' – rather than partly spiritual beings, little lower than the angels. Moreover the medical and agricultural applications of theories of immunology, genetics, and so on, make it hard to take seriously the view fashionable among many literary and sociological academics that scientific theories are merely useful myths, and are destined to be overturned and replaced by others.

As I suggested at the beginning of this essay it is a mistake to think of theories, even in theoretical physics, merely as useful myths. A vulgarization of Thomas Kuhn's ideas has in some quarters led to much relativism about truth and reality. As a corrective to this I have frequently in the past had occasion to refer to an interesting article by Gerald Feinberg[15] in which he claims that 'Thales' Problem', the prob-lem of explaining the properties of 'ordinary matter', has been solved. The properties of the water of the sea, the earth and rocks of the land, the light and heat of the sun, the transparency of glass, and things of that sort, can be explained definitely using only the theory of the electron, proton, neutron, neutrino and photon and their antiparticles if any. This theory is ordinary quantum mechanics supplemented by the inverse square law of gravitation. (Deeper theories, such as quan-tum field theory, are needed to explain the fundamental properties of the electron, proton, neutron, neutrino and photon, requiring dis-cussion of the more recondite and very transient particles produced at high energies, but that is another matter.) This part of physics, Feinberg argues, is complete. It is not likely to be relegated to the scrap heap, as was phlogiston theory. We must remember that even revolutions allow for approximate truth in the proper domain of application of the earlier theories.[16] Newtonian mechanics gives predictions that are correct within observational error for objects whose velocities are not too high or which are not too near very massive bodies. Sometimes indeed there can be a change in ontology. General relativity shows how to replace the notion of gravitational force in favour of the geometrical notion of a geodesic, but much of classical mechanics has no need of this ontology and can be stated in terms of masses and their mutual accelerations.

With these cautions in mind, let us now look more sympathetically at reasons why the 'New Physics' has suggested a more favourable attitude to some sort of theism.

3 The New Teleology and the Old

By 'the new teleology' I mean the sort of teleological argument for the existence of God which rests its case on the wonders and fundamental laws of the universe at large. Such a teleology concedes that the sort of argument used by William Paley[17] in the nineteenth century will not do: we do not need to postulate a designer for a kangaroo, a hawk's eye, or the human immune system, since the evolution of these can be explained by the neo-Darwinian theory of natural selection together with modern genetics which includes neo-Mendelian population genetics and contemporary ideas of molecular biology. Molecular biology gives insight into the chemistry of how genes actually affect embryological development as well as all the other continuing activities in living cells. These last have indeed been given detailed explanations in certain particular cases which have lent themselves to investigation or which have been the object of intense study because of their importance for medicine and agriculture.

The new teleology does not at all rest its case, then, on the appearance that the organs of animals and plants are as if they were designed for a purpose. It rests its case on the grand structure of the universe and the beauty of its laws as discovered by contemporary physics and cosmology. There are also arguments from the appearance of 'fine tuning' in the ultimate laws, such as that the universe is of such a nature that it is suitable for the emergence of intelligent life. Such a teleology need not be in the least controverted by the mechanistic nature of modern biology.

Have I exaggerated the mechanistic nature of contemporary biology? It may be easy enough to catch biologists in their laboratories engaging in apparently teleological talk, e.g. 'What is the purpose of T-cells?' 'What is this enzyme for?' However this is only 'as if' talk. Natural selection mimics teleology. So it is heuristically valuable for biologists who are investigating how an organ or an enzyme works to help themselves by asking what purpose the organ or the enzyme subserves. The biologist does not believe that the organ or the enzyme came about by design, as might a certain feature of an electronic circuit. The feature of the electronic circuit was put in by the engineer who designed the circuit. Someone external, puzzling about how the circuit worked, might be helped by conjecturing the purpose for which the designer put it in. Similarly a biologist might ask heuristically 'What is the purpose of T-cells?' even while recognizing that there was no equivalent of the electronic engineer or of the engineer's purpose. It is useful 'as if' talk.[18] I think that this 'as if' teleology is recognized by most professional biologists, though there are probably some who are not explicitly sure about the philosophical issues, and others, especially in the more peripheral parts of biology, nearer to 'natural history', who may believe in genuine teleology.

Usually it is 'as if' a feature of an organism is for some purpose connected with the survival of the organism, or more accurately (remembering Richard Dawkins' 'selfish gene') of replication of the genetic material, so that, for example, helping a near relative and other altruistic behaviour can lead to such replication, i.e. survival of *gene* types.[19] Of course this heuristics or 'as if' purposiveness can backfire. Recalling the example of the 'sump hole' of the human sinus that is at the top not at the bottom, we should be misled if we thought that it was as if it was there for a purpose, unless of course we were referring to its being as if for good drainage in four-legged mammals from which we are all descended. There can also be features of an organism that have arisen 'purely fortuitously'. I do not of course deny the fortuitous element in all evolution.

Let us therefore put aside the 'as if' teleology in modern biology, together with the earlier theistic teleology of Paley, and return to what I have called 'the new teleology'. To some extent, of course, this is a misnomer, since it is no new thing to echo the sentiment 'The heavens declare the glory of God; and the firmament sheweth his handiwork'.[20] Nevertheless the wonders and beauties of physics and cosmology are now so great and even more striking than was evident in earlier times that many contemporary theoretical physicists are prone at least to theistic *emotions* of admiration, awe and wonder. Theistic emotions are indeed in place. But the question remains as to whether theism itself is intellectually justifiable.

4 Pantheism

In trying to answer this question I think that we can set aside a minimal form of pantheism that simply identifies God with the universe. Such a pantheist does not differ from the atheist in his or her *belief* about the universe, and differs only in his or her attitudes and emotions towards it. Not for nothing was Spinoza described at some times as 'a God-intoxicated man' and at others as 'a hideous atheist'. (However Spinoza was possibly something more than the minimal pantheist that I have in mind. For example John Leslie has seen him as a precursor of his own 'extreme axiarchism' which I shall discuss later in this essay.[21] Moreover Spinoza thought that extension and thought were co-equal and correlative attributes of the world.) A stronger sort of pantheist may hold that the world has a spiritual aspect. One sort of pantheist may think of the universe as a giant brain – stars, galaxies and clusters of galaxies perhaps playing the part of the microphysical particles that make up our own nervous systems. I shall take it that such a form of pantheism is implausible and far-fetched. There is absolutely no evidence that the universe, however large it may be, could be a giant brain.

Closely related to pantheism is the esoteric Hindu philosophy, the Ādvaita Vedānta, of the mediaeval Indian philosopher Sánkara, and foreshadowed in some passages in the Upanishads, such as the Brihad-Āranyaka Upanishad, dating from perhaps about 600 BC. 'Ādvaita' means 'non-dualism': all multiplicity (and hence the world as both science and common sense understand it) is illusion. The metaphysics has a striking resemblance to that in F.H. Bradley's *Appearance and Reality* and even more to the extreme Bradleian view of C.A. Campbell.[22] One advantage of such metaphysics is that the noumenal (Brahman, also identified by the Ādvaita with the Self or Ātman) or Bradley's Absolute is quite inconceivable, and so on the phenomenal level we can pursue science without any danger of religious or *a priori* metaphysical conflict with it. Such metaphysics is in a way impressive but is in the end absurd, since multiplicity is evident in the very propositions we use to state it.

The upshot of this brief look at various sorts of pantheism and near pantheism is, I suggest, that the only obviously plausible form of it is the minimalist one, that pantheism differs from ordinary atheism only in that the pantheist expresses certain emotions towards the universe that the atheist does not. Ontologically there is no difference between such a pantheist and a pure atheist. One may mildly object, however, to the way in which certain scientists in their popular writings often use theistic language in a way that confuses the issue. (Stephen Hawking's 'The mind of God', repeated by Paul Davies in the title of a book,[23] and even Einstein's 'God does not play dice', though I think that it is quite clear that Einstein[24] on the various occasions in which he used the word 'God' was expressing only the minimal form of pantheism.) This use of theistic language by scientists has something in common with the way in which certain Anglican theologians have used Christian terminology to express an essentially sceptical theological position.

5   Fine Tuning and the Anthropic Cosmological Principle

The so-called anthropic cosmological principle entered into recent discussions among certain cosmologists and philosophers because of what seems to be a fortunate and *a priori* improbable 'fine tuning' of some of the fundamental constants of nature. I am of course using the words 'fine tuning' metaphorically to point to the important and improbable relations between the constants of nature without which stars, planets and life would be impossible. I do not use the words so as to imply the existence of design and a 'Fine Tuner'. This last theistic hypothesis would be a further inference, the merits of which will be considered below. In discussing the relations between fundamental constants of physics we have to be concerned with pure numbers. For example, if we say that the mass of an electron is of the order of 9×10^{-31} kilograms we are not talking about a pure number, because the number depends partly on the arbitrary convention of measuring mass in kilograms. However when we say that the ratio of the mass of the proton to that of the electron is 1836 we are referring to a pure number. Our statement is true whatever the units in which we measure mass. The number 1836 would be as familiar to a physicist in Alpha Centauri or wherever as it is to the terrestrial physicist. In fact, trying to get into communication with extraterrestrials would involve sending such numbers as 1836. This would of course depend on sending clues to an arithmetical notation. '.. + ... = ...' and things like that would enable them to guess what '+' and '=' mean. We could also give them a clue to our decimal notation by sending such things as '7 + 5 = 12' (with, say, dot notations for 7, 5, 1 and 2). Now if the extra-terrestrials received a piece of discourse containing '1836' they would guess that the discourse had something to do with protons and electrons. The pure numbers are of cosmic interest, unlike the impure numbers such as 12.5 kilograms, which are terrestrial and conventional. Sometimes the pure numbers are defined in more complicated ways, as with the fine structure constant, which determines the strength of electromagnetic interactions relative to those that explain the other fundamental forces of nature. The 'fine tuning' consists in the relative values of the fundamental constants of physics (constants determined in the end by pure numbers) being in certain ratios to one another. Slight differences in any of these ratios would lead to a universe very different from that which actually exists.[25]

In particular, life as we know it could not have emerged, and without life there could not have been observers. This has led to some curious reasoning in connection with the so-called 'Anthropic Principle' in cosmology. For the moment I shall ignore the possibility of life as we *don't* know it, for example in an environment of ammonia instead of oxygen, or life that is silicon-based (instead of carbon-based), or life in a dust cloud, such as in Fred Hoyle's science fiction novel *The Black Cloud*.[26] Now, the proposition that the universe we observe is such as to contain observers is as it stands tautologous and utterly uninformative. What is informative comes from propositions about the fine tuning which seems to be necessary for the universe to allow for the evolution of galaxies, stars, planets, life, and ultimately observers and theoreticians. The tautologous proposition obviously cannot explain anything but it can draw our attention to interesting facts. If we could show that galaxies, stars, planets, carbon-based life and observers could not exist unless certain relations held between the fundamental constants of physics, we could deduce that these relations *do* exist. Initially, however, the facts about the 'fine tuning' are known independently, and then we see how necessary they are for a universe like ours, and hence for us to be here to know it. Much of it is necessary for there to be, say, stars. So there could be a 'stellar' principle no less than an 'anthropic' one. Also there may possibly be intelligent beings very different from us humans all over the universe, on planets of distant stars. Indeed Brandon Carter, who introduced the term 'Anthropic Principle', has, I think, come to dislike the choice of terminology.

Does the fact that if it were not for the fine tuning we would not be here to know it explain the fine tuning, as some incautious purveyors of the anthropic principle have at least seemed to suggest? Surely not. It is the fine tuning that (partially) explains the existence of observers, not the existence of observers that explains the fine tuning.

Faulty Anthropic Arguments

The matter many be illustrated by a faulty argument of G.J. Whitrow in the appendix to the second edition of a book published in 1959[27] and earlier in a paper in *The British Journal for the Philosophy of Science*.[28] This was some time before Brandon Carter formulated his 'anthropic cosmological principle', and there is some similarity between Whitrow's reasoning and Carter's, and yet an important difference. Carter's reasoning was not faulty in the way (as I shall show) Whitrow's was. This is because Carter connected his anthropic principle with a 'many universe' hypothesis which I shall discuss shortly.

Whitrow begins by assuming plausibly enough that in a space of $s + 1$ dimensions there would be an inverse sth power law of gravitational attraction. (This is the case in Newtonian dynamics and is approximately true in general relativity.) Whitrow also assumes, perhaps plausibly, that life, and hence observers, would not have arisen on a planet which had a very eccentric or unstable orbit. He then goes on to make use of a theorem in classical mechanics that a stable and near circular orbit can occur only in a space of either two or three dimensions. He makes use of an argument to the effect that a brain would not be possible in two-dimensional space: only in a space of three or more dimensions could many neurons be connected in very many ways so as to form a complicated network. (Whitrow acknowledges a suggestion by J.B.S. Haldane and a mathematical discussion with M.C. Austin.) Whitrow thus concludes that 'the number of dimensions of space is necessarily three, no more and no less, because it is the unique natural concomitant of the higher forms of terrestrial life, in particular of Man, *the formulator of the problem*' (Whitrow's italics).

Modern cosmologists play around with theories that space has ten or more dimensions and a complicated topology, but they still hold that macroscopically it has three dimensions and a Euclidean type of topology. (Compare the way in which an oil pipe hundreds of miles long would look like a straight line from far enough away in space, whereas looked at closely its surface is seen to be two-dimensional, with the topology of the surface of a cylinder.) That space has three dimensions at least macroscopically is good enough for Whitrow's argument and we can agree that it *does* follow from Whitrow's premisses, together with some uncontroversial mathematics, geometry, mechanics and natural history, that humans could not exist unless the number of dimensions of space was (macroscopically) three. Nevertheless, insofar as he put the argument as an *explanatory* one, it is quite preposterous. The supposed explanation is back to front.

Surely we should think that it is the three-dimensionality of space that explains the existence of habitable planets containing intelligent life. I do not think of 'explanation' as a very clear notion, and its use depends a good deal on context. I mainly think of it in terms of coherence, of fitting the *explanandum* proposition into our web of belief,[29] but in a scientific or cosmological context at least we should explain the more particular by the more general, the parochial by the cosmic. Whitrow's argument does indeed establish connections between the three dimensions of space and the existence of intelligent life on earth. That space has three dimensions is shown to be a necessary but not sufficient condition of the existence of inhabitable planets and intelligent life.

Is it that explanations come from the giving of necessary conditions, not of sufficient conditions? This will not do, because sometimes it is a sufficient condition that is explanatory. Decapitation is a sufficient condition for the death of Charles I and is explanatory of it. It is not a necessary condition for his death, since he might have died in his bed or by shooting. A cause is sufficient for an effect (given constancy in our contextual assumptions about background states of affairs – e.g. putting a match to a fire causes it to flame, assuming the presence of oxygen, that the wood is not wet, etc.) but is not necessary (e.g. Charles I might have been simultaneously decapitated and shot through the heart.)

These complications make it difficult to say clearly and precisely just *why* Whitrow's putative explanation of the three-dimensionality of space is back to front. I suspect that it is just a matter of the particularity of the suggested *explanans* and of the cosmic nature of the supposed *explanandum*. Let us consider an even more preposterous argument, also due to Whitrow. This is that if space had only two dimensions we could not have any alimentary canal, since we would be divided into two disconnected parts. However, is it not mad to say that space has more than two dimensions because we can eat, instead of saying that the cosmic fact that space has three dimensions is (in part) the explanation of why we can eat?

Brandon Carter who first formulated the anthropic cosmological principle (in fact both a 'weak and a 'strong' version of it) did so in connection with the hypothesis that our universe is only one of a huge variety of universes, a 'world ensemble', in which the fundamental constants of nature, which seem so arbitrary to us, differ randomly from universe to universe.[30] Strictly speaking, of course, 'universe' should refer to everything that there is (perhaps excluding God if we talk of God creating the universe) and so could be taken to refer not to what we think of as our universe but to the ensemble of universes. However, I think that it will not be confusing if I use the word 'universe' ambiguously and rely on context to make it clear whether I am talking of one of the many members of the world ensemble or of the whole lot.

Carter's many universes hypothesis may be held to explain the fine tuning of our universe. If there is a sufficiently large number of universes with the values of the fundamental constants randomly distributed between them, then it could be virtually certain that *some* universes would be such that galaxies, stars, planets, life and intelligence evolved within them. The anthropic principle allays surprise that we are in such a universe. Obviously as intelligent beings we must be in a universe that allows intelligence to arise. This explanation, depending as it does on the many universes hypothesis, does not have the back to front character of the example that we have recently been discussing. But how good is the world ensemble explanation?

An unattractive feature of the explanation is its apparent prodigality. We may be reminded of Ockham's razor, the principle that entities should not be multiplied beyond necessity. 'Necessity' is a bit strong: let us say, 'without more than compensating explanatory advantage'. Ontological parsimony must be balanced against explanatory power. If Carter's hypothesis really does explain the fine tuning of our universe, then perhaps it should be accepted. Simplicity and symmetry are features which make for a good explanatory theory or hypothesis. Now the random distribution of relations between the fundamental constants in the various universes which belong to the huge ensemble of universes restores a symmetry that is missing in our ordinary 'one universe' theory, with its antecedently improbable set of relations between the fundamental constants. A random distribution of the fundamental constants

of nature presumably requires no explanation in the way that a particular and arbitrary looking set of such values would. There is a sort
of symmetry in randomness.

John Leslie has told a 'firing squad' story that illustrates Carter's
point.[31] Suppose that you are put for execution before a firing squad
and to your surprise all the members of the squad, good shots though
they are, all miss. You would be extremely surprised to be still alive.
Suppose, however, that you knew that there were a billion people like
you being executed by firing squad; you might calculate that it was
quite probable that there would be a few lucky survivors, and so you
must be one of them. You should feel surprised and fortunate, but
there would not be the sort of puzzlement that you might feel if you
had been the only candidate for execution. You would feel only the
sort of surprise that the winner of a lottery might feel. In a practically
possible case, of course, there could not be a billion other similar
firing squads and victims and you would guess that the firing squad
had some reason not to kill you, and this would be a sort of analogue
of the design (theistic) explanation of the fine tuning. Leslie's considerations, however, do support the view that Carter's multiple universes hypothesis, or something very like it, could provide a non-theistic
explanation of the fine tuning of our universe, as a serious rival to the
theistic design explanation. If our universe were not one of the tiny
proportion of fine tuned ones we would not be here to tell the tale.
Similarly, if the man is missed by the firing squad he reflects that of
course he must be one of the few to survive.

Some readers will react adversely to the moral drawn from the firing
squad story and so also to the supposed explanatory value of Carter's
many universes hypothesis. Why should your surprise at surviving
the firing squad be allayed by the story of a billion other firing squads?
Certainly with the real world it would not be: we know that there
could not be a billion other firing squads on this small planet. My
answer is that if we rule out the hypothesis that the firing squad had
some reason for trying not to kill you, the question 'Why me?' is not
a proper metaphysical question. Indeed I hold that all indexicals, such
as 'you', 'I' and also tenses of verbs, should be expunged from metaphysical theory.[32] Compare Quine's 'canonical notation'.[33] We should
try to see the world as much as possible *sub specie aeternitatis*, to use
Spinoza's metaphor. Metaphysically 'Why me?' is not an appropriate
question. It could in some cases be a sensible, but not metaphysical,
question. The story assumed that the firing squads were hard-hearted
and incorruptible. If the story is changed 'Why me?' might indeed have

an answer, such as 'The captain of the firing squad is your wife's cousin'. Now the analogy with Carter's idea is quite lost. It is nearer to the design hypothesis: 'God arranged the fine tuning so that conscious life could evolve'.

Carter's many universes were supposed to be completely separate from one another. However Carter's type of argument would work equally well if all the 'universes' were vast parts of one single space–time universe as in a theory proposed by Andrei Linde.[34] Linde's cosmological theory is like a theory suggested by A.H. Guth in 1980 in proposing an inflationary scenario.[35] Linde supposes that the universe expanded exponentially by a factor of something like $10^{1,000,000}$ from an almost point-like beginning to a size comparable to that of a football. In Linde's version of the inflationary story the inflation occurs before the hot big bang in standard cosmology. His theory solves certain problems to do with the flatness and smoothness of space in the early universe. So the motivation was not that of Carter's multiple universes theory, and so there is some independent justification for believing in many universes or sub-universes with random variations in the constants that relate the fundamental forces, which arose from a single proto-force by symmetry breaking. (For symmetry breaking, consider the analogy of a needle in classical mechanics, balanced in a vertical position on its point. There is symmetry about its axis, but the symmetry will be broken by the smallest perturbation, whereby the needle will fall so as to lie in some particular horizontal direction.)

According to Linde's theory what we think of as the universe is only one sub-universe among a huge number of them, like a crystal in a randomly oriented array of such things (as, say, in a metal). Our particular 'crystal', vast as it is, extending beyond the reach of the best telescopes, clearly has values of fundamental constants that are suitable for the evolution of galaxies, stars, planets, life and intelligence. We are obviously *not* in one of the vastly more common 'crystals' or sub-universes that are not 'fine tuned' in this way.

I am of course not competent to assess or even properly understand Linde's theory. However I have mentioned it as a possible way in which something like a 'many universes' theory could get some independent justification. But Carter's and Linde's theories both have the additional advantage of restoring symmetry in the large, Carter's in the world ensemble and Linde's in his total super-universe. This symmetry comes from that of randomness. (But not complete randomness. There are the symmetrical proto-laws, the unified force and scalar field, which by symmetry breaking crystallizes out into the different relations between the four fundamental forces.) This leads me on to a purely metaphysical supposition, that of a completely random universe, without laws or even proto-laws.

Here is the idea. Suppose that the universe was infinite and completely random in the large. Then our huge, apparently ordered universe could be just one infinitesimal part of a disordered whole. We would be living in a Humean world: we would have no reason to suppose that in the next microsecond everything around us would not go into a total chaos rather like a puff of smoke. We of course would do well to suppose that the pseudo-laws, the temporary apparent regularities, would continue to operate. If they do not then no matter – nothing we do matters. But if they do continue to operate it is as well that we plan according to them.

Is not this a chilling thought, that our huge and beautiful universe (as it seems to us) might be a mere speck, a mere infinitesimal random fluctuation into apparent orderliness in what is really an infinite chaos? The image of a monkey typing randomly on a typewriter to produce Shakespeare's *Hamlet* would pale into insignificance beside the awful reality. Carter's and Linde's hypotheses do not quite have the chilling quality of this hypothesis but it is still true that they lack some of the emotional appeal of the design hypothesis. Still, emotional appeal is not proof or rational persuasiveness, and so it is time now to turn to theistic explanations of the 'fine tuning' and to examine their credentials as an argument for the existence of God.

6 The Argument from the Appearance of Design

Contemplating the beautiful laws of nature, many physicists have quite understandably taken them as evidence of design, and, as has been noted above, the apparent 'fine tuning' of the fundamental constants of nature has lent additional weight to this way of looking at things. It should be clear of course that this talk of 'fine tuning' is not to be taken as by itself implying a fine tuner: if so the argument would become both quick and circular. This argument from ostensible fine tuning is the currently fashionable form of the traditional 'teleological argument' for the existence of God. Sometimes this is called 'the argument from design' but this, like a too literal construal of 'fine tuning', would be question begging. Years ago Norman Kemp Smith suggested that the argument should be called 'the argument to design'.[36] Equally we could call it 'the argument from apparent design', or for brevity 'the design argument'.

Unlike some other traditional arguments for the existence of God the design argument was never meant to be apodeictic. In contrast the ontological argument was meant to be quite *a priori* and the cosmological argument almost so, requiring only the assertion that something contingently exists. The design argument is best thought of as an argument to the best explanation, such as we use in science and everyday life. The best explanation for the appearance of design in the world is said to be a designer.

David Hume in his great posthumously published book, *Dialogues Concerning Natural Religion*,[37] obviously thought that there were alternative explanations which are as plausible as that of design. However, he retained a sceptical position, rather than a dogmatically atheist one. Philo, who was probably Hume's representative mouthpiece in the *Dialogues*, said that the universe might as well be compared to an organism as to an artefact, and organisms, *prima facie*, are not designed. They 'just grow'. (Antony Flew has commended the childlike acumen and common sense of Topsy in Harriet Beecher Stowe's *Uncle Tom's Cabin*.[38]) Of course we know from the modern synthesis of the theory of evolution by natural selection together with neo-Mendelian genetics that organisms do not need to have been designed. If we appreciate the huge time-scale of evolutionary processes and the opportunistic way in which they work, our minds need not be intellectually overwhelmed, even though perhaps imaginatively at a loss. However, I am here considering the argument from design in a post-Darwinian context, the new teleology not the old, in relation to the great appearance of design in the laws of physics.

As was just remarked, Hume held that the analogy between the universe and an organism was as good as that between the universe and an artefact. There are possibly many other analogies, equally good or bad. Indeed Hume's *Dialogues* concludes with Philo's concession to his main interlocutor Cleanthes that there is *some* analogy between the cause of the universe and a human mind. This is perhaps in one way a very small concession since with enough ingenuity one can find *some* analogy between almost any two things. However, in another way it is a big concession, namely that the universe does have a cause external to itself.

One trouble with the design argument is that there would have to be a 'cosmic blueprint'[39] in the mind of God. This conflicts with the supposition that God could be a perfectly simple being. At first sight, as Hume seems to have thought, the designer of a universe would need to be at least as complex as the universe itself. It is not clear that this need be so. Complex forms of life evolve as a result of physical law together with the randomness characteristic of mutation and natural selection. Even repeated application of a fairly simple set of rules will allow for very complex but in the large regular patterns, as with the Mandelbrot set which is discussed in chaos theory. Does this mean that the designer of the universe could be *less* complex than the universe that is designed? Such a designer need not be the infinite creator God of the great theisms, at least. Nevertheless the designer's mind would have to have within it a structure at least as complex as the conjunction of fundamental laws and initial conditions. So the question surely arises: what designed the designer? The design hypothesis thus seems to raise more questions (and so is less explanatory) than the atheist one. (I shall reconsider this when I come to discuss John Leslie's conception of God as an ethical principle.[40]) Stephen Hawking has famously, or notoriously, looked forward to a simple 'theory of everything', which would give us knowledge of 'the mind of God'.[41] Of course if God's internal structure were that of the fundamental laws and initial conditions this would make Hawking's metaphor of 'the mind of God' appropriate. Nevertheless, the hypothesis of God, at least as designer, would be redundant, and belief in this sort of mind of God would collapse ontologically into atheism.

If the universe needed a designer which was not identical with the structure of the universe (i.e. laws and initial conditions) we would get into a regress, the designer needing a designer, and so on *ad infinitum*. One may be reminded of Fred Hoyle's fictional interstellar 'Black Cloud'.[42] Hoyle believed in an infinite steady state universe. If one asked where the (highly intelligent) black cloud came from the answer was supposed to be that it was designed by another black cloud, and this by yet another black cloud, and so on *ad infinitum*. Whether or not the cosmology was good (the steady state theory is in fact not generally accepted) the biology was unsatisfying. One expects a complex organism, even a 'black cloud', to have evolved from simpler organisms and ultimately from inorganic life.

Artefacts do not evolve in this way, though it is possible that one day self-replicating robots with occasional random variations in their programming may mimic biological evolution. An engineer designing an apparatus may produce a blueprint. Any complexity in the apparatus will then appear in the blueprint. (If we neglect complexity antecedently inherent in the components, such as transistors, which are the original materials for the engineer's design.) Here I am taking 'apparatus' in the sense of 'hardware'. One may be reminded of Descartes' rather obscure dictum that there must be as much reality in the cause as there is in the effect.[43] (Descartes used the principle in an attempted proof of the existence of God, but my reference to it has a different motivation.) There can be a simple recipe for creating complexity, so long as one does not want to predict the particular *type* of complexity. Illuminate a planet rather like the Earth which is about a hundred million miles from a star rather like the Sun for so many hundreds of millions of years and (with luck) complex organisms, perhaps like elephants or mermaids, will eventually evolve. Still, this is not like the case of designing the universe itself – designing the fundamental laws and boundary conditions. For this there would have to be something like a blueprint in the mind of the designer, and it would have to have a complexity equal to that of a complete specification of laws and boundary conditions. Or can a regional order arise spontaneously out of a universal chaos, the chilling thought of a few pages back? But if we accepted this last idea there would be no need to suppose a designer, or anything else for that matter.

Thus, even if it were supposed that the designer determines only the laws of nature (with non-arbitrary constants in them) and a suitable set of initial conditions, then considerations of simplicity and of Ockham's razor suggest that the supposition was an unnecessary one which should be rejected. Any complexity in the laws and initial conditions would be duplicated in the mind of the designer. (Otherwise I could get no purchase on the notion of design that is involved.)

The matter may take on a different complexion if we look at the apparent arbitrariness of the fundamental constants of nature, as we at present understand them, and the way in which the relations between them are peculiarly fitted for the evolution of a universe which contains life, consciousness and intelligence. There is an appearance of a cosmic purpose which may appeal to someone who concedes the points made in the previous paragraph. It is tempting to think that the arbitrary constants must have been chosen by some purposive agent so as to make the universe conducive to the evolution of galaxies, stars, planets and eventually conscious and intelligent life.

At any rate this purposive explanation of the happy values of the constants of nature and of the forms of the fundamental laws could strengthen belief in a deity whose existence was made probable by some other argument. Of course the view that God designed the universe because he wanted conscious beings in it who would be the objects of his love is a not unfamiliar theological one. I have wondered whether this view could have a touch in it of psychocentric hubris. (I say 'psychocentric' not 'anthropocentric' in view of the possibility that conscious and intelligent life is scattered throughout the universe.) Certainly the Judaeo-Christian tradition sets a high value on humans in the scheme of things, and this value should also be ascribed to minds on other worlds, some of which may indeed be far superior to our human ones. Perhaps there is a bit of human vanity involved in the idea that the universe was created in order for there to be consciousness and intelligence. Bertrand Russell held that vanity is a prime motive for religious belief. Even the horrible view that there is a hell to which the infinite God will consign us for our sins may give us an admittedly miserable sense of importance. Belief in highly superior beings on distant planets may be a blow to our hubris. Of course religious belief in the existence of angels may have had a similar effect,[44] even though in the nineteenth century angels came to be thought of as rather pale creatures, whose main talent was playing the harp. (There did not seem to be reports of super-Einsteins among them.)

Still we should not put too high a value on intelligence. Nor should we forget the sufferings of the non-human animals on earth. As Jeremy Bentham said, 'The question is not "Can they reason?" or "Can they talk?" but "Can they suffer?"'.[45] To see suffering is a corrective to disparagement of a possible 'psychocentrism'. It would be inconsistent of me to object to psychocentrism while at the same time taking seriously – as surely one must – the importance of human and animal suffering when I come to discuss the problem of evil.

Even so, the hypothesis that God designed this huge material universe so as to produce consciousness seems to be *ad hoc*. What a long-winded and chancy way of creating conscious beings. Surely an omnipotent being could have created happy spirits directly, rather than a universe which might produce entities like us, or higher than us, as a result of long and chancy evolutionary processes (see p. 31).

The possibility that the universe contains vast numbers of (and if the universe is infinite, which is of course questionable, infinitely many) stars like our sun, with planets suitable for evolution of life and ultimately intelligent beings, raises interesting theological problems, which have, with some exceptions, been neglected by theologians. Christianity appears to be anthropocentric in its doctrine of the incarnation, that God became man. To avoid this anthropocentrism we should envisage the possibility of incarnations on other worlds throughout the universe, a question to which, with a few exceptions, theologians seem to me to have given insufficient attention.

The new teleology, as I have said, is quite different from that associated with such as Paley. It concentrates on the awe and wonder at the beauties of the laws of physics and the starry heavens above. In its most recent form it focuses on the apparent 'fine tuning', the happy coincidences of the value of the fundamental constants. The ontological extravagance of postulating 'a Designer' could be outweighed by its value in explaining these coincidences. However in assessing the plausibility of such a hypothesis we might also consider the possibility of there being an as yet unknown physical or cosmological hypothesis which might have as its consequence these arbitrary looking values. This would also provide an alternative to 'the many universes' hypotheses.

As a possibly misleading analogy consider the way in which three at first sight unrelated numbers, i the square root of minus one, π the ratio of a Euclidean circle to its diameter and the Euler number e should be related by the simple formula $e^{i\pi} = -1$. Once one knows the proof it becomes almost obvious, though still beautiful. Could the fine tuning one day be deduced from some simple laws, the constants in which do not have an arbitrary appearance? The trouble is that the ratios of the fundamental constants do not look mathematically significant, as do i, e and π. This consideration of a possible theory to explain the fine tuning is more parsimonious than the design hypothesis and than the many universes hypotheses. It partakes, however, of an appearance of wishful thinking, 'something may turn up', to which a theist could rightly object. Furthermore, since i, e and π are all mathematically significant (π can indeed be defined analytically, without geometry) they could be expected, antecedently of the proof, to be related somehow, even if not so beautifully. One trouble with the fine tuning is that the constants involved do not have importance in pure mathematics, and this does support the design hypothesis. There are pros and cons in this part of the debate.

7   God as an Ethical Principle

I now pass on to another concept of God, namely that of God as an ethical principle, namely that value ought to come into existence. This view has been much canvassed by John Leslie, who traces it back to neo-Platonism and indeed back to Plato's Form of the Good itself in the *Republic*.[46] Leslie calls the theory 'extreme axiarchism'. Leslie thinks of 'ought' in ordinary ethical talk as signifying a sort of 'required-ness', which is plausible enough. Unfortunately we often do not do what we think that we ought to do, and so the ethical requiredness in question does not ensure the occurrence of the required act. Still, thinking analogically, Leslie thinks of the axiarchic principle as one which explains the existence and nature of the universe.

The axiarchic principle seems too abstract to account for the details of existence. If God is an axiarchic principle is there anything comparable to a blueprint? Surely not. Simplicity is a virtue in an explanatory posit, but if it is too simple it cannot do the job. The theory also runs up against the problem that disvalue (evils) comes into existence. Another problem arises from the fact that Leslie sees value only in consciousness: a stone or a star cannot have intrinsic value. At first sight one would expect, on the axiarchic principle, that the world would not contain anything other than pure minds. I myself do not believe in pure immaterial processes: I contingently identify conscious states and processes with brain states and processes, but I would say that pure minds are logically *possible*, and would have expected that if the axiarchic hypothesis were true the world would have consisted entirely of these. In his *Value and Existence*, therefore, Leslie struggles with a form of phenomenalism according to which stars and rocks, electrons and black holes, are merely *possible* entities: the world is *as if* they exist. In correspondence Leslie has said that when in phenomenalist mood he is as if he believes just in part of an eggshell, whereas the realist about the cosmos believes in the whole eggshell. He holds that the structure of the part is carried over to the structure of the merely possible whole: the axiarchic principle gives to consciousness the patterns which it would have if it were integrated with the non-conscious cosmos in which the realist believes. Leslie's phenomenalism (if that is what it is) is derived from his axiarchism: it does not depend on the usual bad arguments on which phenomenalists have usually relied (or on which Berkeley relied).

For those, such as myself, who believe that the best explanation of the higgledy-piggledy regularities (or non-regularities) on the observational level is the real *actual* existence of the physical objects postulated by science (and also those implicit in common sense) any sort of phenomenalism is unbelievable. I concede that if one *already* had firm reasons for believing in the axiarchic principle one might have *some* reason for believing in some sort of phenomenalism, but even so it would seem odd that God, or the axiarchic principle, should go about things in such an extravagantly roundabout way, even though it was only an 'as if' way.

The theory of extreme axiarchism has something in common with the more usual argument to design. It has an additional and attractive feature, namely that it purports to account not only for the general features of the universe (the cosmological fine tuning as necessary also for the existence of consciousness, the bearer of value) but also for the very existence of the universe. In this it has something in common with the traditional cosmological argument for the existence of God which I shall discuss in a later section. In this section, however, I shall treat Leslie's axiarchic principle mainly in its capacity as a putative explanation of the apparent design of the world, as an answer to the question 'Why is the world as it is?' rather than to the question 'Why is there anything at all?'

Further Difficulties for Extreme Axiarchism

As I have remarked, if Leslie's hypothesis did all that he claims, it could be intellectually an immensely attractive one. It would explain not only the appearance of design in the world but would explain the very existence of the universe, though perhaps not its own existence. The hypothesis has the advantage of at least the appearance of *simplicity*. It can be stated in a few words. It may be attractive to religious believers who are dissatisfied with too anthropomorphic a concept of God. Plato seems to have had something like a religious attitude to his supposed Form of the Good. Of course Christians typically believe that God is a *person* who can hear and answer prayers. Well, 'religion' is what Wittgenstein called a 'family resemblance' concept.[47] A family resemblance concept is one that (roughly speaking) corresponds to a set of properties, such that we take the word for the concept to apply to something to which a fair number of the properties apply. There need be no necessary and sufficient set of these properties.[48] Thus believing in God is not necessary: consider Theravāda Buddhism. Priesthood and ritual are not necessary: consider Quakerism. Maoism is a border-line case: it had something like a priesthood, a sacred book and a creed. Thus it had some properties that make it not too foolish for us to count it as a religion. Perhaps 'Christian' is a family resemblance concept too. After all there have been what seem to me to be atheist Anglican clergymen and theologians who call themselves 'Christians'.

Is it appropriate to say that a person who believes that God is an axiarchic principle is a Christian, or even a theist? I gather that there are indeed Catholic theologians who hold that Leslie's sort of neo-Platonism is compatible with the notion of God as a person. They can rely on the doctrine of analogical predication which is to be found in the writings of Thomas Aquinas.[49] The idea is that when we apply a predicate to God we do not do so in quite the same sense as we do when we apply it to humans, but nor do we apply it quite in a different sense. There is an analogy between the two uses. So perhaps in an analogical sense an ethical principle can be a person. I myself think that this must be stretching the notion of analogical predication too far. After all it is plausible to suppose that if you stretch analogy enough you can find analogy between any two things. Consider the number 19 and the making of canoes. They have something in common, namely the property of being liked by the headmaster of my school when I was a small boy.

Still, for us metaphysicians the important question is not whether Leslie's hypothesis of God as an ethical principle is compatible with traditional Christian theology. It is whether it is a plausible metaphysical hypothesis. Despite its attractions of simplicity and of being non-anthropomorphic, there seem to be three main objections to it. The first is that good though simplicity may be in a hypothesis, extreme axiarchism is *too* simple to do the job. The second has to do with the problem of evil, which I shall consider in more detail in a later section. The third has to do with the nature of ethics.

(1) We do indeed expect fundamental physical theories to be simple, symmetrical and beautiful. Fortunately our expectations have been satisfied to a great extent, an extent which we had no logical right to expect. Perhaps a simple law might connect with a simple state of the universe at the time it came into existence but with random perturbations and symmetry breaking leading to the complex world that we know. But wouldn't this be an odd way of bringing about value? Would one not expect the axiarchic principle to bring about *directly* a universe of (say) Cartesian immaterial and happy souls? Mind you, the souls would not have all that Leslie and I value. He likes rock climbing and I like bush walking. Souls cannot do these. Whether or not having the illusion of doing these things would do is another matter – there would still be a good deal of indirectness in what comes from the axiarchic principle. In any case the happy souls might have only intellectual pleasures.

(2) Would one expect Leslie's axiarchic principle to bring about a

universe in which *evil* exists? (It is clear that we should understand
the statement of the principle to be glossed as 'the principle that *positive* value comes into existence'.) One of Leslie's replies is that 'it
is no easy matter to bring about ethical requirements in consistent
sets'.[50] This indicates that Leslie's apparently simple concept of God
as an ethical principle must conceal a great deal of complexity. Part of
the complexity might lie in the need for ethical sub-principles saying
what sorts of things have value. Sub-principles may conflict, and then
there must be a trade off. These sub-principles might be propositions
about what means bring about what ends. So Leslie's apparently simple ethical principle does seem to conceal a lot of complexity of the
sort that traditional theologians have associated with God's omniscience. If Leslie's principle corresponded only to God *qua* designer,
then this complexity and perhaps the existence of evil could be put
down to the recalcitrance of the material with which he had to work.
But then there would be a lot that the principle could not explain. Or
does the designer merely work on proto-laws determining only the
values of the fundamental constants that emerge after symmetry breaking? This might conflict with the idea of God as not only designer but
also Creator.

(3) The theory of extreme axiarchism depends on an objectivist
theory about the nature of ethical judgements and speech acts. In the
space available here it will of course be impossible to do proper justice to such theories.[51] First of all we may note theories such as those of
G.E. Moore in his *Principia Ethica*[52] and W.D. Ross in his *Foundations
of Ethics*.[53] According to this sort of theory the mind has an ability to
intuit that things or events that possess certain 'natural' properties or
relations (such as being pleasant or being an instance of truth telling)
also possess 'non-natural' properties or relations (such as goodness
or rightness). Such intuitions would be of synthetic *a priori* truths
about the world, which supervene on purely natural facts. According
to this view ethical judgements would be about objective facts, and
this sort of theory would seem at first sight to be required if we are
to believe in Leslie's axiarchic principle. The Moore–Ross theory fails
to explain the motivating power of ethical belief. Furthermore, the
intellectual intuition of non-natural properties and their relations is
mysterious and incompatible with a neurophysiological account of
the mind. The intuition of goodness or rightness would not be at all
like vision, where we have a theory of photons striking the eye and
thus affecting the nervous system. However Leslie differs from Moore
and Ross because he denies that we intuit or *know* facts about goodness

and rightness. We believe the axiarchic principle because we conjecture it, and part of our conjecture is that it is certainly effective and explains the existence and design of the world. Leslie draws an analogy between ethical and causal requiredness. He holds that the ethical uses of words such as 'must', 'have to', 'are required to', have 'more than punning similarities' to their causal uses. In this way Leslie thinks that his theory of ethics can be objectivist without requiring the postulation of mysterious ethical intuitions. He also thinks that the analogy between ethical and causal requirements overcomes the already mentioned problem for objectivists of the sort of Moore and Ross, that you might intuit that an action is good or right while feeling no motive to do it. So perhaps Leslie's own brand of objectivism about the ethical principle overcomes the main objections to non-naturalistic ethics such as that of Moore and Ross.

Leslie's principle, then, is conjectural, something like a scientific hypothesis, and accepted by argument to the best explanation. But is it the best explanation or even a good explanation? We may accept that there is some analogy between the 'must' of ethics and the 'must' of causal law statements, but there is much disanalogy too. It is notorious that 'ought' does not imply 'is'. If it did the world would be a better place. Leslie would reply that, despite appearances to the contrary, the world is the best that is logically possible granted the value of free will, and in the case of natural evils, granted the fact that 'satisfaction of all ethical requirements simultaneously may well be logically impossible' (ibid., pp. 82–3). He acknowledges that we have no reason to *like* this fact. Seeing a child in pain we need not comfort ourselves with cosy Panglossian optimism. Here of course we are in the midst of theodicy and 'the problem of evil', which I shall discuss in a later section.

Thus the question 'Why is the universe as it is?' (e.g. 'Why the "fine tuning"?') is answered by 'Because it is good that it is'. This is nearer to being an answer to the question 'Why is the universe as it is?' than it is to the question 'Why does anything exist at all?' If the principle is to do the latter job it has antecedently (in a logical, not a temporal sense) to exist itself, and we are back to the 'Who made God?' type of problem. Perhaps it could be said that the axiarchic principle, like God, would be a necessary being. Whatever a principle is, perhaps a *proposition*, the question of whether a proposition is necessary truth must be distinguished from the question of whether the proposition exists. Do we need to postulate propositions? It is already doubtful in what sense the axiarchic principle expresses a necessary truth, and doubtful also whether the existence of such a proposition could itself be necessary. Similar questions will be taken up in the next section, on the cosmological argument for the existence of God, the argument from the contingency of the world.

How could it be that 'It is good that the universe is as it is' *explains* 'The universe is as it is'? The latter statement does not follow from the first, and so there must be a hidden auxiliary premiss. Such a premiss could be 'Because there is an omnipotent being who desires that the world be good'. (On a non-cognitivist theory of ethical language according to which ultimate ethical principles are expressions of desire or attitude the extra premiss would reduce to 'Because there is an omnipotent being who desires that it is as it is'.) Such explanations bring us back to a more familiar type of theism.

Leslie's axiarchism presupposes an objectivist theory of ethics. If one is (as I am with inessential qualifications) some sort of non-cognitivist about ethical language, so that ultimate ethical principles are the expressions of an overriding attitude, then of course extreme axiarchism falls to the ground. So also with some contemporary objectivist theories according to which ultimate ethical properties are natural ones, though they are, as David Wiggins put it, 'lit up' by our emotive attitudes.[54] Certainly our innate attitudes may lead us to notice certain natural properties or combinations of properties. Thus it may perhaps be (I do not know whether it is) that we are innately programmed to notice snakes. It is, however, true that this sort of predisposition often leads to error, as when we take a stick or piece of rope to be a snake. In any case it seems to me that such a theory of ethics has at least some of the difficulties of both naturalism and emotivism. I doubt whether there is *any* plausible theory of ethics that will support Leslie's extreme axiarchism. For example, ethical subjectivism clearly will not do, nor does a theory based on what an impartial spectator would feel, or perhaps a view that the correct ethical principles are those on which impartial spectators would converge in attitude if they knew enough facts. (I myself am sceptical of the possibility of such convergence – consider the lack of rapport between, say, utilitarians and Kantian 'respect for persons' moralists.)

In any case it seems to me that considerations of sociobiology and of anthropology suggest the plausibility of some sort of subjectivist or non-cognitivist theory of the nature of ethics. There does seem to be a genetic basis for a limited altruism. There must be cultural influences too, and cultures also undergo a sort of natural selection which would favour a limited altruism. For example, tribes of people who looked after one another would do well against less altruistic ones. In addition we must not forget the activities of moral reformers with wider sympathies and universalistic bent who push ethics further into what Peter Singer has called 'the expanding circle'.[55] This anthropological and sociobiological way of looking at ethics seems to remove its transcendent appearance and makes less plausible the idea of a creative ethical principle at the back of the universe. Still Leslie's hypothesis cannot altogether be ruled out by these considerations, and I shall have another (brief) look at it at the end of the next section. There the prime focus will not be on design ('Why is the universe as it is?') but on existence ('Why is there anything at all?').

8 The Argument from Contingency

Why, then, is there anything at all? After all, a null universe is the simplest hypothesis. Of course there is a pragmatic paradox in so far as we assert or even entertain the null hypothesis. We must exist in order to assert or entertain the hypothesis and the proposition that the universe is null has to exist in order to be asserted or entertained. Nevertheless the paradox is pragmatic only, and logic does not rule out the empty universe, except for a technicality. In classical first order logic the valid schemata are defined as those that come out true in any non-empty universe. This is for technical convenience, and testing for validity in the empty universe can be done separately, easily and mechanically.[56]

Given that the null universe would be the simplest possible, is it not a matter for great awe that there is anything at all, let alone our vast and complex universe? Despite the fact that I am repelled by Heidegger's style of philosophical writing, there is nevertheless one respect in which I have a sneaking fellow feeling with him. This is his propensity to ask why there is anything at all.[57] Wittgenstein also experienced this amazement that anything should exist at all.[58] In his *Tractatus*[59] he said, 'It is not *how* things are in the world that is mystical, but *that* it exists' (6.44). Admittedly Wittgenstein seems to contradict himself in his next proposition 6.45 where he talks of the mystical as seeing the world as a limited whole, which is surely a matter of *how* it is, rather than *that* it is. No doubt there are grades of mysticality!

One way in which the question 'Why is there anything at all?' is quintessentially mystical is that it apparently has no possibility of an answer. Whatever answered it would have to be something in the world, or else something other than the world, and the question would just reappear over the existence of that other entity. However, we must not go too fast in ruling out all possibility of an answer. Some have sought the answer in the concept of a being whose existence is *necessary*. I shall conclude that indeed no answer on these lines is satisfactory, but nevertheless it is far from my purpose to dissuade anyone, including myself, from asking the unanswerable question. I do think that there is something ultimately mysterious in the fact that the universe exists at all, and that there is something wrong with us if we do not feel this mystery.

As I have just hinted, there has of course been a traditional theistic answer to the question. This is that the universe exists because God created it. The trouble here is that 'universe' must be taken to mean something less than 'everything that there is' (including Carter's many universes, supposing that they exist). There is still the question of God's existence. The usual theistic answer is that God *necessarily* exists, and so there is no need for explanation of his existence. A necessary being is one which just *has* to exist. Or, to put the matter more perspicuously, to say that God necessarily exists is to say that the proposition 'God exists' is a necessary truth.

The Ontological Argument

In this connection it will be instructive to have a quick look at the so-called 'Ontological Argument' for the existence of God, put forward in slightly different forms by Anselm and Descartes. A careful and scholarly discussion of Anselm's and Descartes' forms of the ontological argument may be found in Jonathan Barnes's book *The Ontological Argument*,[60] but here I shall confine myself to what I consider to be the bare bones of the argument. Anselm and Descartes both thought of God as a being no greater than which can be conceived, i.e. a being with all possible perfections. They then thought that existence was itself a perfection, that an existent God is more perfect than a non-existent one, and thence, they thought, it is absurd to deny that God exists. We cannot, that is, have a consistent conception of a non-existent God.

Is 'God' a proper name? Bertrand Russell would have said that it is a description, i.e. equivalent to something such as 'the omnipotent, omniscient and benevolent being'. More exactly, 'God exists' would come out 'There is an x such that for any y, y is an OOB if and only if x is identical with y', or in symbols '$(\exists x)\,(y)\,(OOBy \equiv x = y)$'. The symbols are in fact clearer than the ordinary language version, because of the 'there is an x' which is *not* like 'there is a lion' or 'lion x': 'x' is a variable, whose use is for cross reference, not a predicate. But for the need for cross reference we could just have said 'something'. Thus we could say 'something runs' instead of '$(\exists x)$ runs x'.

The '*is*' in 'God is wise' signifies neither existence nor identity. It is a grammatical quirk, and we can mimic logical notation by writing 'God is wise' as 'Wise (God)'. On the other hand, 'God exists' comes out as '$(\exists x)$ God x'. While we must treat 'God' as a name in 'Wise (God)' we must treat it as a predicate in '$(\exists x)$ God x'. (E.g. '$(\exists x)$ omnipotent x. omniscient x. benevolent x.') The difficulty is clear. In formal logic when names are allowed we can deduce '$(\exists x)Fx$' from 'Fa' where 'a' is a name. The assumption is that names always name something.

We can hardly deduce '$(\exists x)$ strong x' from 'Zeus is strong' because 'Zeus' names nothing. (We could deduce 'someone smokes a pipe' from 'Sherlock Holmes smokes a pipe' but that is within the context of fiction, in which there is a pretence on the part of Conan Doyle and his readers that 'Sherlock Holmes' does successfully name something.) If we are in doubt whether or not God exists we should treat the word 'God' as a predicate, as in 'the one and only x such that x gods'. (To god might be to be omnipotent, omniscient and benevolent.[61])

It is true that we could use a non-standard logic such that names such as 'Zeus' are allowed. In such a logic 'exists' could occur as a predicate. In such a logic quantification ('for all x' and 'there is an x') would be what is called 'substitutional'. According to this '$(\exists x)Fx$' is true if for some name 'a' the sentence 'Fa' is true. Here there is no commitment to existence since 'a' might be, say, 'Sherlock Holmes'. Contrast the (standard) 'objectual' quantification, where '$(\exists x)Fx$' is true only if 'Fx' is true of (or 'satisfied by') something. The usual objection to substitutional quantification is that we get into trouble with 'all rabbits' or 'some rabbits' since we do not have names for all the rabbits. (And if we replace 'rabbits' by 'real numbers' it is even worse, since it is mathematically impossible to have names for all real numbers. It is impossible for finite sequences of symbols to be in one–one correlation with the real numbers.)

It should be noted that in logic '$(\exists x)$' or 'there is a' must be understood as tenseless. We could also take 'exists' as tenseless, too, and replace some such idiom as 'The old town hall no longer exists' by 'The old town hall exists (tenseless) earlier than now'. We put tenses into the predicate and keep 'There is a' as tenseless. In what follows I shall use 'exists' as tenseless.

Still, allowing substitutional quantification, we could deal easily with such a sentence as (to use an example of Jonathan Barnes's) '($\exists x$) (Socrates vowed a cock to x') which is true (substitutionally) because it comes out true when 'Asclepius' is substituted for 'x'.[62] (In standard logic, with objectual quantification, we would deal with the case differently, as perhaps 'Socrates vowed-true of himself "gives a cock to Asclepius"'. Here there is no reference to Asclepius, only the name 'Asclepius', as the quotation marks indicate.)

If we allow substitutional quantification 'exists' could be a predicate in 'God exists'. Even then the ontological argument does not work. We might have the concept of a perfect being, and include 'exists', understood substitutionally, as a predicate contributing to this concept. Nevertheless there would still be the question of whether this concept is true of or applies to anything. Note that 'applies to anything' brings us back to objectual quantification. The ontological argument thus understood is circular and assumes what it sets out to prove.

Barnes tries to show that 'there is a' and 'exist' are not equivalent. Some of his examples involve intensional contexts, as with 'The agents he named under torture were found not to exist'. There are special problems here. I would point out that there weren't any agents that he named, and so 'he named' is not like 'he kicked'. If he kicked any agents there were agents who were kicked. I think that by going metalinguistic one can probably bend these intensional contents into extensional ones, much as one can 'he desired a unicorn' which can be bent into the form 'he desired-true of himself "possesses a unicorn"'.[63]

The upshot of all these considerations is that the ontological argument for the existence of God does not work, which is as much as to say that there is no logical contradiction in denying that God exists. If so the argument from contingency cannot be valid if it is construed as arguing for the existence of a *logically* necessary being.

Not only is the ontological argument invalid, but if its contention that there is a logical contradiction in denying the existence of God were true then the assertion of the existence of God would be trivial. Thus 'p v not-p' tells us nothing about the world and '($\exists x$)Fx v ~($\exists x$)Fx' only that something exists, which we know already.

The Cosmological Argument

We need some suitable sense of 'necessary' other than that of logical necessity, and we need a meaty premiss. The premiss of the argument from the contingency of the world (often called the cosmological argument) is that something exists and that it might not have existed. Now if the argument were a purely deductive one it would obviously be fallacious. The premiss by itself has no interesting logical consequences, certainly no consequences that an atheist cannot consistently accept. However, the argument seems to me best seen as what has come to be called 'argument to the best explanation'. Argument to the best explanation has come to be seen by many philosophers as the fundamental type of inductive argument in science, history and common sense.[64] For example, a detective will make several possible hypotheses about who is the murderer, and will choose the one which gives the best explanation of the footprint in the rose bed, the open window, the unusual demeanour of the butler and so on. The argument from contingency depends on the idea that the best explanation of the existence of contingent beings is the existence of a necessary being. In fact it is held to be the only ultimately satisfactory explanation. The argument was put forward by Thomas Aquinas as the third of his 'Five Ways'.[65] In recent times the argument has been very well put by F.C. Copleston in a discussion with Bertrand Russell.[66] It is the argument most relied upon by modern Thomists.

Copleston reminds us that there are in the world contingent beings. Hence the universe must have a reason for its existence that is external to it. If this thing is itself contingent, the reason for *its* existence would have to be outside *it* also. If we proceed in an infinite regress in this way we are left with an infinity of things which in aggregate still does not contain the reason for its existence. Hence, Copleston argues, the explanation for the existence of the universe must lie in some being 'which contains within itself the reason for its own existence', which *necessarily* exists.

Russell thinks that it is legitimate to ask why any particular event occurs by giving its cause, and so on back indefinitely, but that it is illegitimate to ask for an explanation of the whole infinite chain. This would indeed be so if all explanations had to be in terms of cause and effect, but Copleston reasonably asks why it is illegitimate to ask for an explanation of the whole chain. Such an explanation cannot be causal, but why should all explanations be causal? Could the existence of the universe as a space–time whole be explained by an atemporal necessary being not itself in space or time?

A theologian, such as Aquinas at his best, need not be worried about whether there was a first moment of time, at which God created the universe just before the cosmic 'big bang'. The universe might be finite in earlier time (as cosmologists believe) and yet have no first moment. Time might be like the set of real numbers greater than zero, of which there is no first number, or even like the positive fractions ... $\frac{1}{32}$, $\frac{1}{16}$, $\frac{1}{8}$, $\frac{1}{4}$, $\frac{1}{2}$, 1, 2, ... Of course cosmologists believe that in fact there is a much more sophisticated story to be told about time, or rather space–time. The illustration is simply to show how time could be finite towards the past, and yet there could be no first moment. In the sort of model of the tiny compressed space–time with which the universe began (less than 10^{-33} cm radius) that James Hartle and Stephen Hawking have produced, time-like world lines get bent into space-like directions, and even if each *did* have a first moment there would be no unique such. In any case ordinary notions of space–time break down within such a singularity. Hawking has suggested that these considerations suggest that we do not need belief in a creator God.[67] Aquinas would have had an answer to this. Even if there were no first cause in a *temporal* sense, we would still want to seek an atemporal explanation of the whole *universe*, past and future, which would be in terms of an eternal God outside space and time.

Aquinas could have given a similar retort to the idea that the universe could have come into existence through a quantum fluctuation. The idea is now quite common, and there is talk of our universe spawning baby universes outside our own space–time, perhaps from 'black holes'. However, the idea was put forward earlier in a simple way by Edward P. Tryon.[68] According to Heisenberg's uncertainty principle the energy and time of a system cannot both be determinate. If ΔE is the uncertainty of the energy and Δt is the uncertainty of the time, $\Delta E \cdot \Delta t$ is of the order of magnitude of Planck's constant h and if energy is determinate t is infinitely indeterminate. So if the energy is zero or near zero an infinite or a long-lived universe could have arisen. This could happen if the mass energy (which is positive) and the gravitational energy (which is negative) wholly or nearly cancel out, thus accounting for the coming into being of our universe from nothing at all. Tryon's idea is a very pretty one, but it does not answer the philosophical question 'Why should there be anything at all?' It assumes a structured space–time and the quantum field and also laws of nature (whatever these are). (For example, if laws of nature are regularities there must be the cosmos to exhibit the regularities.) Tryon's idea has evidently been developed in more sophisticated ways, but it seems to me that in much the same way they do not answer the philosophical question, nor come to grips with the idea of whether there must be an atemporal 'cause' for the whole caboodle of a space–time universe.

Are there Suitable Senses of 'a Necessary Being'?

So we are back to our question about whether the explanation of the existence of contingent beings could be, as Aquinas, Copleston and other theologians have thought, a necessary being. Is there a suitable sense of 'necessary'?

One suggestion is that God might be necessary in the sense of not being dependent on anything else for his existence. But then the atheist might say that the universe itself will fill this bill. On the atheist view the universe has nothing beyond itself and so cannot be dependent on anything else.[69] Moreover, if God is a necessary being only in this sense, his existence is no less contingent than is that of the universe as the atheist conceives it. So if this is the sense of 'necessary' in the argument from contingency of the world the argument must be a bad one.

Another suggestion is that 'God exists' might have the sort of necessity that 'There is a prime number between 20 and 24' has. This does *seem* to be a clear case of a necessary yet existential proposition. I think that this analogy between the necessary existence of numbers and that which it is supposed God has is the most promising avenue for the theist to pursue, and yet I can see that there may be problems with it. One problem is to get a grasp of the 'necessary' here. We have logical necessity, which is consistency in first order logic. Then there is physical necessity which includes also consistency with the laws of nature and perhaps also boundary conditions from cosmology. There is legal necessity, consistency with obeying the laws of the land. And so on. My own view, following Quine,[70] is that these forms of necessity, as well as many more mundane uses of 'necessary' or 'possible' or cognate words such as 'must', can be elucidated in a contextual way – as consistency in the sense of first order logic with contextually agreed background assumptions. (Those who believe in so-called 'analytic propositions' can throw them in with the background assumptions.)

Thus we say 'David must have arrived by now' when we can deduce his arrival from background knowledge of his desire to come, the length of the road, the speed of his car, and so on. This seems to account for ordinary language uses of 'must', 'necessary', 'possibly', etc. Modality is explained metalinguistically, nor do we need to go far up in the hierarchy of language, metalanguage, meta-metalanguage, etc. How often do we in real life iterate modalities or 'quantify into' modal contexts in the manner of modal logicians? I do not want to postulate possible worlds other than the actual world in the manner of David Lewis. This proliferation of possible worlds makes Carter's 'many universes' hypothesis look parsimonious by comparison. What Lewis calls 'ersatz possible worlds' are not so bad: I talk of them just as a way of referring to the contextually agreed background assumptions. The definition (some pages back) of logical necessity in terms of inter-pretability in any non-empty universe is not in conflict with my atti-tude here, because for this purpose universes can be defined in the universe of natural numbers, which we can take to be actual and not merely possible. (This is because of the Löwenheim–Skolem theorem.)

Now perhaps we can account for the sort of necessity that we feel about 'There is a prime number between 20 and 24'. The proposition is agreed to follow from unquestioned arithmetical laws, probably not Peano's axioms themselves, since most who believe that there is a prime number between 20 and 24 will not have heard of Peano's axioms. The axioms, Peano's or otherwise, may be regarded as nec-essary because they are so central to our system of beliefs, and anyway each is trivially deducible from itself. They are not definitions, but come rather near to being definitional.

At any rate, the suggestion of mathematical necessity may give some justifiable comfort to the theist. How far this is the case depends on our philosophy of mathematics. It seems to me that there are about five fairly plausible yet not wholly satisfactory philosophies of math-ematics in the field at present, and how we answer the point about necessary existence in mathematics will depend on which of these contending philosophies we accept or think of as the least improbable. Let us take a very brief look at these options. I shall in fact begin with what I regard as *not* an option but which has been very influential in the recent past.

Some Philosophies of Mathematics and their Bearing on Theism

Should we say, with Wittgenstein in his *Tractatus*, that the appar-ent necessity of mathematics arises from the fact (or supposed fact) that all mathematical propositions say the same thing, namely nothing? This would be a way in which mathematics seems to be removed from the chances and contingencies of the world, but it would not help the theist, because to say that God's existence was necessary in this sense would be to say that the assertion that God existed would be completely empty. In the present context I could leave the matter here, since this philosophy of mathematics does not help the theist's search for insight into the way in which God might be said to be a necessary being. However Quine has given reasons why the attempt to exhibit set theory (and hence mathematics) as logic should be rejected.[71] (1) Set theory, unlike propositional logic and first order predicate logic, is *incomplete*. No set of axioms will imply all its truths, though of course any truth will be implied by some set of axioms. Truth in mathematics cannot be identified with provability, still less with provability from some set of definitions or conventions. (2) Set theory, unlike logic, has a constant predicate 'is a member of'. (Logic normally includes the identity predicate, but this is a curious one and can be eliminated if we have a finite primitive vocabulary, which could if we liked include all the predicates in the *Oxford English Dictionary*.) (3) Set theory is Platonistic. There are assertions in it of the existence of sets (and so of numbers), which are not particular objects in space or time. These considerations all make the break between logic and set theory in the same place and answer Bertrand Russell's challenge to say where logic ends and mathematics begins.

The failure of logicism in mathematics should be congenial to the theist, in that the supposed necessity of existential statements in mathematics lives to fight another day as a candidate for shedding light on what God's necessary existence might be like. It should be welcomed by pure mathematicians who would not like to think that their life's work was concocting more and more recondite ways of saying nothing.

I now pass on briefly to some philosophies of mathematics which do seem to be the most plausible, even if not completely satisfying, and see how they might bear on the nature of God's necessary existence.

Quite attractive is Quine's form of Platonism. His Platonic objects are sets. In line with the pioneering work of Frege and of Whitehead and Russell he holds that set theoretical entities can do duty for all the entities postulated in classical mathematics. He points out that a physical theory contains mathematics and empirical physics seemingly inextricably intertwined with mathematics. Since theories are tested holistically, if we believe physics we must believe the mathematics needed for it. (Quine concedes that some pure mathematics may go beyond what is quite needed. This is especially true, of course, of the more esoteric reaches of set theory. This can be seen as 'rounding out' and might even be justified ontologically on the score of a sort of simplicity.) Thus we believe in mathematical objects by the ordinary hypothetico-deductive method of science: we believe in the entities postulated by the theory that is best explanatory of observations. Thus Quine's Platonism does not require talk of mysterious powers of direct intuition of Platonic objects. (I see no reason why sophisticated robots might not apply the hypothetico-deductive method.) Quine's Platonism is thus not in conflict with modern mechanistic biology as traditional Platonism seems to be. It is possible that if the world (including space–time) had a discrete grain we could get by without the real numbers and with difference equations instead of differential equations. Thus there is *some* empirical constraint on the mathematics we need to postulate. Nevertheless because of the slack between hypothesis and observation mathematics is very much immune to revision, and this may give it a sort of necessity. However this necessity would be epistemological, not ontological.

It should be conceded that the more traditional form of mathematical Platonism, according to which the mind has direct intuitive contact with the mathematical entities, is congenial to many mathematicians.[72] Roger Penrose has indeed used this supposed feature of mathematics to argue towards a new view of mentality and of how the brain works.[73] Diffidently, because Penrose after all is an eminent cosmologist and the son of a great neurobiologist, I go the other way. If Penrose's view is accepted it could give some comfort for the theist. It is just conceivable that the brain may need for its full understanding recondite quantum mechanical principles, such as of non-locality, but it seems to me that since neurons operate mainly electrochemically the brain is probably more like a computer or connection machine. Even with the recondite principles it is hard to be convinced that intuition of Platonic entities is possible for it.

Another philosophy of mathematics that is a leading contender in the field is the fictionalism of Hartry Field.[74] He holds that mathematics is a fiction: all its existential statements are false. The universal ones are true but vacuously so, since 'everything is such that' in this case is equivalent to 'it is not the case that something is not such that'. According to Field mathematics merely *facilitates* scientific inferences which could be carried out in a more complicated way nominalistically. (He makes use of space–time points of which there are as many as there are real numbers.) To show this in detail he needs to reconstruct physical theories nominalistically and has done so for certain theories.

Field's fictionalism would hardly appeal to the pure mathematician, who would not like to think of himself or herself as a sort of Dickens or Thackeray. (Or worse, since in novels there are many existential sentences which are not only pretended to be true but which are true!) Still, that's not an argument. Field's theory is ontologically parsimonious and is in that way appealing. It is a no nonsense sort of theory. One worry about really believing set theory, I think, is the fact that the set membership relation between a set and its members is *too* intimate: there is something mysterious about it.

If Field's theory is accepted we must say that there are no true existential mathematical sentences, and *a fortiori* no necessary ones. So Field's theory does not help in the theist's possible hope that mathematical necessity throws some light on what God's necessary existence might be like.

One philosopher who has strongly felt the mysteriousness of the set membership relation is David Lewis, who in his *Parts of Classes*[75] treats the relation of set to subset as the whole/part relation. (Classically, of course, this is done by defining *subset* in terms of set membership.) However the notion of set membership still obtrudes in one place, the singleton relation, the relation of a thing to the set of which it is the only member. In an appendix with John P. Burgess and A.P. Hazen (explaining two methods due to these logicians) he gets over this problem but at a certain cost of empirical assumption as to what is in the universe, and also of structuralism, where one talks indifferently about many different subject matters. He also needs plural quantification, which is familiar in ordinary language as in 'some critics admire only one another'. This sentence cannot be rendered into first order predicate logic without talking of sets of critics. George Boolos[76] gives the semantics in terms of second order logic, but Lewis cannot take this option because he is trying to replace set theory and he thinks of second order logic as 'set theory in sheep's clothing', as Quine has put it. (One trouble I have with structuralism is that I can think of a structure only in set theoretic terms.) Lewis's theory may be the philosophy of mathematics of the future, but because of its reliance (especially in the Appendix) on some general empirical assumptions about the world it does not provide the sort of sense of 'necessity' which might help the theist.

Properties may seem less mysterious than sets, because physicists postulate properties of mass, length, charge, spin, charm, colour (these words not to be taken in their ordinary sense!) and so on. We might take 'this has a mass of 2 kg' as expressing a relation between this, the standard kilogram, the property mass, and the number 2. Note that they are not the bad old properties to which Quine has objected, as if using the predicate 'tall' committed one to the property 'tallness'. No, they do not come from a bad philosophy of language and meaning, but from what science tells us. I am myself inclined only to believe in those properties which fundamental physics and cosmology need to postulate. This sort of scientific realism about universals was pioneered in Australia by D.M. Armstrong[77] and has led to various ideas in the philosophy of mathematics, as by Peter Forrest and Armstrong[78] (who have their differences) and most notably by John Bigelow in his book *The Reality of Number: A Physicalist's Philosophy of Mathematics*,[79] which needs to be taken very seriously. There are differences: Bigelow and Forrest believe in uninstantiated universals, Armstrong only in instantiated ones. But because of the empirical basis of these theories, it once again does not give any help to the theist in the search for some analogue of God's necessity in that of mathematical existence.

Probably, therefore, the theist's best bet might after all be to try to defend the old fashioned form of mathematical Platonism, with its direct intuitions of a super-sensible reality (universals), which exist eternally and in some sense necessarily. If this sense of 'necessarily' could be made intelligible then God might be said to exist necessarily in this sense. We are led into obscurities and it is, as I have said, hard to fit Platonic intuitions into modern epistemology and neurobiology.

When all is said, however, it might be best for the theist to say simply 'God exists necessarily' in the way that the number 23 does. Would this be a sort of polytheism with many necessary beings? Or would 23 be somehow *part* of God? I leave this question to theologians. The atheist will feel well relieved of these intractable problems.

Eternity and Sempiternity

In discussing the cosmological argument I took it that Aquinas was at his best in thinking of God as eternal, in the sense of not being in time at all. In this way the existence of God would be said to explain the existence of the whole space–time world (as we think of it) without being an efficient cause at the first moment of the universe's existence, a concept which has no clear sense in modern cosmology. As I noted, the universe can have a finite past and yet have no unique first moment. Furthermore there is no unitary time. The special theory of relativity tells us that there is no preferred set of axes in Minkowski space. Still, perhaps a preferred set could be got by going outside the theory, e.g. in preferring space–time axes with respect to which the cosmic background radiation is equal in all directions. Even so, because of the expansion of the universe, these local times would lie in different space–time directions from galaxy to galaxy. Also time-like world lines get bent up in black holes (as at the beginning of the universe) and black holes may possibly spawn baby universes with their own different space–times. We should therefore be cautious about talking of God as in time, sempiternal not eternal. In *what* time would a sempiternal God be sempiternal in? These considerations reinforce, in my mind at least, the interpretation of God's eternity as atemporal rather than sempiternal. In what follows I shall use 'eternal' in this atemporal sense and shall contrast eternity with sempiternity.

William and Martha Kneale have explored the issue of eternity versus sempiternity in two scholarly and instructive papers.[80] They bring out the tensions in Aquinas's thought. On the one hand Aquinas had a classically inspired preference for the 'eternal' conception of God, which William Kneale traces back to Parmenides and Plato, but *not* to Aristotle, who was on the 'sempiternal' side. Kneale suggests that the 'eternal' conception was naturalized in Christian theology through Boethius. According to this conception God is outside time altogether. On the other hand there is talk of God as a living being and as performing actions. This suggests sempiternity. My difficulties about the notion of sempiternity make me wish to advise the theologian (I hope *without* being a devil's advocate) to go the 'eternity' way. How would an eternal being act on the world? Perhaps in this way: a certain relation between the atemporal God and a temporal act (say someone's prayer) is correlated with another relation, say between the atemporal God and a temporal state of grace or whatever. Some such answer might be given as to how John Leslie's axiarchic principle could act on the world or bring it into existence. There would be some sort of relation between an atemporal thing (as I conceive that an axiarchic principle, proposition or rule must be) and a space–time universe. One other problem with Leslie's idea of an axiarchic principle actually bringing the world into existence is analogous to those brought up a few pages back. This is that we can ask what explains the existence of the axiarchic principle. Leslie holds that the axiarchic principle is a necessary proposition, but need the existence of a necessary proposition itself be necessary? Perhaps it is if the existence of universals is necessary, but I have noted that this is at least controversial.

Once more the atheist may feel grateful for being excused from such conundrums, fascinating intellectual problems though they are.

9 The Argument from Religious Experience

With the argument from contingency philosophers and theologians
were endeavouring to argue for a creator God, not merely a finite 'big
brother' God. The latter would merely be a higher part of the universe
though not immediately observable, which we can assist in the fight
against evil.[81] The same might be said about the argument to design,
even though strictly speaking this argues only for a designer who
works on already existing material. Those who argue from religious
experience could be arguing for the creator and designer God of the
great monotheistic religions, though some might be arguing only for a
'big brother' God. Let us examine the argument.

The argument is that since many persons report that they have
experiences as of acquaintance with God this raises the probability
that God exists. Religious people usually talk of 'certainty', not of probability. This claim to certainty would not necessarily be conceded by
an inquiring person who heard the reports. Such a person would be
pleased with a mere raising of probability. However, William James
considered the question of whether a believer's religious experience
could give a good reason for his or her own religious beliefs, even
though this reason is not interpersonally persuasive. The believer
may think that these experiences enable him or her to cope better with
the problems of life, and perhaps become a better person. The idea
that this may constitute an intellectually respectable *reason* for belief
is connected with James's pragmatism, which assimilates the notion
of truth to that of the useful or what works. I do not think that it is
necessary nowadays to take up space in refuting this confused notion
of truth. This is not, however, to say that we can totally ignore pragmatic considerations, as in the well-known matter of Pascal's Wager,
which I shall consider shortly.

When people talk of religious 'experience', the word 'experience'
tends to be somewhat protean in meaning. In the first place, they
may be claiming that they have something like perception. However,
there are clearly no special religious sensations as there are visual,
auditory and tactual sensations. Nor do they correlate with interpersonally perceptible situations, as visual, auditory and tactual sensations
do. Furthermore, in the last century or two there has come to be increas-
ing physical and neurophysiological knowledge of how perception
works. There is nothing like this in the case of religious experience,
at least if this is thought of as a sort of spiritual perception. Do spiritual

photons come from God to some neurophysiological organ? Perhaps this is an unfair question. God might be everywhere, even in the synapses of the brain, and in the previous section I have played with a notion of how an external (atemporal) being might be said to act on the world. Still, there does remain some difficulty in seeing sense perception as a fit model for the notion of religious experience.

Experience of God has sometimes been described as the feeling that there is a 'presence'. This feeling is not connected with a special perceptual sensation. Thus two explorers in the wilderness may say to one another that they feel that there is someone nearby whom they cannot see. In fact they know that no other explorer or native of the region is nearby. Nevertheless, I suppose, the feeling can be strong and shared interpersonally. A psychologist would put it down to an illusion brought on by loneliness and privation. Similarly a vague feeling of a Presence, such as some mystics have reported, need not be taken as veridical. If a person of mystical bent does take it as veridical, a sceptic need not accept the mystic's claim. The principle of theoretical economy favours the sceptic's explanation in terms of some sort of illusion. Not that the sceptic will convince the mystic. At the beginning of this essay I put forward scientific plausibility as a guide in metaphysics and the mystic will refuse to go all the way with this guide. There is thus likely to be deadlock here. At any rate I think that the sceptic can say this, that religious experience provides no *objective* warrant for religious belief unless the possibility of a naturalistic explanation of the experience can be ruled out as implausible, and it is hard to see how this requirement could be met.

There are all sorts of possible explanations of the numinous. Here is an example. I love the hills. Hills at the top of a glen can look a bit like huge crouching animals, and this may make us feel towards them as one would towards conscious beings, even though we know that they are solid rock and have no personality whatever. With this 'as if' feeling there can be one that I am inclined to describe as numinous. It presumably arises from some neurological harmoniousness that comes from the fact that the structure of our brains is largely that of our early prehistoric ancestors and so is adapted to surrounds of wilderness, or something like wilderness (even though the hills had been cleared for sheep). I do not put this forward as a serious piece of psychology, as a good explanation for the sort of case that I have in mind. I am neither a psychologist nor an anthropologist. It obviously will not do as a general explanation, since many mystics have hardly been hill persons or lovers of wilderness. I put it forward as a suggestion that naturalistic explanations of mystical experiences need not be too hard to come by. I do not want to decry the experiences: the experiences can certainly be valued, and as I said in an earlier section, contemplation of the laws of nature can certainly induce religious *emotions*, and these should be prized. As a philosopher I often wonder what it would be like to spend all one's life on practical and human-centred concerns, such as politics, economics, town planning, and all sorts of business, administrative and managerial activities, with no time and leisure to indulge the philosophic and scientific impulse to contemplate the universe at large. It is fortunate indeed that most people do not have this impulse, for they are the people who make the world go round. In hospital I do not want too dreamily philosophical a nurse or physician. One of the virtues of organized religion is that whether it is true or false it does to a certain extent cater for the speculative and even to some extent cosmic impulses in a wide section of the population, despite a certain anthropocentricity in some features of some of the world's religions.

Religious experience does of course often take specific forms depending on particular religions or cultural circumstances. Catholic peasants may report an encounter with the Virgin Mary, whereas Muslims, Jews or Buddhists would hardly do so. Again particular circumstances may have something to do with it, as in the case of Paul on the road to Damascus, feeling turmoil and guilt about his previous activities of persecuting Christians, seeing a great light and seeming to hear the voice of a risen Jesus. (Acts xii, 3–19; xxii, 6–21; xxvi, 12–18. In the first of these passages Paul's companions are said to hear the voice, but not in the second. Perhaps the light could have been an unusual light in the atmosphere. A sceptic would have to take the companions having heard the voice too as an embellishment of the story in later years, or of the companions' recollection soon afterwards.) Joan of Arc heard voices, and some have put this down to tuberculosis affecting her brain. The point is not that these explanations are indeed the correct ones: it is that someone who has naturalistic preconceptions will always in fact find some naturalistic explanation more plausible than a supernatural one. The words 'in fact' in the previous sentence are important. I am talking about the world as I believe it is. Suppose that I woke up in the night and saw the stars arranged in shapes that spelt out the Apostles' Creed. I would know that astronomically it is impossible that stars should have so changed their positions. I don't know what I would think. Perhaps I would think that I was dreaming or that I had gone mad. What if everyone else seemed to me to be telling me that the same thing had happened? Then I might not only think that I had gone mad – I would probably *go* mad. Well established astronomical knowledge is not so easily abandoned. Of course I am here trespassing over the border between the discussion of religious experience and that of miracles. The topics clearly overlap and I shall return to the discussion of miracles in a later section.

Sometimes religious experience can consist of a sudden feeling of certitude, peace, joy, fear, the presence of God. A good example can be seen in Blaise Pascal's report of his own conversion experience.[82] Such a report can be very impressive, though there is no valid inference from the fact that the thoughts are had to the proposition that God in fact exists. To *feel* certain need not be to *be* certain. The converted person believes that the thoughts have a supernatural cause, but the naturalist will prefer some naturalistic explanation in terms of the psychological history of the person in question.

The word 'experience' can have a less 'inner' or 'subjective' connotation, as when a person is said to have had 'experience of life', 'military experience', even, as we read in job advertisements, 'experience in marketing'. In this sense a monk (for example) certainly has religious experience, but he need not have any specifically religious experiences. In this connection we should consider the question of whether a person's religiously motivated life, say as a Christian, is evidential value for others. The person's religious beliefs may be a source of many excellent traits of character and of motivation to beneficial and effective action. This may be so, but it does not bear on the truth of the beliefs. There are also good and admirable persons who profess mutually incompatible religions and (more importantly) no religion at all. Scepticism helped David Hume to be *le bon David*. More to the point, there have been self-sacrificing atheist saints. Waiving this point, I must insist that it is important to distinguish between the question of whether a belief is true and the question of whether it is useful to have it.

It could be that the religious experience of a person, in the sense of 'experience' appropriate to the above mentioned example of the monk or that of 'military experience', might be undertaken precisely *in order to induce religious belief*. This is the course advocated by Pascal, in his notion of a wager. Pascal's Wager will be discussed in the next section. The argument of the wager purports to prove that one should by a sort of brain washing, going to masses, using holy water, and so on, induce belief in the Catholic religion. Pascal, as already a believer, would probably disapprove of the term 'brainwashing'. It is not clear whether he would regard the acquisition of belief after immersing oneself in Catholic practices as explicable naturalistically. He might have held that these practices somehow attract the grace of God. To the sceptic of course the whole thing must initially appear as a sort of brainwashing. Such psychological mechanisms are indeed possible. One might cultivate the company of conservatively religious persons, avoid reading books such as Bertrand Russell's *Why I am not a Christian*,[83] and confine one's philosophical reading to St Thomas Aquinas, or better still avoid philosophical reading altogether and stick to electronics or pure mathematics, or other theologically neutral subject matter, and to practical activities. Whether it would be rational to submit to such non-rational processes is another matter. To decide this we must wait on our discussion of the wager.

10   Pascal's Wager

Pascal, the important seventeenth-century mathematician and physicist, became an adherent of the austere Jansenist group of Catholics who were rivals of the more worldly Jesuits. Pascal held that the existence of God could not be proved by reason. (Later, the First Vatican Council was to condemn this opinion as a heresy.) He implicitly conflated belief in God with belief in the Catholic religion, including its doctrine about bliss in heaven and infinite torment in hell. So for him the only two 'living options', as William James called them,[84] were Catholicism on the one hand and atheism on the other hand. For example, he would not think of Islam and a Muslim would not think of Catholicism. Moreover, there are other options, though not ones that Pascal would have considered. Nevertheless in evaluating Pascal's argument we must consider other options.

Still, let us for the moment pretend that Pascal's two options are the only ones and follow his argument which can be put simply as follows. Pascal argued that Catholicism has a non-zero probability. He concedes that it is possible that one might have many pleasures in our earthly life which would be lost to us if we embraced a strict religious life. However Pascal points out that such happiness could only be finite. Even the smallest finite probability of infinite torment in hell would outweigh it, since it would give an infinitely negative 'expected utility' (to use a present day terminology). The product of an infinite unhappiness with even the smallest non-zero probability of its occurrence will still be infinite. So it is prudent to embrace the religious life.[85]

As I have suggested, one thing wrong with the argument is precisely in the supposition that there are only the two options. Pascal could compare only those options that were live for him, but options might be live for us though not for Pascal. Furthermore Pascal makes the assumption that the only alternative to atheism is Catholicism with its additional doctrines of heaven and hell. These assumptions could be questioned and we could shed doubt on the factual assumptions behind the argument.

One assumption of Pascal's argument is of the existence of an after-life and of the possibility of eternal damnation if we reject the Christian religion, perhaps even just its Catholic version. But maybe it is some other religion that will be rewarded by God. Just as conceivable as Pascal's assumption, as Antony Flew has remarked, is that 'there is a hidden God who will consign all and only Catholics to the fate they so easily approve for others'.[86] (Still it might be judged much less probable than the orthodox belief – if so the argument could perhaps be sound.) Similarly, as William James remarked, there might be a Deity, who took 'particular pleasure in cutting off believers of this pattern [i.e. on the basis of Pascal's Wager] from their infinite reward'.[87]

Modern views about hell fire, even in the Catholic church, though not in some Protestant sects, and certainly in the Church of England whose theology becomes more and more indefinite in other ways as well, have softened considerably. If God is not only omnipotent and omniscient but also benevolent he would surely not consign people to hell fire. Of course the doctrine of hell fire is often regarded as mythical, implying only the pains of guilty feelings and alienation from God. We could raise the question of whether an omnipotent, omniscient and benevolent God would allow even these pains. Furthermore literal belief in an afterlife at all has weakened among many Christians. In evaluating the argument I have set aside these softening considerations. It seems that even on its own terms the argument of Pascal's Wager has the flaw of unconsidered assumptions, and with these assumptions added there is too much indeterminacy with opposing positive and negative infinities to be balanced up.

The argument of Pascal's Wager is an example of a pragmatic argument for belief. The argument is that belief is *useful*, not that it is *true*. Though Pascal's argument is flawed and in any case is stated in terms that do not appeal to the contemporary theological mind, similarly pragmatic arguments suggest themselves. If belief (in God or in some particular religious system in detail) makes us happier, why should we not try to inculcate it into ourselves, if necessary by non-rational means? A friend of mine, an exceptionally admirable philosopher of long-standing positivist bent, said to me that it was a pity to deprive people of their religious beliefs, since these gave them solace, and he said that he himself regretted not being able to share these beliefs. Now consider the case of a hypothetical person Mary who believes that if she continues the study of philosophy she would lead an unhappy life, missing belief in God and perhaps belief in an afterlife. Should she abandon philosophy and confine her studies entirely to (say) electronics or pure mathematics? Mary might feel that there would be something shameful in taking such a course, but it is not easy to see how from a consequentialist and prudential point of view it would not be the right one.

Of course consequentialism is not (and in my opinion ought not to be) purely prudential. It needs to consider not only one's own happiness but that of all sentient creatures. Now Mary might consider that her religious beliefs, solacing though they are for herself, are indirectly harmful. She might point to various consequences of religious belief that she considers harmful. Religious wars might be one of them, overpopulation with the probability of mass starvation, disease and eventual world population collapse, might be another, with religious beliefs making population control hard to bring about. So Mary might think in a consequentalist way that arguing herself out of her religious belief might improve the general happiness even though not her own happiness. Alternatively she might think that knowing the truth is one of her intrinsic values. She might want the truth at all costs, even at that of her own happiness. Let us for the sake of argument suppose that Mary's beliefs about the bad social consequences of religion are false or that the evil effects are outweighed by the good social works undertaken in the name of religion. What about the prudential considerations?

Once again, we might consider that Mary could be wrong about the empirical facts. In my experience arguing oneself out of one's religious beliefs can bring about peace of mind, since one does not need all the time to square one's religious beliefs with continuing developments in cosmology, biology and for that matter philosophy. (Some deny that there is nowadays conflict between science and religion but I have challenged this view on pp. 9–13.) The philosopher and logician Arthur Prior once confirmed to me in conversation that this sort of peace of mind can indeed come from rejection of one's previous theological beliefs.

In his essay 'The Will to Believe' William James expressed a good deal of distaste for Pascal's argument, holding that Pascal's talk of believing by our volition seems 'from one point of view, simply silly' and 'from another point of view it is vile'.[88] Silly because for a Protestant the remedy of masses and holy water would not be a live option, and vile because of its difference from the scientific attitude of testing hypotheses by evidence. Nevertheless, James did think that if we are concerned with a forced option of how to live our lives then the option of faith and a leap in the dark is an appropriate one to take. So despite his reservation about Pascal his own attitude was not really so different. Indeed James held that if we take the leap of faith belief will follow. (Or indeed not so much follow as be there already, given James's largely behaviourist theory of belief.) It may be that James's pragmatism was a source of his view in 'The Will to Believe' since the notion of working in practice in the sense of leading to a worthwhile life could easily have been confused in his mind with verification of a hypothesis by observation. Explicitly, I think, he did distinguish the two things but even within this one essay he was not always a very self-consistent writer, and this makes him hard to interpret. His views are probably not as outrageous as a superficial account of them might suggest. Be that as it may, his 'Will to Believe' does suggest something like the decision to brainwash oneself.

Religious apologists do sometimes defend a leap of faith by saying that science itself depends on a giant leap of faith. They might point out that since Hume raised the philosophical problem of induction it has appeared that we have no reason to believe that the future will be like the past. According to Hume laws of nature are mere regularities whose continuance in the future cannot be justified by reason. Nowadays we might put it by saying that hypotheses are always underdetermined by observation. The apologists could seek a similarity between attempted pragmatic justifications of induction (or scientific method) and the religious pragmatism of William James. These attempt to show that if any method of predicting the future works then induction (the scientific method) works. (Of course science is concerned not only with prediction but with explanation and with theoretical knowledge, and there is a question of whether the pragmatic vindication of induction could be taken beyond vindicating it as a mere prediction device.) There does nevertheless seem to be an important difference. Many people have no difficulty in living without religious belief but no philosophical sceptic about induction could continue to live if he or she really believed this scepticism. The spectacular advances of science, and its applications to technology and to medicine, would seem to me to make impossible a really sincere philosophical scepticism about scientific method. Even fundamentalist Protestant sects in the USA who promulgate a two-thousand-year-old view of the universe do so unblushingly with the aid of modern electronics of radio and television and their medical missionaries make use of the most sophisticated biological techniques of contemporary medicine. The religious leap of faith is therefore a leap additional to that of the scientist, not an *alternative* to it. I conjecture that the sort of religious apologist that I am considering here would have to be an instrumentalist in the philosophy of science, and a realist in theology. It is an uncomfortable position. By contrast an atheist who was a scientific realist need not be an instrumentalist about theological statements: he or she might simply give them the truth value 'false'.

11   Miracles

The discussion in section 9 on the argument from religious experience led on naturally to a brief discussion of Pascal's Wager and James's 'Will to Believe'. It should also lead on to a discussion of miracles, in so far as if one did witness a miracle, this would surely count as having a religious experience. Still if there really are miracles, perception of them would usually be by the usual organs of perception, eyes, ears and so on. So 'experience' here would not refer to a special mode of acquiring knowledge, though the knowledge acquired (if it *was* acquired) would be of something naturalistically inexplicable. Discussion of the reality of miracles, and of if or how we could be assured that a miracle really occurred, usually concerns itself with the reliability of witnesses and this will lead on in section 12 to some remarks on the New Testament.

One type of alleged miracle is that of 'conversion experience', as in the case of St Paul already mentioned. These, as William James remarked, certainly occur.[89] On the other hand a sceptic will put the experience down to natural causes, and so while agreeing that the experience existed will deny that any supernatural cause of it existed or that putative perceptions involved were veridical. Conversion experiences are inevitably subjective, and our attitude to reports of them will depend on our views about the argument from religious experience. The sceptic may agree that the experience is in fact had but will doubt that it constitutes a perception of anything external. On the other hand there are claimed to be inter-subjectively observable miracles, for example the feeding of the five thousand or the appearance of angels at the battle of Mons, to take two very different examples.

Such a miracle as the feeding of the five thousand clearly involves a violation of the laws of nature. Some philosophers have contended that this makes the notion of a miracle a self-contradictory one, on the grounds that an exception to a putative law of nature would show that the putative law was not really a law and that laws are universal regularities. This objection can be got over by supposing a clause in the statement of any law of nature 'except when there is divine intervention'. Or to put it otherwise, the laws of nature tell us how the universe regularly works, even though there can be miraculous exceptions. A theist might say that the laws of nature are imposed by God on the universe as a whole by one comprehensive creative act, whereas miracles would be exceptional events imposed by God for particular reasons at particular locations in space–time. Such a notion is not obviously contradictory though I sense a problem of whether a truly omnipotent and omniscient God would not be able to create a universe in which the laws of nature would be such that the desired exceptional events occurred without breaking a suitably chosen set of laws, and whether God, for aesthetic reasons if for no other, would not want to do the job this way. Perhaps a theist could indeed say that this is how the universe really is: that miracles are only events that *appear* to be contrary to the laws of nature.

Anyway, whether subsumable under law or not, miracles must be remarkable events serving some divine purpose. Sometimes it has been held that one purpose of miracles is to induce faith in those who saw or heard of them. We wonder then why God does not perform miracles for all to see, not just for a favoured few. To refer to a previous example, perhaps the stars could be so placed as to spell out the Apostles' Creed in Greek. Alpha Centaurians would see the stars in different patterns from those that we see, but perhaps somewhere in the sky they would see a pattern of verses in Alpha Centaurian.

Because miracles are, or appear to be, exceptions to the laws of nature there is a *prima facie* reason for doubting any report of a miracle. There is always the possibility of explaining away such reports by reference, as Hume remarked, to the well-known phenomena of the credulity and knavery of humankind. Nevertheless someone who *already* believed in an omnipotent being would have some possibility of rational belief in a miracle story. At least such a story would cohere better with his or her system of belief than would be the case with the system of belief of a sceptic or atheist.

At one place in his very well-known essay on miracles, section 8
of his *Enquiry Concerning Human Understanding*, David Hume put
forward his scepticism about miracles with a qualification: he said
that 'a miracle can never be proved *so as to be the foundation of a
system of religion*' (my italics). The interpretation of this very readable
and at first sight very lucid essay has given rise to surprisingly many
scholarly problems, as can be seen, for example, from Antony Flew's
learned chapter in his *Hume's Philosophy of Belief*.[90]

As I read Hume he is concerned to establish the weaker point, that
a miracle cannot be proved 'so as to be the foundation of a system of
religion'. He does not quite claim to prove that a miracle could not be
proved, but he does hold that a miracle cannot be proved so as to be
the foundation of a system of religion. Nevertheless he argues that in
fact, with the background knowledge that educated theists, atheists
and sceptics should be expected to have in modern times, such a proof
of a miracle encounters great obstacles, even though by 'proof' here
is meant something less than apodeictic proof but only the sort of
establishment that scientific hypotheses are capable of. He does think
that 'there may be miracles or violations of the usual course of nature,
of such a kind as to admit of proof from human testimony' but he adds
that 'perhaps it will be impossible to find any such in all the records
of human history'.

Sometimes when we find a miraculous fact extremely well attested we
do not need to say 'Ah! a miracle', but look for a naturalistic explanation. This happens with reports of miraculous cures of disease. It is
possible to suppose that the original diagnosis was incorrect. Again,
many diseases have spontaneous remissions which are not regarded
by medical experts as miraculous. Furthermore our understanding of
psychosomatic medicine may allow us to explain some apparently
miraculous cures of illness. Sometimes we doubt the fact itself. The
man raised from the dead may not really have been dead. On the other
hand, to allude to an example discussed by Hume, if a one-legged
man is reported to have been made two-legged, we judge that there
must have been some error in the testimony. There can hardly be
misdiagnosis of the number of a man's legs, and there could be no
medical or biological explanation of the sudden sprouting of a previously amputated human leg. Hume puts the point in too empiricist a
way. He holds our doubt of the report of such a sprouting of a leg to
be 'because it is contrary to our experience'. The credulity and knavery
of humankind (and perhaps love of the marvellous for its own sake)
provides a ready enough explanation. However, by just saying 'contrary

to experience' Hume does not do justice to the importance of *theory* in our scientific background knowledge. Consider the explosion of an asteroid eight kilometres above a fortunately uninhabited part of Siberia early in this century, flattening trees over 2,200 square kilometres. Fortunately the observation of such an occurrence is not a common experience, but our knowledge of the astronomy of the solar system is such that an occurrence of this sort is quite intelligible and to be expected to occur occasionally.

We must remember that in his discussion of miracles Hume was not in his mood of extreme epistemological scepticism, according to which anything could be followed by anything. That is, Hume is not concerned with mere *logical* inconsistency. Hume was of course aware that there is no logical inconsistency in supposing that a one-legged man suddenly sprouted a new second leg. We must suppose that Hume is concerned with physical possibility or impossibility. Now our notion of physical possibility has to do with the question of whether a phenomenon fits coherently into a web of belief. Of course there are anomalies in science, but these are not regarded as miracles. A good example from the past is that of the advance of the perihelion of Mercury, which could not be fitted in with Newtonian mechanics and gravitational theory, but which later was accommodated by the general theory of relativity. Normally a scientist will not abandon a theory until there is a better theory to replace it. (Compare Bruce Bairnsfather's First World War cartoon, of 'Old Bill' with another soldier sitting in a shell hole with all sorts of stuff bursting around, and saying 'Well, if you knows of a better 'ole, go to it'.) Alternatively the scientist may be sceptical of reports of a refractory phenomenon. People who are *too* empiricist, accepting observation reports too readily, join forces in the credulity stakes with those who are not empiricist enough, and are ready to believe any theory however inadequately it has been tested.

Need the concept of a miracle involve that of a violation of the laws of nature? Not always, because the notion of a miracle, as with other non-trivial concepts, has what Friedrich Waismann has called 'open texture'.[91] I think that it would be perfectly proper to give the name 'miracle' to a religiously significant and unusual event, such as the parting of the Red Sea which allowed the Israelites fleeing from Egypt to pass through, even though the event could be given a naturalistic explanation. The term 'miracle' would be even more appropriate if it were claimed that God had set up the universe to contain the event, even though it occurred in accordance with deterministic laws.[92] Similarly

God might have set up the universe so that the event occurred indeterministically but without violating quantum mechanical laws.

Even so, if the event was naturalistically possible but very improbable we might be justified in doubting the truth of the report of it. Its very significance in a religious context might increase the probability that this highly improbable event never occurred, and that the report of it was fictional, part of a story told (and even believed by its narrator) in a more credulous age. It is indeed often foolish to believe one's own eyes, as is shown by the existence of clever conjurors. In fact the existence of conjurors illustrates the fact that things can often occur in a natural way, even though we have no idea how they occurred.

Here we are obviously passing from the topic of the conception of the miraculous to that of the assessment of testimony, and thus to questions in the philosophy of history, and in particular to that of the higher criticism of the New Testament. Historical evidence of course goes beyond documents and verbal reports: we must also consider relevant archaeological information and other evidence, such as from astronomy.[93]

12　Higher Criticism of the New Testament

This section is particularly concerned with the Christian form of theism. Adherents of Judaism and Islam would claim that they have the purest form of monotheism because of Christianity's difficult notion of the Trinity. Like Christians, however, they are people of a Sacred Book and questions in the philosophy of history and of testimony in general, which have arisen in the higher criticism of the New Testament, may have some applications in the study of these other religions. I shall not investigate this further matter here.

Certainly many Christians believe in God and the divinity of Jesus because they believe in the literal truth of the Old and New Testaments. It also works the other way (often in the same people): people believe in the historical truth of much at least of the New Testament because they believe in God and his veracity. Thus in some cases the argument can become circular. Of course many people believe without argument.

The higher criticism of the New Testament is essentially a matter of looking at the documents and other evidence (for example, archaeological evidence) as a good historian would do in any other field of history. It is true that there are good, even outstandingly excellent, historians who do not carry over their normal methodologies to the evaluation of the New Testament. This need not be an all or nothing affair. A historian may make place for the supernatural when he or she evaluates the New Testament even though he or she would not do this when writing on, say, the Wars of the Roses or the first Reform Bill. Nor need there be any brash abandonment of reverential language. Thus Dennis Nineham in a fine commentary on St Mark's Gospel[94] regularly refers to Jesus as 'our Lord', and yet his arguments are in many ways quite sceptical. There is a variety of positions between supernaturalist and totally naturalist opinions about the historical Jesus and where a commentator comes down here must depend to a great degree on his or her implicit or explicit notions of the metaphysical possibilities.

This was the theme of F.H. Bradley's first publication, *The Presuppositions of Critical History* (1874).[95] Bradley was stimulated to write this work on the philosophy of history as a result of the new critical work on the New Testament and the beginnings of Christianity by F.C. Baur, D.F. Strauss and C. Holsten. His arguments are sometimes a bit like those of Hume on miracles, but while Hume as an empiricist spoke of the unusual or what is contrary to experience, Bradley was rightly more coherentist about warranted assertability, stressing the way our experience is laden with theory and other background beliefs, whether scientific or metaphysical. He refers to Paley's protest against 'prejudication' and states on the contrary that all history must rest in part on prejudications.[96] His idea is that our historical conclusions come from inference, which is 'never a fragmentary isolated act of our mind, but is essentially connected with, and in entire dependence, on the character of our general consciousness'.[97] Stripped of his idealist language I think that Bradley's talk here is much the same as Quine's talk of 'a web of belief', which I have adopted earlier in this essay. It should be noted that in his essay Bradley is concerning himself purely with testimony and documents. Historians also make use of archaeological evidence, but in the present context I shall neglect this complication.

Bradley recognizes that historical testimony that may not be accepted at one time because it did not fit into a web of belief may become accepted later because the web has been expanded and modified. He mentions Herodotus's disbelief in the Phoenicians' story of their circumnavigation of Africa because they said that they had seen the sun to their north. Modern geographical and astronomical knowledge fits this fact about the sun beautifully into our web of belief so as to make us feel completely sure of the truth of the Phoenicians' claim to have sailed round the south of Africa. Bradley also refers to the alleged phenomena of stigmata which might more recently have come to be regarded as medically possible, and to the report of African confessors who spoke even though their tongues had been cut out, which had, he says, come to be regarded as physiologically possible.[98]

C.A.J. Coady, in his valuable book *Testimony: A Philosophical Study*,[99] worries that Hume's and Bradley's criteria would have ruled out acceptance of many historical propositions that we now regard as quite certain, such as reports of human sacrifice or of trial by ordeal, Socrates' acceptance of death rather than freedom, and the astonishing feats of Napoleon Bonaparte. In connection with the last case he quotes from Archbishop Whateley's witty *Historic Doubts Relative to Napoleon Bonaparte*.[100] In reply I would urge that though Napoleon was unusual and so were many of his deeds and sufferings, we are aware of the great variability of human character, talents and abilities, and so in a sense the humanly unusual is usual. At any rate it fits well into what we know of human genetics, plasticity of brain function and so on. The case is different with the resurrection of Jesus. Similarly with Coady's examples of human sacrifice and trial by ordeal. These may be unusual in our experience, but are perfectly compatible with what we know of human nature. This example shows the importance of the notion of coherence in this connection, rather than those of 'the usual' or 'the analogous'. (Bradley did use the latter term, but he need not have.)

Of course in science we do have anomalies. Consider the advance of the perihelion of Mercury which was unexplained until Newtonian gravitational theory was succeeded by general relativity. In such cases, however, we are dealing with repeated or repeatable observations or experiments. Moreover scientists do not despair of a naturalistic explanation of anomalies: they wait until a better theory explains them. (Except in cases in which doubt is cast on the observations or experiments, but in these cases we do not have a proper anomaly.) Indeed this came about in the historical case of the Phoenicians and the circumnavigation of Africa. We might give a naturalistic explanation of Jesus appearing to his disciples after his death but then it would lose its main religious significance. There have indeed been theories that Jesus did not die on the cross but appeared to be dead and was entombed in a state that mimicked that of death, later recovering and being seen on the road to Emmaus. I do not want to put any weight on such speculations.

If a person already has positive beliefs about the supernatural many of the supernatural elements in the Gospels may well be easily assimilated into his or her web of belief. However, if one is already sceptical about the facts of the historical Jesus then one will have a very different attitude to the Biblical documents. Some scholars might indeed assess the documentary evidence in a more straightforward fashion, though not necessarily uncritically, as the work of many outstanding Christian New Testament scholars will testify. Orthodox commentators will be interested in explaining the existence of inconsistencies and other oddities in the documents, doing linguistic analyses of style and vocabulary to shed light on authors and sources. Nevertheless they will disagree with those of more naturalistic bent, who will go much further in getting behind the Gospel stories at what they conceive of as the historical Jesus. Of course one might eliminate all the supernatural from the Gospel stories and still remain a theist. Nevertheless I think that the higher criticism of the New Testament is after all relevant to theism, since belief is holistic and changes in one area can influence strength of belief in other areas. For other theistic religions of course it is not necessary to believe in the divinity and resurrection of Jesus, though analogous problems may exist elsewhere.

Revelation may be more plausible to one who already finds belief in the supernatural plausible, but it should be obvious that revelation by itself cannot without circularity be used to justify its own validity.

There are many reasons for distrusting much in the Gospel stories. The earliest Gospel to be written was that of St Mark and is dated by scholars many years after the crucifixion. Matthew and Luke incorporated the gist of almost all of Mark into their Gospels, in which scholars have detected another hypothetical documentary source, called 'Q'. Mark also would have depended on oral tradition. It is commonplace that oral tradition can lead to distortions and exaggerations as words are passed from one mouth to another. There were stories of virgin birth and resurrection elsewhere in the middle east, neo-Platonic influences from Greek philosophy, and historians in ancient times were not as scrupulous about literal truth as are modern ones. There is the puzzle of the different authorship (discovered by philological investigation) of the final verses of Mark. Changes, both intentional and unintentional, can also creep in as manuscripts are transcribed. These considerations already give some latitude to a sceptical commentator, but there are other important matters of methodology. For example, if a passage seems to be inconsistent with the author's evangelical purpose it is likely that it is true: the evangelist could not omit or change it because it was so well known. What I want to concentrate on here, however, is the sort of consideration emphasized by Bradley, namely that of metaphysical presuppositions. Suppose that, as I do, you regard the best touchstone of metaphysical truth to be plausibility in the light of total science, how will the gospel stories look to you? This attitude seems to me to be reasonable, since science tries to attain *well tested* theories. There are of course areas of controversy. Nevertheless, it is the case that there is a huge body of well tested and uncontroversial established fact and theory.

The historical Jesus has proved to be elusive. All sorts of accounts have been made, ranging from the literalist and supernaturalist to the sceptical and naturalistic. A naturalistic account that has appealed to me as plausible is that of S.G.F. Brandon.[101] However I am not a historian or a New Testament scholar, and so I suggest that the cautious reader should take what I say about Brandon's theory as merely illustrative of the possibility of a plausible naturalistic theory and also illustrative of Bradley's view about the importance of presuppositions (mine being naturalistic) in critical history.

Brandon's hypothesis is that Jesus was closely connected with the zealots, Jewish resistance fighters against the Roman occupation. This explains his trial at the hands of Pilate, which must have been for sedition, not for blasphemy. Blasphemy was a matter for the Jewish religious establishment and the penalty for this was not crucifixion but stoning. That Jesus' trial was for sedition explains Pilate's involvement: if it had been for blasphemy it would have been in a Jewish court. Mark had a motive for wanting to transfer responsibility from the Romans to the Jews. Mark was writing largely for the Roman Christians, whose position was uncomfortable as it was at the time of the great Jewish revolt and the consequent destruction of Jerusalem, and he would have been at pains to conceal the connection of the original Christians with zealotry and hence sedition, for fear of bringing harm to the Christians in Rome. At least one of the disciples actually was a zealot, Simon the zealot. Luke, writing later after the fuss over the Jewish revolt had died down, explicitly called Simon by the Greek word 'zelotes', whereas Mark more cagily used the Aramaic word, 'Cananaean', which would not be easily understood by the Roman Christians. The two 'thieves' who were crucified with Jesus were probably zealots, since the Romans referred to zealots as 'lestai' (brigands).

The above is merely meant as a very small *sample* of considerations brought forward by Brandon in a book full of technical philological and historical scholarship. The interested reader is referred to Brandon's work itself. 'A pretty tall story', an orthodox believer might say, 'Jesus a leader of revolutionaries, something like modern mujahideen? Poppycock! Jesus said "Turn the other cheek".' Yes, one might reply, but he also said that he did not come to bring peace but a sword. The disciples in Gethsemane were armed. And so the dialogue might go on. What should we believe, the orthodox story or the naturalistic one or something in between? (Or of course some other possible naturalistic story?)

Brandon's theory might be shown to be implausible, but could it be *less* plausible than the orthodox story that Jesus performed miracles and not only claimed to be the son of God (and even this has been doubted) but *was* the son of God, and after the crucifixion rose bodily into heaven? A balancing of plausibilities is needed and the metaphysical presuppositions of the reader will largely determine which way the balance falls.

There is a common argument for the literal truth of the Biblical account of the Resurrection of Jesus. The naturalistic metaphysician will of course wonder about the very biological possibility of resurrection or immortality as commonly conceived. So the argument had better be a very good one. The argument relies on the sudden transformation of the disciples after the crucifixion from a fearful group of people huddling in an upper room to a brave and successful lot of evangelists and martyrs. How could this have happened, it is asked, if they had not really seen the risen Jesus? The transformation was indeed wonderful, but the workings of the human brain are extremely complex and can be expected to issue in surprises. In any case the transformation may not have been all that surprising. Experience of millennarian sects has given us instances of how resistant their devotees can be to empirical disconfirmation when their millennarian expectations do not eventuate. *Ad hoc* excuses are made: they had got the date wrong, and so on. A sect may be smugly sure of being the chosen few who will be saved while all others are engulfed in a general deluge and will not proselytize. However, when the prophecy fails there will be an inner doubt, despite the *ad hoc* excuses. Proselytizing will suddenly become congenial because it widens the circle of people who give reassuring agreement with the sect's tenets. A sect which behaved in this sort of way has indeed been studied and their behaviour given a sophisticated psychological explanation roughly on these lines, by the American psychologists Leon Festinger, Henry W. Riecken and Stanley Schachter.[102] Another partial explanation of the spread of Christianity was the activities of St Paul, who grafted on ideas characteristic of Greek and near eastern philosophy, and who has been described by some scholars as the inventor of Christianity.

13   The Problem of Evil

After this brief excursion into the philosophy of history as it applies to New Testament theology, let us return from Christianity to theism in general. The concept of God as it is understood in the main monotheistic religions is that of an omnipotent, omniscient and altogether *good* being. Then the problem arises: how can there be evil in the world? For the atheist there is no problem: there is the amount of goodness and evil that we observe, and both are explicable. We think that altruism is good and (as was suggested on pp. 34–5) there are sociobiological and evolutionary explanations of at least a limited altruism, and intellectual pressures, such as analogy with scientific law, that can push towards a universalistic altruism. Nor is evil a problem for the atheist. As was suggested in an earlier section a biologist can talk in 'as if' purposive terms. There is natural selection for various traits of character, or rather tendencies to these traits, since character depends also on education and environment. For example, human combativeness is a very bad and dangerous trait in our H-bomb age, but it presumably had survival value in prehistoric times. (Perhaps the combative man is more likely to be killed, but if he helps to preserve his near relatives some of his genes will be passed on. In any case attack may be the best method of defence.) The more aggressive tribes may kill off the less aggressive ones. So what is a bad trait in an H-bomb era has evolved. (Just as the bad placement of the sump hole of our sinuses evolved when our ancestors had four legs and held their heads downwards.) Moreover, bad traits can arise in special cases without selection. If we think of human biology in an 'as if' or pseudo-teleological way we can think of ourselves as machines that simply go wrong, as all machines tend to do. There are more ways of going wrong than there are of going right.

So we should not be at all surprised at the existence of human criminality and general badness. Nor need we be surprised, as naturalistically minded people, at natural evils. There are earthquakes, volcanoes, hurricanes and bacteria and viruses that harm us. Would it not surprise us if the world were *not* such as to contain things that harm us 'poor forked creatures'? There is no problem for the atheist in the existence of good things and bad things alike.

On the other hand for the theist evil is a big problem. If God is omniscient he knows how to prevent evil, if he is omnipotent he can prevent evil, and if he is benevolent he wants to prevent evil. The theist believes that God is omnipotent, omniscient and benevolent. If the theist's beliefs are correct, how then can there be evil? Unless the theist is prepared to settle for a finite 'big brother' God, his or her problem seems insoluble. However, as I observed earlier, a finite 'big brother' God would be just one big thing in the universe, not the infinite God of the great monotheistic religions, the God who created the universe.

There have indeed been countless attempts to solve this apparently insoluble problem for theism. The literature of these attempts is called 'theodicy', derived from the Greek words for 'God' and 'just'. Whole books have been written on this subject, and it is impossible in a short space to deal with all the attempts that have been made. It looks as though the theistic hypothesis is an empirically refutable one, so that theism becomes a refuted scientific theory. The argument goes: (1) If God exists then there is no evil, (2) There is evil, therefore (3) It is not the case that God exists. Premiss (1) seems to follow from our characterization of God as an omnipotent, omniscient and benevolent being. (2) is empirical. We can hardly reject (2). It seems therefore that the theist has to find something wrong with (1) and this is not easy. I shall discuss only some standard ways in which philosophers and theologians have tried to reconcile the existence of God with that of evil. The discussion will suggest that there is a real problem for the theist here, and that probably no *plausible* solution of the problem exists.

Since God creates not only the universe but the laws according to which it operates, he is not bound by any merely physical necessity. The only necessity that binds him is logical necessity; for example, he cannot create a universe in which pain both exists and does not exist. This is no real inability: since logical principles assert nothing about the world, so that whatever the world was like they would still apply, they do not constitute a constraint on God's power.

Nor do we need here to consider trick cases, such as whether God can make a box that he cannot open. These do not describe a real constraint on God's power. However, something a bit like this sort of problem will arise shortly when we consider 'the free will defence'.

Since God is not constrained by physical necessity there is no need for him to use painful means to attain a good end, as a dentist may have to when drilling a tooth.

The Free Will Defence

A common argument that is meant to reconcile God's omnipotence, omniscience and goodness with the existence of evil is that evil is due to misuse of the free will with which God has endowed us, and that the value of free will itself is so great as to outweigh the evils that proceed from it. The idea is usually combined with a libertarian theory of free will according to which free will is incompatible with determinism, and that even God could not create free beings who were always caused by their beliefs and desires to act rightly.

One weakness of the free will defence is its reliance on a libertarian theory of free will. I shall consider this shortly. Another weakness is, *prima facie* at least, that it totally ignores *natural* evils. Consider a two-year-old child dying painfully of cancer. To whose misuse of free will could this be put down? Even if free will had value, and if it was the misuse of free will by explorers that led to epidemics (as measles was brought to Australia and the South Pacific whose people lacked immune resistance to it), was the value of the free will comparable to the disvalue of the subsequent suffering? What about earthquakes, volcanoes, hurricanes which cause suffering due to no one's fault? What about the very existence of dangerous bacteria and viruses? It would betoken a mediaeval mind to put natural evils down to a wrong choice made in the Garden of Eden by Eve, and what a strange sort of God would have allowed such a choice to be so harmful. The story of Adam and Eve is of course capable of some allegorical truth. The apple brought the knowledge of good and evil, and certainly human increase in knowledge in general has brought many sufferings, as the invention of nuclear weapons will testify, as well as of course many benefits. There is something in the notion of original sin, but I think that this should be thought of in terms of the defectiveness of our genetic endowment. Thus, as I already mentioned, pugnacity may have been much more appropriate in a prehistoric tribal environment and the genes for it may have been selected, but it is very inappropriate to a contemporary situation in which opposing nations have deadly weapons. Also many harmful genes or combinations of genes have been due to mutations or to recombinations and have not yet been weeded out by natural selection.

Natural evils thus provide a formidable difficulty for the free will defence. They have nothing to do with free will. It is true that some philosophers and theologians have put down the existence of natural evils to the free and malevolent choices of fallen angels. Such an explanation smacks of being *ad hoc* and it is thoroughly implausible. There are perfectly naturalistic explanations of the mutations of influenza viruses, volcanic eruptions, tidal waves and other disastrous things or events.

I now want to go on to say that even if we ignore natural evils the free will defence does not work. This is because an omnipotent, omniscient and benevolent being would make a universe in which everyone chose in a morally perfect manner. It might be that with the best will in the world a person might act wrongly because of imperfect knowledge of cause and effect (consequences of action) but at least God could have created beings without positive wickedness. Or perhaps God could have created a world of both bodily and spiritually incorruptible angels who would exercise their free will in purely intellectual or aesthetic choices which were such that bad consequences were impossible. This seems possible even on a libertarian or indeterministic theory of free will.

Even in a world such as ours where bad consequences may occur through lack of knowledge, free but wicked choices might be impossible. God could have created beings with purely moral desires, from which they would always act. Even on a libertarian theory of free will it is logically possible that everyone would always *in fact* act rightly. God, who surveys all time and space, could have created such a world.

If this is thought to be a contentious assertion, I can go on to say that this idea of a universe with all indeterministic choices being right is not necessary for my argument. This is because I will not grant the theist the notion of libertarian free will, which seems to me to be an absurd one. Let me explain. I hold that any sensible notion of free will is compatible with determinism. Indeed one could go further and say with R.E. Hobart, in a famous essay,[103] that not only is determinism *compatible* with free will but that at least a fair approximation to determinism is necessary for there to *be* free will. Of course, as Hobart recognized, modern physics is indeterministic, but approximates to determinism on the macro-level. Our nervous system is susceptible of quantum effects, which are indeterministic, as for example our retina and visual system is sensitive to the arrival of a single photon, but it does not seem plausible that this indeterminism is important in affecting behaviour: it is doubtful whether our behaviour would be significantly different if our neurons were *completely* deterministic in their operation. In cricket a batsman facing a fast bowler has to have a very fast and reliable lot of computations going on in his brain or he would not be able to get his head out of the way of a fast moving ball. It is true that the person in the street tends to equate free will with indeterminism, if he or she is asked to make a philosophical comment about it. The question, however, is whether the concept of free will that is implied in everyday talk is or is not compatibilist. There is no clear answer here because there is not a precise boundary between everyday talk and metaphysical talk. Compatibilism seems right in relation to any sensible account of free will. Indeterminism does not confer freedom on us: I would feel that my freedom was impaired if I thought that a quantum mechanical trigger in my brain might cause me to leap into the garden and eat a slug.

It really is extraordinary how many physicists in their popular writings come out with the idea that quantum mechanical indeterminacy leaves room for free will. Roughly speaking – I shall make a qualification or two shortly – we feel free in so far as we are determined by our desires (together of course with our beliefs).

Some help here may come from J.L. Austin's suggestion that 'free' is really a negative word, used to rule out one or another way of being positively unfree.[104] We set a prisoner free and she goes wherever she wants. Before that she was unfree in that she wanted to go elsewhere, but could not do so. In a shotgun marriage we say that the bridegroom did not want to marry the bride but wanted even less to be shot by the prospective father-in-law. In another context the bridegroom could be said to be free, because he is doing what he wanted, that is to avoid being shot. In one way an alcoholic is free to stop drinking: he is not bound hand and foot and having the drink poured down his throat. On the other hand he may say that he is not free (or not able) to stop drinking. He wants to overcome his craving for drink but cannot do so. Here is a case in which he is thwarted in respect of a higher order desire (to modify his desire to drink) by the sheer inalterability of his lower order desire. We can modify the relative strengths of another person's desires in various ways: reasoning, rhetoric, persuasion, threats, promises. None of these are incompatible with determinism: indeed they all presuppose it, or at least (remembering quantum mechanics) an approximation to it. This is the notion of free will and responsibility of most use to the law. The main reason for punishment is deterrence. Deterrence is the imposing of conditions that change the relative strengths of a person's desires, such as not to be fined or sent to prison. If our actions were not determined by our desires attempts at deterrence would be futile.

It is sometimes said that we can act from a sense of duty against our strongest desire or combination of desires.[105] Such an objector forgets that sense of duty is itself a desire (to do one's duty). This is a desire that parents, teachers, friends, clergy and commanding officers are keen to inculcate. (Immanuel Kant distinguished 'willing' from 'desiring' but this was to make a metaphysical mystery of something that can be naturalistically explained.)

Another thing that has commonly been said is that libertarian free will is acting from reasons, not from causes. This does not help. In one sense a reason *is* a cause. 'What was your reason for asking for coffee?' 'I just wanted coffee rather than tea.' Here the desire for coffee was greater than that for tea and the desire caused the action. On another occasion asking for a reason may be asking for a justification. 'Why did you do that?' 'I promised my wife that I'd do it.' Here there is implicit reference to a rule of promise keeping. The rule (or 'reason' in this sense) is not something that acts on us. The upshot is that acting from reasons is not something different from and possibly in conflict with acting from causes. The justificatory story is perfectly compatible with the causal story.

Because free will is compatible with determinism God could have set up the universe so that we always acted rightly, and so for this reason alone the free will defence does not work. I do have some sympathy with the view that the compatibilist account of free will does not quite capture the ordinary person's concept of free will. This, however, is because the ordinary person's concept of free will, if one gets him or her arguing in a pub, say, is inconsistent. The ordinary person wants the action to be determined, not merely random, but undetermined too. The compatibilist can say that if this is the concept of free will we clearly do not have free will, just as I don't have a round square table in my study. Once more the free will defence fails.

I hold, therefore, that the free will defence does not hold even for moral evils, evils due to the misuse of free will. In any case natural evils provide the biggest difficulty for the theist. Unconvincing replies are sometimes brought up. If people starve in a drought they are blamed for lack of foresight. This is a cruel reply and anyway presupposes a retributionist God. Moreover what wrong choice has been made by a child dying of cancer? As to the reply that natural evils are due to immoral choices by fallen angels, the reply seems to be quite fanciful. Furthermore, if my remarks about free will are correct God could have arranged it that angels acted freely and never fell. Waiving all these points also, one wonders how an omnipotent God would allow the fallen angels to get away with it. A benevolent government with sufficient power would arrest, imprison, or even execute a very devilish criminal who otherwise would kill millions.

Two other weak responses are the following. (1) God has a reason for allowing evil but we do not know what it is. Well, we know that God does not have a reason for allowing round squares because the notion of a round square is an inconsistent one. So if this answer is to work it must depend on one of the other defences. (2) It may be said that evil can enhance goodness, just as ugly chords can enhance a piece of music. I doubt whether the mother of the child dying of cancer would be impressed by this idea. A closely related idea, on which I touched when discussing Pascal's Wager, is that if the universe contains an infinite amount of goodness then a finite amount of badness leaves us with still an equal infinity of goodness.

Let a be the total amount of badness in the world, and let there be an infinite series of good things, $b + b + b + \dots$. Then it may be held that $-a + b + b + b + \dots = b + b + b + \dots$. In Cantor's set theory the union of a finite set with an infinite set has the same transfinite number as the infinite set. The set that contains all the stars in our galaxy together with all the integers is no bigger than the set of all the integers itself. So if (rather absurdly) we were to assign a value v to each star and also to each integer, the value of the set containing both the stars and the integers would be no greater than that of the set containing only the integers. (There would be other curiosities, such as that the value of all the even integers would be equal to the value of all the even and odd integers.) I conclude that analogies inspired by Cantorian set theory are unhelpful, even if not positively absurd. We should say that the value of the universe containing positive evils is less than that of the infinitely good universe containing no positive evils. So God would perhaps have allowed the $b + b + b + \dots$ universe but would not have allowed the $-a + b + b + b + \dots$ universe. He would not have allowed the universe with the child dying of cancer.

This consideration that even an infinitely good universe should contain no positive evils within it enables me to deal with another, and more interesting, defence of theism.[106] This is that it is unfair to ask of even an omnipotent God that he should create the best possible universe, since of any universe we can conceive of a better. This might lead us to some interesting speculations related to the theory of transfinite cardinal numbers, but let us for the sake of argument concede the point. If it is logically impossible that any universe is the best possible, then indeed even omnipotence could not create such a universe.

Nevertheless, surely we would expect an omnipotent and benevolent God to have created a universe without positive evils.

Contemplating evil, I feel the attractions of a philosophy, such as that of the Ādvaita Vedānta, according to which reality is very different from what it seems or what we could possibly know, and that the world as we think we know it, including both good things and bad things, is illusory. However such a philosophy cannot be stated without absurdity. Though I feel its attraction it is compatible neither with orthodox theism nor with the sort of scientific realism that I am compelled to defend.

14   Historical Theism and Metaphysical Theism

By 'Historical Theism' I mean theism as integrated into the great monotheistic religions. By 'Metaphysical Theism' I mean theism which is independent of all considerations of time and place, such as a chosen people in Palestine or of the birth and crucifixion of Jesus. Islam is rather different, and is very austere in its concept of God, as is shown by its prohibition of pictorial representations. Nevertheless it does have its sacred places and the revelation of the Koran to a particular prophet, Mohammed. The difficulty for many modern would-be believers is therefore that a lot of the religious imagery is highly particular. One finds oneself in a mental world in which the earth is at the centre of the universe and where even particular places and times are supposed to be of immense importance.

Of course theologians can claim that theological conceptual schemes can advance and be modified just as philosophical and scientific ones can. However, the particularity of what are not necessarily the essential features but of the general ambience of the scriptures of the great monotheistic religions may be worrying to traditional theists. Obviously those who persecuted Galileo were worried. Even the heliocentric universe was tiny compared with the universe as it is known in modern cosmology. Perhaps the discovery of the galaxies by Hubble would have been even more scary to those who fear the vast cosmic spaces.

Suppose that there are a hundred thousand million stars in a galaxy and that there are perhaps a comparable number of galaxies. That is a lot of stars in the universe. Planetary systems much like our solar system are likely to occur only around main sequence stars similar to our sun. Among main sequence stars at least two-thirds are double (or triple) stars, and life is not so likely to emerge in planets of these type of stars. The chance of *intelligent* life emerging is even less. Evolution on earth could easily have taken a different turn. It is likely that an impact by an asteroid 65 million years ago led to the earth being covered by dust clouds and so to something like an envisaged 'nuclear winter'. It is believed that this was the cause of the extinction of the dinosaurs, and so indirectly led to the dominance of mammals. Our planet Earth is the only one in the solar system which is suitable for the evolution of intelligent life. So even if there are very many other planetary systems in our galaxy, few might have been suitable for the evolution of intelligent life. Even our solar system is due to a series of happy accidents. Stuart Ross Taylor, in his book *Solar System Evolution: A New Perspective*[107] explains recent ideas which go as follows. An irregular bit of a larger molecular cloud broke off in such a way that it took a special form and was rotating about its centre. This irregularity allows an escape from the problem of the distribution of angular momentum between planets and the sun which beset La Place's nebular hypothesis and its descendants. The dust grains accreted gravitationally into planetesimals and these into planets, the whole process involving collisions between the various bodies. Collisions indeed form an important part of the story, and account for many of the varying characteristics (such as differing inclinations to the ecliptic plane of the various planets). A large planet-sized object is supposed to have collided with the earth. The resulting splash of molten material formed the Moon, about 80 per cent of whose mass comes from material from the impacting body, so that the Moon's constitution is dissimilar to that of the earth. The impacting body was destroyed in the collision and the collision stripped away the early atmosphere, which eventually was replaced (through gas emanating volcanically from the earth) by an atmosphere suitable for the evolution of life. This collision was a lucky accident for the prospect of life. Another lucky accident is that of the formation of the huge planet Jupiter in its position outside the asteroid belt, since it forms a gravitational barrier to comets. Without Jupiter perhaps a thousand times as many would impact on the earth making conditions for life very difficult.

The main matter of interest is how the formation of the solar system depended on a lot of accidents, and how uniformitarian theories of its origin are out of place. All the planets are importantly different from one another. So even if there are many such systems in the galaxy, few might be suitable for life and still fewer would develop intelligent life. Indeed Taylor is of the opinion that we are alone in the universe.[108] Remember that we need not only to multiply together all the probabilities of lucky astronomical accidents which led to our solar system containing a planet suitable for life, but we have to multiply this very small probability with the probabilities of all the lucky biological accidents in the biological evolutionary process. We then need to compare the reciprocal of this very small number with the huge number of stars like our sun in the galaxy, multiplied again by the huge number of galaxies. It is obviously very hard to estimate the probabilities and the final answer.

Before I heard a lecture by Ross Taylor and read his book I was of the fairly conventional opinion put forward by astronomers that there are probably hundreds of millions of planets with planetary systems suitable for the evolution of life and that we are far from being the only intelligent beings in our galaxy, let alone in the universe, and that probably there are vast numbers of planets with intelligent beings technologically far in advance of ourselves. At any rate Ross Taylor's considerations suggest that although planetary systems might be common, those with a planet suitable for the evolution of intelligent life are extremely rare, and that the prospects of the current programme SETI (search for extraterrestrial intelligence) are very poor.

This is probably to some extent a temperamental matter, because so much guesswork and quantifying of probably unquantifiable probabilities is involved, but I find it hard to believe that we are alone in the universe, or even in our galaxy. Even if the emergence of intelligent life is rare in the extreme, the number of galaxies is comparable to the number of stars in our Milky Way system. The reason I am inclined to believe that there is much other intelligent life in the universe (in which case a lot of it will be very advanced compared to ourselves) has to do with something like Leslie's 'firing squad' argument (see section 5) being at the back of my mind. Furthermore, the probability of intelligent life in the total universe of everything that there is would become a certainty if the universe were infinite or if there were infinitely many of Carter's many universes, discussed in section 5.

While not entirely closing our minds to the possibility that we are in fact alone in the universe let us look at the question of how the existence of life on other worlds would affect the Christian doctrine of the Trinity. Suppose (for the sake of argument) that there is an incarnation on ten million other planets. Does this mean that the Third

Person of the Trinity is multiply incarnated? Or would the Trinity be a (ten million and one)-ity? As far as I have been able to discover the orthodox view (such as that of E.L. Mascall) would be to take the former alternative.[109] This is a hard matter which raises a lot of philosophical problems, but no more so, perhaps, than the original doctrine of incarnation itself.

The problems that arise from the possibility of life on other worlds does seem to have been somewhat neglected by theologians. However, recently John Hick has considered the subject in his book *The Metaphor of God Incarnate*, Chapter 9, where he also refers to several other theological writers who have discussed the matter.[110] Hick's theory is quite attractive, though conservative theologians might not like the notion of incarnation to be treated as metaphorical. A very odd way out was put forward, admittedly in the imaginative context of a fanciful novel, by C.S. Lewis.[111] This was that among countless other planets containing intelligent life ours is the only one on which its inhabitants sinned and so needed a Redeemer. One may find some difficulty in believing that our planet is the only one on which intelligent life exists, but it is far more difficult to believe that if there are millions of other planets containing intelligent life, ours is the only one in which sin existed. Even if intelligent life had existed for millions of years and evolved into angelically good beings they would have had to pass through the sinful stage in any evolutionary process that is at the least likely. As was explained on p. 66, unfortunate tendencies of character (such as combativeness) are likely to persist because they had survival value at an earlier stage of evolution, and also because there are so many more ways in which a machine can go wrong than there are ways in which it can go right.

Metaphysical Theism

Let us return from the special case of Christianity to the general question of theism itself. My arguments in this essay against any form of theism have not been apodeictic. As I remarked in section 1, there are no knock-down arguments in philosophy. Premises and even methodology can be questioned. For example I have not surveyed all the many ways in which philosophers have tried to deal with the problem of evil. Such would involve a voluminous work. What I think we can do, instead of aiming at an apodeictic argument, is to push the person who disagrees with us into a more and more complex theory, involving more and more disputable premisses. There may be disagreement on the relative plausibilities of premisses. In the end we may agree to disagree, while nevertheless sticking to the assertion that there is an objective truth of the matter, whether or not we can agree on what it is. Sometimes a Wittgensteinian dissolution, rather than solution, of a philosophical problem may occur, but the history of philosophy since Wittgenstein has made it appear unlikely that if we think hard and long enough we will show the fly the way out of the fly bottle.[112] Metaphysics cannot be avoided. But it need not be apodeictic or entirely *a priori*.

A philosopher who thought he had an apodeictic disproof of the existence of God was J.N. Findlay. He thought that all necessity was a matter of linguistic convention, and that there was no sense in which God's existence could be necessary.[113] Any being that was not necessary might, he says 'deserve the δουλεια canonically accorded to the saints, but not the λατρεια that we properly owe to God'. In reply G.E. Hughes rightly rejected this view of necessity.[114] (Recall the discussion in section 8 of logical and mathematical necessity.) And indeed in his reply to Findlay's reply to him he concedes that 'proofs and disproofs' hold only for those who accept certain premisses. So ultimately we must, I think, resort to persuasion and considerations of relative plausibility.

Let me return to what I called 'the new teleology', the consideration of the 'fine tuning' and the beauty and wonders of the laws of nature, and the emergence of conscious beings such as ourselves. Paul Davies, in his *The Mind of God*,[115] holds that the universe is not 'meaningless' and that the emergence of consciousness in some planet in the universe is not a 'trivial detail, no minor by-product of mindless, purposeless forces'. The trouble with this is that a purpose must be a purpose of some person or super-person. Talk of 'meaning' or 'purpose' here therefore begs the question in favour of theism. The evidence that Davies has is that the laws or proto-laws and the initial conditions in the universe (or collection of universes as in Carter's hypothesis) imply that conscious life is pretty sure to emerge somewhere, perhaps many times over. If no more than this is meant there is no argument for theism. ('Pretty sure' above is a bit strong if Ross Taylor is right that we are probably alone in the universe. It would be a matter of luck.)

I concede that theism is an emotionally attractive doctrine. Perhaps it even is true. But if it *is* true then the problems that I have put forward in the case of traditional theism make it likely that such a theism would have to be understood in such a way that it would differ little from what we at present regard as atheism.

Notes

1   J.J.C. Smart, 'Why Philosophers Disagree', in Jocylyne Couture and Kai Nielsen (eds), *Reconstructing Philosophy: New Essays in Metaphilosophy* (Calgary, Alberta: University of Calgary Press, 1993), pp. 67–82.
2   T.S. Kuhn, *The Structure of Scientific Revolutions*, 2nd edn (Chicago and London: University of Chicago Press, 1970).
3   See pp. 60–6.
4   See for example, Richard C. Jeffrey, *The Logic of Decision*, 2nd edn (Chicago and London: University of Chicago Press, 1983), pp. 185–7.
5   J.L. Mackie, *The Miracle of Theism* (Oxford: Clarendon Press, 1982).
6   Paul Davies, *The Mind of God* (London: Simon and Schuster, 1992).
7   John Leslie, *Universes* (London: Routledge, 1989).
8   Ludwig Wittgenstein, *Philosophical Investigations* (Oxford: Blackwell, 1953), sections 66–7.
9   Paul Davies and John Gribbin, *The Matter Myth* (Harmondsworth: Penguin Books, 1991).
10 For speculations contrary to my own on this point, see Roger Penrose, *The Emperor's New Mind* (Oxford: Oxford University Press, 1989) and *Shadows of the Mind* (Oxford: Oxford University Press, 1994).
11 For details, see J.O. Burchfield, *Lord Kelvin and the Age of the Earth* (London: Macmillan, 1975).
12 See Silvanus P. Thompson, *The Life of William Thomson, Baron Kelvin of Largs* (London: Macmillan, 2 vols, 1910), p. 1094.
13 For the speculations and objections, see John Horgan, 'In the Beginning . . .', *Scientific American*, 264 (February 1991), 100–9.
14 See, for example, the first three essays in Stephen Jay Gould, *The Panda's Thumb* (Harmondsworth: Penguin Books, 1980).
15 Gerald Feinberg, 'Physics and the Thales Problem', *Journal of Philosophy*, 63 (1966), 5–17.
16 See the title article in Isaac Asimov, *The Relativity of Wrong* (Oxford: Oxford University Press, 1989).
17 William Paley, *Natural Theology* (London, 1802).
18 On this topic see the perceptive methodological article by the neurophysiologist G. Adrian Horridge, 'Mechanistic Teleology and Explanation in Neuroethology', *Bio Science*, 27 (1977), 725–32.
19 Richard Dawkins, *The Selfish Gene* (Oxford: Oxford University Press, 1976).

20 Psalm 19, Old Testament Revised Version, 1884.
21 John Leslie, *Value and Existence* (Oxford: Basil Blackwell, 1979), pp. 211–3.
22 F.H. Bradley, *Appearance and Reality* (Oxford: Clarendon Press, 1897). C.A. Campbell, *Scepticism and Construction* (London: Allen and Unwin, 1931).
23 Paul Davies, *The Mind of God* (London: Simon and Schuster, 1992).
24 Cf. quotation from letter from Einstein to Born on p. 176 of Born's article in P.A. Schilpp (ed.), *Albert Einstein: Philosopher-Scientist* (New York: Harper Torchbooks, 1959).
25 For a summary of the 'fine tuning', see John Leslie, *Universes* (London: Routledge, 1989), pp. 2–5 and 25ff.
26 Fred Hoyle, *The Black Cloud* (London: Heinemann, 1957).
27 G.J. Whitrow, *The Structure and Evolution of the Universe*, 2nd edn (London: Hutchinson, 1959).
28 G.J. Whitrow, 'Why Physical Space has Three Dimensions', *British Journal for the Philosophy of Science*, 6 (1955–6), 13–31.
29 See J.J.C. Smart, 'Explanation – Opening Address', in Dudley Knowles (ed.), *Explanation and its Limits* (Cambridge: Cambridge University Press, 1990), pp. 1–15. The metaphor of the web of belief is due to Quine. See W.V. Quine and J.S. Ullian, *The Web of Belief*, revised edn (New York: Random House, 1978).
30 Brandon Carter, 'Large Number Coincidence and the Anthropic Principle in Cosmology', in M.S. Longair (ed.), *Confrontation of Cosmological Theories with Observational Data* (Dordrecht: D. Reidel, 1974). This article is reprinted in John Leslie (ed.), *Physical Cosmology and Philosophy* (New York: Macmillan Publishing Company, 1990).
31 John Leslie, *Universes*, pp. 13–14.
32 See for example, J.J.C. Smart, *Essays Metaphysical and Moral* (Oxford: Blackwell, 1987), Essay 10 'Under the Form of Eternity'.
33 W.V. Quine, *Word and Object* (Cambridge, MA: MIT Press, 1960).
34 Andrei Linde, 'The Universe: Inflation out of Chaos', *New Scientist*, 105 (1446), 7 March 1985, 14–18. Reprinted in John Leslie (ed.), *Physical Cosmology and Philosophy* (New York: Macmillan, 1990). Linde has a later theory in which universes give birth to baby universes. This does not affect the philosophical points that I wish to make. See Andrei Linde, 'The Self-Reproducing Inflationary Universe', *Scientific American*, 271 (November 1994), 32–9.
35 See A.H. Guth and P.J. Steinhardt, 'The Inflationary Universe', *Scientific American*, 250 (May 1984), 116–28.
36 Norman Kemp Smith, 'Is Divine Existence Credible?', *Proceedings of the British Academy*, 17 (1931), 209–34.
37 Norman Kemp Smith (ed.), *Dialogues Concerning Natural Religion* (Edinburgh: Nelson, 1947).

38   Antony Flew, 'Arguments to Design', *Cogito*, 6 (1992), 93–6.
39   Cf. title of book by Paul Davies, *The Cosmic Blueprint* (London: Heine-
     mann, 1987).
40   John Leslie, *Value and Existence* and John Leslie, *Universes*.
41   Stephen W. Hawking, *A Brief History of Time* (London and New York:
     Bantam, 1988).
42   F. Hoyle, *The Black Cloud*.
43   René Descartes, *Meditation* III.
44   On changes in our beliefs about angels, see Enid Gauldie, 'Flights of
     Angels', *History Today*, 42, December 1992, 13–20.
45   Jeremy Bentham, *Introduction to the Principles of Morals and Legis-
     lation*, ch. 17, section 1, sub-section 2, footnote. In Wilfrid Harrison (ed.),
     *A Fragment on Government and an Introduction to the Principles of
     Morals and Legislation* (Oxford: Basil Blackwell, 1948).
46   John Leslie, *Universes* and in his earlier metaphysical treatise *Value and
     Existence*.
47   See note 8.
48   See Ninian Smart, *Reasons and Faiths* (London: Routledge and Kegan
     Paul, 1958).
49   Thomas Aquinas, *Summa Theologica* I q. 13.
50   Leslie, *Universes*, p. 166.
51   For my own views on this matter, see J.J.C. Smart, *Ethics, Persuasion
     and Truth* (London: Routledge and Kegan Paul, 1984).
52   G.E. Moore, *Principia Ethica* (Cambridge: Cambridge University Press,
     1903).
53   W.D. Ross, *Foundations of Ethics* (Oxford: Clarendon Press, 1939).
54   David Wiggins, *Needs, Values, Truth*, 2nd edn (Oxford: Blackwell, 1991),
     p. 137. The theory that Wiggins canvasses here contains subtleties that
     I here ignore as not germane to the present problem. For a discussion of
     the theory as I understand it (which may not be very well) see J.J.C.
     Smart 'Value, Truth and Action', *Ethics*, 100 (1990), 628–40, especially
     pp. 632–3.
55   Peter Singer, *The Expanding Circle* (Oxford: Clarendon Press, 1981).
56   See W.V. Quine, *Methods of Logic*, revised edn (New York: Holt, Rinehart
     and Winston, 1959), p. 97.
57   See for example M. Heidegger, 'What is Metaphysics?' (last sentence), in
     D.F. Krell (ed.), *Basic Writings of Martin Heidegger* (New York: Harper
     and Row, 1977).
58   As reported in Norman Malcolm, *Ludwig Wittgenstein: A Memoir* (Oxford:
     Oxford University Press, 1958), p. 20.
59   *Tractatus Logico-Philosophicus*, translated by D.F. Pears and B.F.
     McGuinness (London: Routledge and Kegan Paul, 1961). See also Nicholas
     Rescher, *The Riddle of Existence* (Lanham, MD: University Press of Amer-
     ica, 1984), pp. 4ff.

60 Jonathan Barnes, *The Ontological Argument* (London: Macmillan, 1972).

61 Thus W.V. Quine parses names as predicates in order to put language into the canonical notation of his *Word and Object*.

62 Jonathan Barnes, *The Ontological Argument*, p. 57.

63 Compare W.V. Quine, Word and Object. Compare also some of the papers by Donald Davidson, such as 'On Saying That', in which Davidson embarks on the project of showing that the underlying structure of intensional sentences is indeed that of classical first order logic. Donald Davidson, *Inquiries into Truth and Interpretation* (Oxford: Clarendon Press, 1984).

64 See Gilbert Harman, 'The Inference to the Best Explanation', *Philosophical Review*, 74, 88–95, and Gilbert Harman, *Thought* (Princeton: Princeton University Press, 1975). For a recent treatment see Peter Lipton, *Inference to the Best Explanation* (London: Routledge, 1991).

65 *Summa Theologica*, I, qa. 2, art. 3.

66 See Bertrand Russell and F.C. Copleston, 'A Debate on the Existence of God', originally broadcast by the British Broadcasting Corporation, 1948, and included in John Hick (ed.), *The Existence of God* (New York: Macmillan, 1964).

67 Stephen Hawking, *A Brief History of Time*.

68 E.P. Tryon, 'Is the Universe a Vacuum Fluctuation?', *Nature*, 246 (1973), 396–7.

69 See C.B. Martin, *Religious Belief* (Ithaca: Cornell University Press, 1959), p. 156.

70 See W.V. Quine, 'Necessary Truth', in his *Ways of Paradox and Other Essays* (New York: Random House, 1966).

71 To prevent misunderstanding I should make it clear here I count so-called 'higher order logic' as 'set theory'. Quine has called it 'set theory in sheep's clothing', *Philosophy of Logic* (Englewood Cliffs, NJ: Prentice-Hall, 1970), pp. 66–8. Whether it be called 'logic' or not the point I make about set theory applies to it, once allowance is made for the 'sheep's clothing'. Quine calls first order logic simply 'quantification theory'.

72 Especially to pure mathematicians. See G.H. Hardy, 'Mathematical Proof', *Mind*, 38 (1929).

73 Roger Penrose, *The Emperor's New Mind* (London: Vintage, 1989).

74 Hartry Field, *Science without Numbers* (Oxford: Blackwell, 1980) and *Realism, Mathematics and Modality* (Oxford: Blackwell, 1989).

75 David Lewis, *Parts of Classes* (Oxford: Blackwell, 1991).

76 'To Be is to be the Value of a Variable (or to be Some Value of Some Variables)', *Journal of Philosophy*, 81 (1984), 430–49.

77 D.M. Armstrong has pioneered such an empirically based theory of universals. See for example his *Universals: An Opinionated Introduction* (Boulder, Colorado and London: Westview Press, 1991).

78   Peter Forrest and D.M. Armstrong, 'The Nature of Number', *Philosophical Papers*, 16 (1987), 165–86.

79   John Bigelow, *The Reality of Number: A Physicalist's Philosophy of Mathematics* (Oxford: Clarendon Press, 1988).

80   William Kneale, 'Time and Eternity in Theology', *Proceedings of the Aristotelian Society*, 61 (1960–1), 87–108, and Martha Kneale, 'Eternity and Sempiternity', ibid., 69 (1968–9), 223–38. The Kneales come down on the side of sempiternity.

81   Cf. William James, *Varieties of Religious Experience* (New York: Random House, 1929), final chapter and postscript.

82   See the article on Pascal by R.H. Popkin, in Paul Edwards (Editor in Chief), *The Encyclopedia of Philosophy* (New York: Collier-Macmillan, 1967).

83   Bertrand Russell, *Why I am not a Christian* (Simon and Schuster, 1957). Edited by Paul Edwards with an Appendix on 'The Bertrand Russell Case'.

84   See William James, 'The Will to Believe', in his *The Will to Believe and Other Essays in Popular Philosophy* (London: Longmans Green, 1931), especially p. 6.

85   See Pascal, *Pensées*, edited by Louis Lafuma and translated by H.T. Barnwell (London: Dent, 1973).

86   Antony Flew, *The Presumption of Atheism* (London: Pemberton Publishing Company, 1976), ch. 1, p. 16, also ch. 5 ('Is Pascal's Wager the Only Safe Bet?'). Flew indicated that the idea of Pascal's wager can be traced back to the Islamic philosopher Al-Ghazali.

87   William James, 'The Will to Believe', p. 6.

88   Ibid.

89   William James, *Varieties of Religious Experience*, p. 22.

90   Antony Flew, *Hume's Philosophy of Belief* (London: Routledge and Kegan Paul, 1961).

91   See F. Waismann, 'Verifiability', in Antony Flew (ed.), *Logic and Language*, First Series (Oxford: Blackwell, 1951).

92   I am here indebted to an unpublished paper by W. Ginnane.

93   Thus my father calculated that there were neap tides at the time of the Spanish Armada. He did this on behalf of J. Holland Rose. See the latter's paper 'Was the Failure of the Spanish Armada due to Storms?', *Proceedings of the British Academy*, 22 (1936), 207–44, especially p. 226. (There is a misprint in the second footnote, where 'E.M. Smart' should be 'W.M. Smart'.)

94   D.E. Nineham, *The Gospel according to St Mark* (Harmondsworth: Penguin Books, 1972).

95   Reprinted in F.H. Bradley's *Collected Essays*, vol. 1 (Oxford: Clarendon Press, 1935).

96   Ibid., p. 20.

97 Ibid., p. 20.

98 Ibid., pp. 63–4.

99 C.A.J. Coady, *Testimony: A Philosophical Study* (Oxford: Clarendon Press, 1992).

100 First published 1819 anonymously. Quoted in Coady, *Testimony: A Philosophical Study*, p. 187.

101 S.G.F. Brandon, *Jesus and the Zealots* (Manchester: Manchester University Press, 1967). Also 'The Jesus of History', *History Today*, 12 (1962), 13–21, and 'The Trial of Jesus', *History Today*, 16 (1966), 251–9.

102 See Leon Festinger *et al.*, *When Prophecy Fails* (Minneapolis: Minnesota University Press, 1956).

103 'Free Will as involving Determination and Inconceivable without it', *Mind*, 43 (1934), 1–27.

104 J.L. Austin, *Philosophical Papers*, 2nd edn (Oxford: Clarendon Press, 1970), p. 180.

105 See for example, C.A. Campbell, 'Is "Freewill" a Pseudo-Problem?', *Mind*, 60 (1951), 441–65. For reference to controversy about this between Campbell and myself see J.J.C. Smart, *Our Place in the Universe* (Oxford: Blackwell, 1989), ch. 6.

106 See George Schlesinger, 'The Problem of Evil and the Problem of Suffering', *American Philosophical Quarterly*, 1 (1964), 244–7.

107 Stuart Ross Taylor, *Solar System Evolution: A New Perspective* (Cambridge: Cambridge University Press, 1992).

108 Using somewhat different reasoning John D. Barrow and Frank J. Tipler have concluded that we are probably alone in our galaxy. Still, there are a lot of galaxies, and so we could be far from alone in the universe. See Barrow and Tipler, *The Anthropic Cosmological Principle* (Oxford: Clarendon Press, 1986), ch. 9.

109 See E.L. Mascall, *Christian Theology and Natural Science* (London: Longman, Green, 1957), p. 43.

110 John Hick, *The Metaphor of God Incarnate* (London: SCM Press, 1993), ch. 9.

111 C.S. Lewis, *Perelandra* (London: Bodley Head, 1967).

112 Wittgenstein, *Philosophical Investigations*, section 309.

113 'Can God's Existence be Disproved?', in Antony Flew and Alasdair MacIntyre (eds), *New Essays in Philosophical Theology* (London: SCM Press, 1955).

114 Ibid. See also the reply by A.C.A. Rainer. Rainer thinks that we know God's necessity by analogy and only God himself directly apprehends this. Findlay thinks that this is stretching the doctrine of analogy a bit far.

115 Paul Davies, *The Mind of God*, p. 232.

2

Atheism and Theism

J.J. Haldane

1 Introduction

It is a pleasure to find myself debating with Jack Smart an issue of fundamental theoretical and practical importance. Smart is one of the most distinguished and respected philosophers of his generation and his work has long been associated with the intellectual virtues of clarity, honesty, fairness and modesty. Early in his introduction he avows his commitment to scientific method, and more generally to the idea that 'plausibility in the light of total science is an important guide to metaphysical truth'. I shall be discussing this idea later; but for now I note that he goes on to say that he would attempt to 'explain or explain away putative non-scientific ways of knowing' among which he includes appeal to 'the assumptions of common sense'. There is some irony in this since one thing that Smart has often brought to philosophical discussions is sharp reminders of what we ordinarily believe and of what is implicit within this, reminders intended to deflate and perhaps even to refute what have seemed to him the wilder claims of metaphysics.

An example of this comes later in chapter 1 where he objects to the philosophical thesis that material objects are just constructs of subjective experience, offering the counter that the best explanation of the regularities in our observation is 'the real *actual* existence of the physical objects postulated by science (*and also those implicit in common sense*)' – the latter emphasis is mine. When push comes to shove Smart would probably give priority to science over common sense, a policy I shall question later; but I observe that for him common sense is at least a reasonable, if not an infallible resource when it comes to assessing metaphysical theses.

In this respect, and in the robustness of his own sense of the real, he reminds me of figures in our common intellectual ancestry, *viz*. the Scottish 'Common Sense Realists' – most famously Thomas Reid (1710–96) whose best known writings are directed against the philosophical scepticism of his fellow-Scot, and arguably the greatest British born philosopher, *viz*. David Hume (1711–76). In those days, particularly in Scotland, philosophers debated issues of general importance in styles that were intended to be accessible, so far as possible, to the educated reader. In this century, however, and especially since the Second World War, philosophy has become resolutely academic and professional. There have been clear gains from this and from the associated trend towards specialization; but there have also been real losses, one of which is the unwillingness or inability of many philosophers to engage in wide-ranging but serious discussions in a manner accessible to those who are not already familiar with a specific agenda or technical vocabulary. Smart is an exception to this, and chapter 1 is a good example of how one can range far, making points that are of general interest, while observing professional standards of clarity and rigour. I shall try to emulate his good example.

We would hardly be 'in debate' if we did not hold opposing views, and given the depth and extent of the issues encompassed by atheism and theism it will be no surprise that there is much about which we disagree. Nevertheless I want to begin by emphasizing a point of common conviction. I do so not for the sake of initial courtesies, but because the point in question is a central philosophical thesis, now much controverted, and because it is intimately connected with my commitment to theism – and, indeed, with Smart's attachment to atheism. This is the belief in *metaphysical realism*: the idea that there exists a world independent of any finite mind and that the nature of this mind-independent world is something it possesses independently of and prior to its description by common sense, science or philosophy.

Smart is a metaphysical realist and so am I. We differ in what exactly we think reality is like and more relevantly we differ over the question of whether reality is to be explained as the creation of a divine being or is something whose existence and fundamental character call for no explanation. But although these are major disagreements we find ourselves united in opposing a strong anti-realist current in contemporary philosophy. Anti-realism is the view (or rather, a grouping of views) that 'reality' is not independent of us, in particular of our ways of thinking. One kind of anti-realism is the 'phenomenalism' discussed by Smart and mentioned above. Another is 'ontological

relativism' – the idea that there is no saying what exists independently of some scheme of classification. This is not the harmless claim
that unless we have the means to describe things – the relevant concepts and words – we can't describe them; but rather the striking
thesis that the things in question *do not exist* unless and until, and
only so far as, they are 'delineated' by some classificatory scheme.

There are some things for which it is plausible to make this claim.
Imagine, for example, an artist, 'Graphico', who chooses to depict in
his work only objects within certain arbitrary ranges of shapes, sizes,
sources and surface textures. Perhaps he operates other criteria also,
so that his work portrays a very wide variety of items that are not
otherwise significantly related to one another. Engaged by his unifying
vision we might then refer to the depicted objects – pieces of stone,
bundles of leaves, table tops, patches of grass, cloud formations, sections of human skin, etc. – as 'Graphics'. Here, then, we are in the
position of being able to say that 'Graphics' do not exist independently of human beings. We can be anti-realists about 'Graphics'; but,
of course, what we mean by this is that they do not exist *as Graphics*
independently of our classification. *This* identity is an artefact of human
interests, in particular those of Graphico and his admirers; and we
might add, therefore, 'but of course the things in question may, and
in most cases do, have a prior identity that is not of our making, a
mind-independent nature'. What the metaphysical anti-realist maintains is that there are no such prior natures; everything is a practical
or theoretical artefact in one way or another. Alpha particles, beech
trees, cats, diphtheria, electrons, fish, *et cetera ad infinitum*, are all in
this philosophical sense 'mind-dependent' entities.

This is what Smart and I are united in opposing.[1] Contemporary
anti-realism comes in a variety of forms many of which make their
claims about mind-dependence not in terms of concepts but in terms
of truth. That is to say they hold that what 'depends on us' is whether
something is true or not; truth being understood epistemologically, i.e.
in terms of what is knowable through empirical confirmation or reasoning. A typical version of this formulation of anti-realism might
have it that a claim is true if and only if it is, or can be, confirmed.
Truth, therefore, is immanent within and not transcendent of actual
and potential enquiry. Setting aside what are certainly important issues
about how anti-realism is most aptly expressed, and related issues about
the best formulations of realism, Smart and I maintain that the world and
truth are not in general of our making, and further hold that reality is
a possible object of practical, scientific and philosophical investigation.

Set against this background of significant agreement, however, is our opposition over the question of whether there is a God; and this difference is made more interesting, I believe, by the fact that we would each connect our realism with our perspective on the theism/ atheism issue. Smart has made clear his view that understanding of the world as it is in itself does not call for and indeed is at odds with theism. My belief, by contrast, is that reflection on various matters, including the existence of the world and of minds that can comprehend, appreciate and act within it, leads to the conclusion that there is an immaterial, intelligent, uncaused cause of reality, and that this – as St Thomas Aquinas (1225–74) says – 'is what we call God' (*et hoc dicimus Deum*).

Jack Smart is well-known for his direct and consistent espousal of a scientific, naturalistic version of realism. He is a straightforward atheistic realist. Let me, therefore, add at this stage what readers should also know, both as a matter of 'declared interest' and as a fact relevant to the style of argument and defence I shall present, namely that I am a Christian of a largely 'unreconstructed' sort. More precisely, I am an orthodox Roman Catholic believing in such Credal doctrines as the Trinity, and by implication the Divinity of Jesus Christ; his crucifixion, death and resurrection; the establishment and divine protection of one holy, catholic and apostolic church; the forgiveness of sins; the resurrection of the dead and the life of the world to come. This is clearly not 'minimalist' theism; but nor, as I shall try to show, is it religious fundamentalism of the sort that distrusts or is antagonistic towards philosophy, science and historical scholarship. Indeed, it has been a feature of Catholic Christianity since the days of the Church fathers (the Patristics) that it lays great emphasis on the reasonability of theism in general and on the defensibility of Credal belief in particular.

Of course, there are other views among practising Christians and those who take a philosophical but uncommitted interest in the nature of religion. That which is most clearly opposed to my own approach is one associated with trends emerging out of nineteenth-century Protestant theology – though, along with more or less everything else, it is prefigured in the Middle Ages and in antiquity. On this view (or better, family of views) religion is an autonomous mode of personal engagement with the world. That is to say it is a 'way of going on', the point and coherence of which does not depend upon historical, scientific or philosophical reasoning. The religious person is one whose words and deeds express an orientation of the will towards a set of spiritual values. For this reason the approach is sometimes known as religious 'voluntarism' (L. *voluntas*, will or inclination) or as 'fideism' (L. *fides*, trust or faith).

One appealing feature of this account is that it makes personal character, in particular spirituality, essential to religious commitment; and this contrasts with the image of the soulless scholastic who, though he may debate the metaphysics of angels, the possibility of God's restoring virginity, and the logic of the Trinity, is devoid of religious sense and inclination. A second attraction of voluntarism is that it is more or less (according to its character) immune to rational criticism. Since it does not rely upon reasoned truth it cannot be brought down by philosophical, scientific or historical investigations. In the modern period, and particularly in the eighteenth and nineteenth centuries, traditional theism was subjected to a battery of criticisms from these quarters: Kant's 'refutation' of natural theology, Darwin's scientific alternative to creationism, and scholarly demythologizing of scripture all being cases in point.

However, to the extent that it is invulnerable to such criticisms it seems to diminish in anything other than emotional or assertive content. If one's world view makes no metaphysical or historical claims then it has nothing to fear from these quarters, but equally it has nothing to contribute to them either; and this raises the question of what people think they are doing when they engage in personal prayer or sacramental worship. If Christianity is compatible with Christ's having been a confused, trouble-making zealot whose bones now lie beneath the sands of Palestine and whose 'exploits' are no more than the self-serving fictions of people ignorant of the real events of his life, and with there being no reason to believe, and some reason not to believe, in the existence of a divine creator, then its claims to our attention are only those of a self-contained lifestyle and not of a true account of reality.

Moreover it is a mistake to oppose metaphysics and spirituality. As a general methodological principle one should not presume that because one mode of description and assessment is available it follows that another is excluded. Not only might they be compatible but one may have to draw on both to construct an adequate account. Praying for the dead is a characteristic religious activity expressing a commitment to the value of human life. Saying this does not make metaphysical questions about the possibility and nature of an afterlife irrelevant. On the contrary, it is plausible to hold that the meaning of this activity is given in part by the idea that death may not be the end of the story. Thus if there are insurmountable difficulties in the ideas of disembodiment, reincarnation or resurrection, then the meaning of the religious practice is threatened. As St Paul says, with great seriousness, in his first letter to the Corinthians:

> But if there is no resurrection of the dead, then Christ has not been raised; and if Christ has not been raised, then our preaching is in vain and your faith is in vain . . . If for this life only we have hoped then we are of all men most to be pitied. (1 Corinthians 15: 13–20)[2]

Religion: metaphysical or spiritual? I answer 'both'; but in doing so I am not claiming that every good and true believer needs to be able to offer proofs and refutations. I do maintain, though, that unless religion is in principle rationally defensible then belief is unwarranted; and further that the appropriateness of doctrinal commitment depends upon membership of a (historically extended) religious community within which there are theologians and others competent to provide reasonable defences of these commitments. This is analogous to what is sometimes termed 'the division of intellectual labour'. Testimony, theological competence and teaching authority are essential to doctrinal religion, for without them most believers at most times would be unsupported in their faith.

Once again, however, I should warn readers who may not be aware of it that such a view is not universal among Christians of all denominations. Many would insist upon the necessity and sufficiency of a personal, interior conversion; a finding of God within oneself, in prayer or in the reading of the divine word in scripture. This seems to me to be as unreasonable as a corresponding demand that someone engaged in astronomy establish everything for himself (not consulting textbooks, research material or authorities) including the reliability of his equipment and the methodology of his procedures. Under those conditions few will ever come by much in the way of astronomical knowledge. Similarly, the demand that one establish for oneself the full credentials of one's belief is likely to result in little faith and much disagreement – as, I believe, history shows. If there are no doctrinal authorities then there can be no reliable doctrines and without the latter there can be no significant religious content.

For theists of my persuasion and background it is natural to look to the example of the philosophical theology of the Middle Ages and in particular to the towering and enduring achievements of Aquinas as embodied in the *Summa Theologiae* and many lesser known writings.[3] Like Smart, however, I am a product of English-language philosophy

and feel most at home with analytical styles of argument. Far from
regarding these allegiances as sources of tension, however, I feel
them to be mutually supportive. Indeed on other occasions I have
coined the expression 'analytical Thomism' for the philosophical-cum-
theological approach I find myself following – one, incidentally, that
draws more on the spirit than on the details of Thomistic philosophy.[4]
I am not a historical Thomist. Readers need not be unduly cheered or
troubled by these particular commitments; it is enough to take stock of
the fact that my contribution is that of a straightforward theistic realist.

However else our arguments may be thought to fall short, therefore, neither of us is likely to seem evasive. Smart observes that there
are those whose purported theism amounts to no more than polite,
religiously-affected, atheism; and I have argued that one result of ac-
commodations to modernity has been to drain many accounts of religious belief and practice of any ontological significance. Odd though
it sounds, therefore, there are indeed religious anti-realists; and more
strikingly yet some of them are to be found within religious denominations. So far as the historical self-understanding of Christianity is
concerned the existence of professing atheists within these churches
is at best a mark of profound confusion and at worst a cause of scandal
and despair. If one should come to think that 'God' is a human construct – be it ever so noble and inspiring a one – better to say what
one then truly believes: that there is no God and that faith is in vain.[5]

2   Theism and Science

An important tradition within Western philosophy believes in the
primacy of natural science as a guide to truth. This is sometimes met
with the charge that such an allegiance amounts to 'scientism' – the
view that the only things that 'really' exist are those recognized by
fundamental physical theory; and that the only forms of genuine
knowledge are scientific ones. I shall try to show that a commitment
to fundamental science as the *sole* arbiter of the real is indeed a form
of unwarranted reductionism. But such a case has to be made. Name-
calling is not a method of argument, and it is no less unsatisfactory to
deride atheist materialism as 'scientistic' than it is to abuse theist anti-
materialism by calling it 'superstitious'. If important questions are not
to be begged one has to *show* that a rejection of all else other than scientific ontology and epistemology is unreasonable.

It might be so for a variety of reasons. First, it may be that the materialist's arguments against other ways of thinking are fallacious; second, it may be that while they avoid fallacies they are inconclusive and that this leaves other possibilities as rational options; and third, it may be that the materialist runs into difficulties in stating and arguing for his or her own position. It may even turn out that part of what he or she wants to say only or best makes sense given certain non-materialist, non-reductionist and perhaps even theistic assumptions. I shall be returning to these several ideas at various points but at this stage let me offer a brief illustration.

Smart's belief in science involves the kind of realism mentioned above. That is to say he assumes that the best explanation of our having certain ideas about the structure of the world, such as that it is constituted by material elements located in space–time, is that these ideas are the products of a history of interactions between elements in such a world and subjects who are themselves parts of it. This view rests on a number of further assumptions. First there is the claim that the constituents of the world are possessed of more or less determinate natures and that these are intelligible to human beings. For that to be so many things have to be true of them and of us. On the side of the objects, for example, it is necessary that their intrinsic natures be relatively stable and that they be describable in qualitative and quantitative terms. Assuming that the world is dynamic, the patterns of interaction also need to exhibit a fairly high degree of regularity. Unless these various conditions obtained no sense could be made of biological, genetic, cosmological, chemical and physical theories, or of the forms of observation and experimentation out of which they have developed. Regular orbits of planets around stars and of electrons around nuclei involve stable energy levels and angles of momentum; and considerable intellectual powers of conception, discernment and inference have been exercised in socially shared and continuous histories of scientific enquiry in order to get us to the stage we are at today.

Stability, regularity and intelligibility in world and mind are underlying assumptions of even the most limited claims of scientific realism. But suppose we ask what reason we have for making these assumptions. The general answer cannot be that they are *conclusions* of scientific enquiry, since they are part of what makes it possible. Rather we should say that assumptions concerning the intelligibility of objects and the intelligence of subjects are preconditions of empirical enquiry revealed by reflection on thought and practice. This recognition raises a number of issues including that of whether such preconditions serve to establish the existence of a God. I shall examine this in due course; but for now I only want to observe that science involves an absolutely fundamental and extensive commitment to the nature of reality; one that is presupposed rather than derived from it; and one that makes ineliminable reference to the idea that what there is is intelligible.

So viewed, it should now seem odd to *oppose* scientific and religious ways of thinking about the nature of reality. On the contrary, it is plausible to regard them as similar; for a central idea of theism is that we and the world we inhabit constitute an objective order that exhibits intrinsic intelligibility. What is added is the claim that both the existence and the intelligibility of this order call for an explanation and that this is given by reference to a mindful creator. Thus science is faith-like in resting upon 'credal' presuppositions, and inasmuch as these relate to the order and intelligibility of the universe they also resemble the content of a theistic conception of the world as an ordered creation. Furthermore it seems that the theist carries the scientific impulse further by pressing on with the question of how perceived order is possible, seeking the most fundamental descriptions-cum-explanations of the existence and nature of the universe.

It will not do to respond that this further search is unscientific, for that is simply to beg the question against the theist. Assuming that by 'science' we understand investigation of and theorizing about the empirical order then properly scientific attitudes and interests are certainly compatible with theism. Indeed the Judaeo-Christian-Islamic doctrine of creation serves to underwrite science by assuring us that its operative assumptions of order and intelligibility are correct and by providing a motivation for pure science, namely understanding the composition and modes of operation of a vastly complex mind-reflecting artefact.

Let us pursue this approach a bit further. Smart's version of scientific realism is *reductionist*. He dismisses a familiar version of the design argument on the grounds that the apparent teleology of living systems is explicable by reference to the blind and purposeless operations of evolution – random mutation plus 'selection' of features having adaptive utility. This is something to which I shall return in the next section, but as above my concern at this stage is to query whether Smart's conception of science is not ideologically driven. Consider, then, the insistence upon reductionism. Like so many other expressions used by philosophers this is a term of art in need of definition. To begin with let me distinguish between ontological and conceptual-cum-explanatory reductions. These can go together but they need not.

An ontological reduction maintains that one purported category or class of entities is a construct and that the things belonging to it are derived from some more basic category. So, for example, the *average weight* of members of a population is an artefact derived from a series of *actual weights* upon which a mathematical operation has been performed: average weight W = the sum of real weights (w^1, w^2, w^3, ... w^n) divided by the total number n in the population. Therefore, we might say there are no such things as average weights over and above real weights. Certainly some individual's weight may in fact be equal to the average; nevertheless his weight is real in a way that the average is not. This comes out in the fact that there need not be anyone whose weight equals the average; the latter is not an actual scale-impacting weight but rather an intellectual construct abstracted from such. At this point, however, the ontological reduction might be pressed further, since it may be claimed that *actual weight* is not a fundamental category either, but is itself an artefact reducible to 'real' features such as mass and gravitational acceleration. At some stage, however, the reductions will have to come to an end and this amounts to an identification of the class of basic entities.

In order to appreciate the difference between ontological and explanatory reductionism it is useful to distinguish between, on the one hand, things or natures and, on the other, concepts or terms. Ontological reductionism holds that what are identified as Xs are really Ys; explanatory reductionism maintains that talk of 'Xs' can be replaced without loss of content by talk of 'Ys'. In the philosophy of mind, for example, there are at least two kinds of behaviourism both of which involve reductionism. Some behaviourists argue that mentalistic concepts such as 'belief' and 'desire' classify patterns of actual and potential behaviour, and moreover that these concepts can be replaced by overtly behavioural ones without loss of meaning. In short, to say that A 'believes' something is not to describe or attribute a state additional to his or her behaviour. It is precisely to refer to that behaviour, and the same reference could be made using undisguisedly behavioural terms. This claim combines ontological and explanatory reductions by insisting both that there are no mental attributes over and above patterns of behaviour, and that mental concepts can be translated into or replaced by behavioural notions. However, while having reason to suppose that there are no relevant facts additional to behavioural ones someone might hold that mental concepts have a content that cannot be reduced to that of behavioural terms. In this event one might advance ontological but not conceptual or explanatory behaviourism.

Every fact about 'minds' is a fact about behaviour but not every (or any?) mentalistic description is equivalent in content to a behavioural one.

The philosopher-theologian Bishop Butler (1692–1752) coined the maxim 'Everything is what it is and not another thing' and thereby pointed to a general difficulty for reductionism. If some class of entities does not really exist why are there terms purportedly referring to them? This question becomes the more pressing in a context in which someone insists upon ontological reduction but concedes that conceptual or explanatory reductions are unavailable. In the case of average weights the question is easily answered by indicating the convenience of averages so far as certain of our interests are concerned. But here the insistence upon ontological reduction is accompanied by an adequate explanatory reduction. Consider instead the philosophical example mentioned above, namely that of behaviourism. If, as is now generally accepted, mentalistic vocabulary *cannot* be reduced to behaviouristic terms, what can motivate and sustain the insistence that this fact notwithstanding there is really only behaviour, with apparent reference to mental states being an artefact of a way of speaking? One response would be to show that, appearances to the contrary, there are no irreducibly mental states because there could be none. The very idea, let us say, is contradictory.

In Smart's essay we find him arguing that a properly scientific view has no place for teleologies, not because he has an argument to show that there could be no such things as purposes but because he believes that such teleological talk can be shown to be like the case of average weights, a convenient *façon de parler*. However, from the terms in which he invokes neo-Darwinian theories of natural selection to set aside 'old'-style teleological arguments, it also seems that he accepts that were there irreducible purposes in nature that fact would support a case for theism. For my part I contest the claim that purposive descriptions and explanations are out of place in science. Not only do I believe that many teleological concepts are irreducible, I think that a commitment to the reality of objective natures, functions and associated values is presupposed by scientific enquiry and speculation. In effect, therefore, I am suggesting that Smart's approach is unwarrantedly 'scientistic' inasmuch as it is motivated by a prior concern to avoid non-natural explanations and its concept of nature is an austerely physicalist one. I shall try to show how it is possible to respect and value science without being scientistic and thereby to develop a less restrictive and more extensive understanding of nature.

3 Some Varieties of Explanation

In the following two sections I shall explore a series of design arguments, including that which Smart takes most seriously, *viz.* the argument from 'fine tuning'. I do not have equal confidence in each, in part because of my own ignorance of the relevant scientific data but also because I doubt that the current state of our philosophical development is such that we are yet in a position finally to decide upon them. The latter point arises from the variety of forms of description and explanation, a variety that the reductionism of modern philosophy has tended to obscure.

With the seeming exception of the ontological argument which maintains that it is part of the very concept of God that that concept is necessarily instantiated, all theistic arguments involve claims about *causation*. I shall not discuss ontological proofs because to the extent that I have a settled interpretation of them I am in essential agreement with the sorts of objections Smart presents. That said, and I believe this may have been the view of St Anselm (1033–1109) himself, ontological reasoning might have a legitimate role in philosophical theology in serving as a bridge between the conclusion – reached by non-ontological arguments – that there is a cause of things, and further claims about the nature of that cause, such as that it is perfect.[6]

The other sorts of arguments – from natural regularity and purpose, from contingency, from change, from the existence and nature of special features such as minds and values, and so on, are all species of *causal* arguments. They maintain that the natural order, or something encountered as, or inferred to be, part of it, could not exist save for the existence and *efficacy* of something else that is not itself part of that order (or not essentially so – for Christians believe that in the person of Jesus Christ God the Creator entered into His own creation).

In antiquity and in the Middle Ages philosophers held that there were a variety of distinct types of causes. That is to say, their reflections led them to identify a range of productive factors that might be cited in descriptions or explanations. Following Aristotle these philosophers identified four causes, or four kinds of 'because' explanations,[7] the so-called '*material*', '*formal*', '*efficient*' and '*final*' causes; but this taxonomy always had the appearance of artificiality (not to say numerology: the number 4 has been held to be a 'significant' number – but then again so have the numbers 3 and 5), and once one begins to consider the variety of statements in which one thing is explained by or related to another it is not at all clear how many basic types of 'cause' there may be. Consider, for example, the following: '6 is even *because* it is divisible by two'; 'I am still alive *because* my heart and brain are still functioning'; 'my heart and brain are still functioning *because* I am still alive'; 'the quadrangle seems exposed *because* the design of the north-east corner is unresolved'; 'Mary is happy *because* she is contented'; 'the figure is trilateral *because* it is triangular'; 'the villain was cruel *because* of his selfishness'; 'the rules were breached, the audience was offended, the baby cried and the alarm went off all *because* he started shouting', and so on.

In some sense(s) these various claims are causal ones; certainly one can reformulate them using the word 'cause' rather than 'because'. But it is a matter of enduring philosophical controversy how they should be understood; and this difficulty is not resolved by insisting, as many contemporary philosophers do, that there is only one kind of causation, namely efficient causation, the paradigm of which is one object colliding with another and starting it in motion. Whatever else might be said it is obvious that the number 6 is not even because it can literally be sliced in half by the number 2, and however his shouting caused the rules to be breached it was not, as with the setting off of the alarm, by setting up motions of air molecules that then impacted a surface.

Uncertainty about the nature and varieties of causation is bound to affect (itself another type of causing!) interpretations and assessments of causal arguments, particularly if these involve more than one kind of cause. It is in part for this reason that I entered the qualification about our ability to make conclusive assessments of non-ontological proofs of theism. In particular the design arguments that I am interested in here posit an extra-natural cause from somewhat different perspectives and the nature of these viewpoints bears upon the sense of the causal claim involved. The arguments in question are from functional natures, from enabling pre-conditions and sustaining conditions, and from intellectual understanding. The first two are discussed by Smart.

Most forms of scientific enquiry are non-microscopic. Most of what people study in university and pursue in non-academic fields and laboratory research concerns categories of phenomena above the level of physics. Such studies are generally concerned with dynamic systems. These enquiries are certainly mindful of the fact that the entities in question are composed out of matter but the focus of their interest is *organization*, in particular functional organization. They want to know what has happened, is happening or will happen and what the active and passive powers of the various 'elements' are. For example, environmental studies may combine astronomical, meteorological, botanical and various other sciences in the effort to understand the development of a system. In doing this it uses a series of taxonomical and explanatory schemes in which reference to natures and functions is extensive. It would be a mistake to suppose that such branches of scientific study could purge themselves of these sorts of notions, since they and the observational and theoretical methods that go with them are constitutive of these very forms of enquiry. Botany can no more dispense with notions of structure, function and growth than cricket can purge itself of the ideas of innings, runs and wickets.

There is a general point of some importance here. Reductionists often confuse formal nature and material composition. In their concern to show that ultimately there is nothing more than 'atoms in the void' or 'energy plus space–time', they overlook or underestimate the significance of the hierarchy of forms within which matter is held together. I am not at all suggesting that one go in the opposite direction and say that what individual things are made of, and what, if anything, *everything* in the cosmos is made of, is unimportant for an understanding of the natural order; but I am claiming that real science, as contrasted with the reductionist philosopher's ambition for it, is happy to recognize a variety of features and levels of natural being, and can proceed very well without progressive elimination of one sphere after another, collapsing the structure of science down to the atomic core that is physics.

It might be conceded that the concepts of the life sciences, for example, cannot be reduced to physics; but Smart and others will want to insist that there is nothing in biology that is incompatible with a wholly physicalist world view. Nothing in the higher levels of organization of matter involves real properties or forms of causation that are non-physical or non-mechanistic. Here more could be said about how the terms 'physical' and 'mechanical' may be interpreted but it is not in the interest of the debate between Smart and me to be too liberal about this. We are concerned with whether the physical and the real are one, and subject to details which he explains (about the best interpretation of mathematics and set theory, for example) Smart says they are and I say they are not. So when he makes his claim on behalf of physicalism, he denies that reality contains anything over and above what physics recognizes.

4 'Old' Teleology

The case of biology is a significant test of attitudes, for, as Smart notes, living systems were long cited in design proofs and neo-Darwinian theory is supposed to have put an end to this. My earlier point about actual sciences being built around the recognition of distinctive forms of organization of matter tells against reductionism as a general policy and applies to the relation between chemistry and quantum mechanics as much as to that between zoology and general physics. But the traditional teleological argument is concerned with a special claim of irreducibility, *viz.* that of purpose to mechanism. Teleologists maintain that organisms exhibit beneficial order: that is to say both in their general organization and in the functioning of their parts they generally operate in ways that are, in one or another way, good for them. For example, the lungs absorb oxygen, the heart pumps blood, the kidneys remove waste products, the genitals enable procreation and so on. Naïvely, it seems natural to say that these parts and functions exist for the well-being of the animals, be they individuals or species, and, assuming that they are not intelligent entities prudently directing their own behaviour, that the existence of such well-organized structures points to a benign designer.

This, in essence, is the last of Aquinas's famous five ways (*quinque viae*) or proofs set out in response to the second question 'whether there is a God' of the *Summa Theologiae* (Ia, q. 2, a. 3.). The text is brief and worth quoting in full to give a flavour of the directness of Aquinas's style:

> The fifth way is based on the guidedness of nature. Goal-directed behaviour is observed in all bodies in nature, even those lacking awareness; for we see their behaviour hardly ever varying and practically always turning out well, which shows they truly tend to goals and do not merely hit them by accident. But nothing lacking awareness can tend to a goal except it be directed by someone with awareness and understanding; arrows by archers, for example. So everything in nature is directed to its goal by someone with understanding and this we call God.[8]

St Thomas's formulation can be applied to the issue of fine tuning but at this stage I am concerned with apparent purpose in the organization and activity of living things. Belief in real teleology and in the need of a purposeful agent to create and sustain it has been held to be refuted on the basis of the theory of natural selection. Given replication, inheritance, variation, environment and time the range of animate species is explicable in physico-mechanical terms. So it is said, but the issue is not quite so clear.

First, a concession to the anti-teleologist or mechanist. It is right for him or her to argue that the traditional design argument is challenged by the mere possibility of evolutionary explanations. If the existence of such complex animals could be the result of natural mechanico-evolutionary processes then any argument to the effect that they could only have come into existence through a special creation is thereby refuted. This is correct, but note where the concession leaves the debate. Unless the evolutionist has an argument to show that creation is excluded we are faced with competing hypotheses. Indeed the dialectic is subtler still, since the theist may not want to exclude evolutionary theory as an account of the history of species development but only to reject it as a complete explanation. However, even this position requires that he or she produce reasons for thinking that natural selection cannot be the whole story.

I think there are three places, or points of transition, at which such reasons may be found. First, the step from non-living to living entities; second, the step from basic 'life forms' to reproductive species; and third, the transition from mindless to minded life. I shall deal with the last of these later and at some length but take the first and second together now.

The Emergence of Life and the Origins of Reproduction

Old style vitalism, the dualistic idea that living things are composites of two substances, a quantity of inanimate matter and a motivating *élan vital* or life force, has little to be said for it. Indeed, from the point of view of the Aristotelian picture I favour it is quite the wrong way to think of the nature of living things. On this preferred account the difference between an inanimate object and a living thing is not that the latter is a lump of matter plus an immaterial agent resident within it; rather it is that the latter has an intrinsic functional organization in virtue of which its movements are explicable in terms of ends towards which they are directed. Notice that this is an avowedly non-reductive and teleological characterization. That is not a problem for me; rather it presents a challenge to the anti-teleologist to provide a non-teleological account of the difference between living and non-living things.

Appeal to their matter alone will hardly do. First, the pure reductionist will not want to rest his account at any level that is not further reducible to physics, so an ineliminable chemical theory will be problematic. Second, bracketing this point, no merely compositional account seems adequate since it need not be an issue of contention what non-living and living things are made of. The question is what makes one and not another *alive*. To deploy the Aristotelian terminology it may be agreed that inanimate A and animate B have the same kind of material cause (physical substratum), the issue is whether this is sufficient to explain their natures as kinds of things, living and non-living respectively. According to the neo-vitalist account each has a formal cause, that which makes it be the sort of thing it is, and the latter has a final cause – its organic well-being or efficient functioning – towards which it is moving.

I began this contrast in terms that suggest comparing two objects sitting side by side on a table – or more realistically two specimens beneath a microscope or in some other apparatus. But any purported naturalistic account of the nature of vitality will want to serve in a historical account of the origins of life. That is because the naturalism in question is materialist and involves the familiar idea that life itself has evolved from non-living matter. Thus the difference between the living and the inanimate has first to be specified, and then it has to be shown how there could be a natural transition from one kind of state to another. There will be no principled obstacle to success in the latter task if the former leaves no vitalist or teleological residue. For then one will only have to show how one spatio-temporal arrangement of microphysical particles led to another. But notice that this course involves the denial that there are any such entities as living things and that there was ever any such process as the emergence of life. In reality, the situation is no different from that obtaining before the earth and the sun were formed.

This 'eliminativist' conclusion is at odds with what is generally supposed to be the case, including the presuppositions of most working scientists. We do believe there are living things and that they exhibit features additional to those of matter as that is characterized by physics. The nature of such features is precisely what the life sciences are concerned to describe and understand. Moreover, nothing in elementary physics forces us to say that this is an illusion; there is nothing in physics that is incompatible with biology, even teleology.

It is only the philosophical imperative of reductionist materialism that requires the denial of ontological and explanatory irreducibility.

Suppose then that this point is conceded, but it is maintained that the existence and emergence of life do not call for any explanation beyond that available to naturalism. My objection is now this: if these accounts eschew eliminativism and allow the veridicality of biological characterizations, then they have to show why descriptions of beneficial teleology are not also warranted, and how the laws of nature operating on inanimate matter could generate life. The former is so to speak a 'stopping' problem, the latter a 'starting' one. If the existence of complex living forms is allowed why not grant what appearances also suggest, namely that these forms exhibit beneficial order? Why stop with mere life? And if even mere life is granted how did it start? The latter question is intended as a philosophical one. I am not asking what the natural mechanism is but how it is even conceivable that there could be one. Since no conjunction of descriptions of purely physical states together with non-biological laws entails a description of biological states any account of these issues is going to be open to a vitalist interpretation. The advocate of neo-vitalism, in the Aristotelian sense explained above, can claim that what has been described is the material-causal substratum of life not something that is of itself sufficient for it. It may be countered that this is ontologically extravagant, to which I would respond that it is not superfluous if a materialistic explanation seems incomplete, and that only a non-scientific insistence on reductionism motivates the thesis that it must be no more than mechanism even where there could be no deductive explanation of how it is so.

The next stage in the defence of teleology concerns not the origins of life but its evolutionary history. First, however, let me observe that contrary to some popular expositions evolutionary biologists do not try to show that every advantageous characteristic is the direct product of natural selection. Genetic mutations rarely have single effects and if some of these improve the reproductivity of breeding populations then while they will tend to be selected for, other collateral effects may be preserved so long as they are not seriously disadvantageous. Thus features may emerge that were not themselves selected, and some of these may be good, some indifferent, and some bad – though not so bad as to be fatal. In other words, even within the sphere of contemporary evolutionary theory it is conceded that not every significant characteristic, organ or power is an evolutionary adaptation.

That selection is not a necessary condition of species development may not be so troubling given the general presumption of evolution. More problematic is the suggestion that it might not be sufficient: that a further cause may need to be operative. The standard evolutionary account of speciation is in terms of cumulative selection. That is to say, very roughly, it is supposed that the origination of one species from another is not by a single step (that would defy belief) but by progressive sifting and sorting as the product of one selection is then subjected to further selection, and so on. Think, for example, of a gardener who wants to grow large, strong vegetables but currently has only small, frail flowers. He could try planting the seeds from the latter and waiting until spring but it would be a miracle if these seeds developed into what he wanted. However, if he were patient and lived long enough, then he might proceed by gathering seeds from the largest and strongest of the flowers, planting these, training and nurturing the seedlings eliminating the weaker ones; then gathering the seeds from the largest and strongest plants, and so on. It would be less surprising if eventually cumulative selection proved effective in leading to the development of a species of the desired sort.

Purged of intention and agency this is how evolutionary theory explains development. Notice, however, that cumulative selection presupposes some form of replication possessed by the original and intervening living entities. They need to have some mechanism of reproduction. This is a feature to be explained by selection no less than others, but it is hard to see how it can be. Selection purports to explain adaptive features of which replication is prime; but it operates over generations, and successive generations only come into existence because of the replicative powers of their ancestors. These powers cannot themselves be the product of cumulative selection. So, contrary to its implausibility, the claim has to be that their emergence occurred in a single step; somehow non-replicating entities just turned into reproducing species.

A likely rejoinder to this observation will be the claim that the initial step was not to full-scale reproduction but to proto-replication. Organic reproduction proceeds asexually or sexually. In the first case parts of the organism become detached and form new individuals; and in the second, special cells (gametes) are formed within individuals, and the joining of these in fertilization yields a cell that develops into an individual of the same type as its parents. The selection of advantageous parts and powers is made possible because of the inheritance by one generation of features possessed by the previous one, and the transmission of the same or relatively similar characteristics to its offspring. One way of regarding this process is in terms of the transmission of organizational information through enduring and reliable channels to which the various parties have access. The present worry is that any theory claiming that communication produces the channels – along with everything else – faces the objection that without the channels there could be no communication. They are part of what the organizational information creates. The envisaged reply is that initially something arises which is less than a power of transmission but enough to get the process of communication started.

One way of framing the worry I have about this is that it seems to be trying to account for a significant qualitative difference in terms of a merely quantitative one. Let me illustrate what I mean, and indicate why I think there is a problem, by switching to a parallel case concerning the nature of mental phenomena. I shall be saying more about the philosophy of mind and theism shortly; at this point the feature to focus on is simply the structural analogy between the case I am about to discuss and that of reproduction.

A few years ago I wrote an essay in the course of which I criticized the efforts of Daniel Dennett to give an adequate reductionist account of mental representation.[9] The problem is this. Thoughts are intentional in the technical sense that they are directed towards, or are about, something or other (from the Latin '*intendere*': to aim or direct). How is this possible? One much discussed suggestion is that to think 'There is a tree in the garden' is for one's mental system to be in a computational state involving a representation – a sentence in the mind and/or in the head – the content of which is that there is a tree in the garden. Very crudely indeed, one might thus suppose that someone thinks that p when his or her information processing system entertains a mental sentence 'S' the meaning of which is that p.

Much could be said about this, but here simply note that it involves a homuncular regress ('*homo*' (man), '-culvs' (little)). The problem of mental representation has not gone away. It has just been moved from the personal to the subpersonal level: I think that p because (in some sense or other) there is something – a 'processing module' – in me that can interpret a symbol 'S' that means that p. To his credit, Dennett sees that this proposal is hopelessly regressive if treated in realist terms, i.e. as maintaining that representational power is derived from a representational subsystem, and so he offers an alternative reductionist-cum-eliminativist version of it. He writes:

[You] replace the little man in the brain with a committee [whose members] are stupider than the whole; they are less intelligent and 'know' less. The subsystems don't individually reproduce all of the talents of the whole. That would lead you to an infinite regress. Instead you have each subsystem doing a part, so that each homuncular subsystem is less intelligent, knows less, believes less. The representations are themselves, as it were, less representational . . . a whole system of these stupid elements can get to exhibit behaviour which looks distinctly intelligent, distinctly human.[10]

Engaging as it is, I suggest that this proposal fails because of a fallacy of equivocation committed in the sentence: '*The representations are themselves, as it were, less representational.*' To say that something is 'less representational' is ambiguous between claiming that it represents less and maintaining that it is less a representation. Dennett hopes to 'discharge the homunculi' by progressive reduction of representational content; but the fact that some representations contain less information does not on that account make them any less representations. The *non-representation – representation* distinction is not the same as the *much representation – less representation* distinction; and one cannot explain the former in terms of the latter, since however little intentional content a representation carries it is still on that very account a representation.

Commenting on this objection Kathy Wilkes proposes that it can easily be set aside:

> For Haldane, intentionality, or the existence of representations, is all or nothing . . . I find this impossible to believe . . . We need only look to neuroscience; where time and again the 'homuncular strategy' is bearing fruit. Low-level function can be called 'expecting/comparing', 'detecting', 'synthesizing'; as we go down the hierarchy the degree of intentionality fades, the representations do indeed (*pace* Haldane) become more limited (cf. the primary visual cortex, where cell-columns 'detect horizontals', or 'detect colour contrasts').[11]

However, if one compares this passage with that from Dennett it should be clear that it invites exactly the same response. The intentionalizing of low-level functions may be methodologically convenient, but if a regressive homuncularism is to avoided it has to be discharged. Mention of 'fading' intentionality does not begin to achieve this when, as here, it is explained in terms of the representations becoming more limited. If one process detects both horizontals and verticals, and another detects only horizontals, then the second is to that extent more limited, but it is not thereby any less a process of detection.

Recall now the response that although the evolution of species proceeds by cumulative selection which presupposes reproduction, which itself could only plausibly be the product of cumulative selection, nonetheless the process could begin with proto-replication. What is envisaged is quantities of primitive organic matter 'giving rise' in one way or another to further quantities that resemble the originals, and so on. The inescapable question, however, is whether this initial process involves the exercise of powers of reproduction, be they ever so limited. To say that it does, intending by this a realist non-reductionist interpretation, is to ascribe teleology to the process and to admit the failure of mechanistic evolutionary theory. However, to say that it does not leaves it unexplained how reproduction could emerge out of successive non-reproductive events.

Admittedly, there are many conceivable circumstances in which chance forces act upon something in such a way that the effect is the production of things like the first. Imagine, for example, the improbable but not impossible situation in which three pieces of slate fall in succession and at different angles on to a cube of clay cutting it into eight smaller cubes. Interesting as this might be, it is not the exercise by the cube of a power of reproduction. Similarly, the mere sundering of organic matter into several pieces is not a form of asexual reproduction, and nor is it made such by repetition. Certainly if a number of distinct individuals of relevantly similar sorts participate in processes that systematically give rise to the existence of further individuals of the same sorts, which in turn lead to more of the same or similar and so on, then it becomes reasonable to attribute powers of replication. But this is not an explanation of reproduction; it is a description of it. And if to avoid this conclusion one says that each successive stage is really like the first, not reproductive but 'reproductive' or 'proto-replicative', i.e. the product of chance, then not only does evolutionary biology have no account of systematic reproduction, which is the basis of its theory of speciation, but what was an initial improbability is now multiplied unimaginably many millions of times over.

On this account anything could result from anything at any time. It is not even that one would be saying that the reproductive process can sometimes go wildly wrong. The idea of going wrong presupposes a background of operational normality, and the idea of a reproductive process is that of something different in kind from a mere statistical pattern. Certainly it is not logically impossible that every single step of evolutionary history should have been a biological accident in the radical sense now envisaged, as if falling slates kept quartering cubes here, there and everywhere, many millions of times. No *contradiction* is involved in this supposition. Nonetheless it is incompatible with a realist interpretation of general biology, let alone special evolutionary theory; and to borrow a delightfully low-key phrase from Richard Swinburne it is 'not much to be expected'; or as a Scot might say (with greater effect, if perhaps less accuracy) 'nae chance'.

I am not arguing the case for creationist science, the not logically impossible but foolish view that there is nothing to evolution; that God made the world as we find it today, a few thousand or a few hundred thousand years ago, complete with the fossil record. Early in chapter 1 Jack Smart writes of how his beliefs about reality are formed in the light of total science. As would be expected I cannot agree that this is a wholly adequate methodological principle (at least as he interprets it). Yet I certainly think that reason supports the claim of the empirical sciences to be a major source of our knowledge about reality, and no one who takes scientific canons of enquiry seriously should be willing to suppose that the world came into being in the period suggested by literal biblical creationists. Further, I acknowledge that there is a history of evolutionary processes and that our evidence and inferential grounds for thinking this also provide reason for linking humankind with pre-human species. What I have been arguing, however, is that biology, including its evolutionary dimension, cannot be understood or adequately accounted for in purely mechanical non-teleological terms. The emergence of life and the start of speciation call for explanations and what reductionism has to offer fails to provide these, giving at best a blank cheque to chance, which is to say offering no intelligible explanation at all.

Mind over Matter

Consider next, then, the special case of *Homo sapiens*. One of the enduring problems of philosophy concerns the nature of mind and its relation to matter. Over the centuries a variety of possibilities has been canvassed, but these can all be placed within a general and exhaustive distinction between materialist and non-materialist views. Smart is a materialist; I am a non-materialist. There are different forms of each position. Earlier I discussed eliminativism as a view about biological phenomena. This holds that there are no such things as biological states and that we are misled if we think that biology implies that there are. Anything true that it has to say can, in principle, be otherwise and better said in the language of some more fundamental science – ultimately physics. Similarly eliminative materialists in the philosophy of mind maintain that there are no such things as mental states. I regard this view as not much more plausible than it sounds, which is to say wildly implausible; and on other occasions I have tried to argue this in debate with one of its best-known proponents, *viz.* the Canadian-born philosopher Paul Churchland.[12]

Here I shall not pursue the details of our dispute, but it is appropriate to offer the following brief defence of common-sense, or as it is sometimes disparagingly referred to, 'folk' psychology. First, then, it is uncontested between critics and defenders that we have an idea of ourselves as subjects of consciousness, thought and agency. We describe ourselves as acting and we explain and evaluate our actions by citing reasons for them. Our reasons are taken to involve beliefs and desires, or more generally to have cognitive and conative aspects or elements. These latter we take to involve representations of our common environment; further, it is supposed that in language and through other forms of symbol manipulation we communicate our beliefs and feelings to one another. The eliminativist's claim is that all of this is a myth, an erroneous account of the nature and causes of behaviour. We are in the grip of a false theory of human beings. All that really exists is bodily movement arising from neurophysiological events; instead of being thinking agents we are organic machines. Against this I contend that ordinary psychological descriptions, including self-descriptions, are not parts of a proto-scientific theory of the unseen and unknown inner causes of movement, but (often observational) accounts of thought and action – in the latter case interpretations of intentional behaviour.

According to the eliminativist the apparent action described as 'Kirsty's writing a sentence' is in truth no more than a sequence of causally related physical events. Since 'writing' is an action-term implying intention, and 'sentence' is a grammatical description presupposing common linguistic conventions, the eliminativist is committed to the possibility of replacing these with non-psychopersonal terms in his account of events. It is now generally agreed among philosophers that 'type–type' psychophysical identity theories will not work. That is to say any hypothesis to the effect that psychological items of type Ψ (*psi*) are identical with physical items of type Φ (*phi*) falls foul of the fact that instances of the former type can be associated with many different sorts of physical set-ups. There are, for example, indefinitely many ways of writing a paragraph and it would be crazy to think that this action type could be correlated with any specifiable type of bodily movement, or even with a disjunction of these, preparatory to identifying the former with the latter (and eliminating the one in favour of the other). That is to say, any suggestion of the form 'action type Ψ is identical with physical type Φ, or with one or other of the physical types Φ^1, Φ^2, Φ^3, Φ^4, ...' is refuted by actual or easily imagined cases of the former that are not cases of the latter.

What I now want to add to this is the suggestion that it is equally impossible to sustain a 'token–token' identity theory. Such a theory would insist that while action types cannot be identified with physical event types, nevertheless individual instances (or tokens) of the former can be identified with instances of the latter. In other words I am claiming that actions cannot be identified with, reduced to, or eliminated in favour of movements of quantities of matter. Imagining an appropriate scene, ask yourself the question what is the physical event that is the reality otherwise described as 'Kirsty's writing a sentence'? No doubt some bodily movement, but which? As one begins to think about individuating a series of events within a region of space–time the nature of the problem starts to become clear. Consider all the movements involving Kirsty's body that might have occurred in the specified region: heartbeats, hair quiverings, eye blinkings, nerve impulses, muscle contractions, desk impactings and so on. There is no prospect, not even 'in principle', of identifying relevant movements save by non-dispensable use of action concepts involving reference to Kirsty's intentional behaviour. The relation between the movements thereby identified and the action itself is not one of identity but composition. Actions are more than movements; persons are more than bodies. Eliminativists and other reductive materialists are led to suppose otherwise because they bring to the issue a prior presumption that all there is, and so all that can be involved, is matter in the physicalist sense.

Let me note here that while Smart is certainly a materialist he does not, I believe, go along with those who claim that it is possible, in principle, to give definitional or deductive equivalents of psychological terms, and nor does he agree with Churchland that psychological descriptions can be eliminated. His view is that notwithstanding the impossibility of reductions or eliminations it is plausible to hold that there are no genuine mental properties, no features over and above those acknowledged by physics. How can someone defend such a view? After all if it is allowed that talk of beliefs, desires, intentions and so on is appropriate, and that it is not equivalent to talk about physical states, is this not reason to acknowledge that there are irreducible psychological attributes? Indeed does it not involve an implicit commitment to the reality of the mental as a distinct category?

If I have him aright, Smart's view is that some kind of property dualism or mental emergentism would be the appropriate conclusion were it not for other considerations. More precisely, he believes, first, that the circumstances in which we find ourselves attributing psychological states to one another, and the styles of those attributions, encourage an identification of the former with states of the brain; and second, that we have reasons not to posit non-physical properties, these being the sufficiency of physics and the difficulty of reconciling other sorts of facts and explanations with it.

In discussing the problem of evil towards the end of chapter 1 Smart describes and defends determinism. I shall have reason to come back to both issues later; for now, however, I want to pick up what he has to say about the explanation of actions. In keeping with a widely shared view he holds that in citing an agent's reasons we are giving *causes* of his actions. This will seem to support the identification of psychological with physical states if we also assume that the brain fits into the explanation of behaviour in a similar way. Let us suppose Kirsty wrote her sentence *because* she wanted to communicate her ideas. In writing it her body moved in various ways *because* of events in her brain and nervous system. Putting these two together we might conclude that there was one sequence of behaviour describable psychologically and physiologically, and one cause (or subset of causes) specified in the first case by talk of reasons and in the second by talk of events in the central nervous system. This inference constitutes the first of the considerations against property dualism. The second is less an argument than an extended assumption. It is that physics is all we need and that since the recognition of any other kind of reality would *ex hypothesi* be inexplicable physicalistically, it would be at odds with physics.

Taking these in reverse order, the issue of whether the physicalist world-view is adequate is precisely what is in question and so it cannot be assumed as part of a case against any alternative. Equally the idea that acknowledgement of mental attributes is incompatible with physics is only true if by 'physics' one means not physical science but physicalism, the doctrine that there is nothing other than what physics deals with. Certainly the latter is incompatible with acceptance of *sui generis* psychological states and features, let alone the existence of an immaterial deity, but again the truth of physicalism is what is at issue. It cannot be part of an argument in favour of itself.

As regards what one might term 'the argument from causation' recall my earlier comments about the variability of causal ('because') explanations. When we say 'Kirsty wrote because she wanted to communicate' and 'her body moved because of events in her brain' it is by no means obvious that the two 'becauses' signify the same kind of relation. In the second case we are dealing with efficient causation; very crudely, a case of an energy transfer communicated from one place to another through the intervening physical medium, sections of the body. But in the first case what 'because' introduces seems to be an item from the rational and not the physical order; in Aristotelian–Thomistic terms it is a formal-cum-final cause. Compare this with the difference between saying 'the circular stain on the table is there because of a coffee mug', and saying 'the area of the stain is not equal to that of a square of the same breadth because it has a circular boundary'. In the first case the base of the mug left an impression on a surface, but in the second circularity is not doing any impacting or pushing, the relation in question is an abstract geometrical one. So from the fact that 'because' features in explanations of writing and of bodily movements we cannot immediately proceed to the conclusion that both are statements of efficient causation, and then look for this single inner causal factor.

Moreover the causal argument I sketched helped itself to an ambiguity in the term 'behaviour'. We can say the writing was a piece of behaviour on Kirsty's part and that during the relevant period her body was behaving in various ways. But it would be another hasty inference to suppose that what is referred to is the same in both cases, and thus that if the cause of the latter was a set of brain events then *ex hypothesi* this was the cause of the former. Writing is intentional behaviour, i.e. action; bodily movements may or may not be intentional. So although there is an appropriate use of the term by which we may speak of the behaviour of muscles and bones it would be a fallacy of equivocation to infer that movements and actions are the same. Of course, this fails to show that they are not the same; for all I have just said they could be. The point was rather to defuse an argument that assumed they were and on that basis inferred that actions are nothing other than bodily movements effected by brain events.

Now, however, I want to go further and argue that there are grounds for not regarding action and psychological explanation more generally as a species of causal explanation in the sense required by the physicalist argument. Assuming the law-like nature of efficient causation, and the claim that giving reasons is giving efficient causes, it ought to be the case that there are psychological laws connecting psychological states to one another and (as reasons) to actions. As Paul Churchland has been concerned to emphasize there are indeed well-established psychological generalizations of an apparently law-like form – what he calls the 'explanatory laws of folk psychology'. Consider the following examples:

(1) *For any subject x and any propositional content p: if x fears that p then x desires that it not be the case that p,*

and

(2) *For any subject x and any propositional contents p and q: if x believes that p, and believes that if p then q, then barring confusion, distraction, etc., x believes that q.*

Notice first that while (1) is an unrestricted generalization it is patently false, and when one tries to accommodate counter-examples, cases where someone fears that p but does not desire that not p, by introducing a *ceteris paribus* clause, or, as in (2) by various exclusions, it quickly becomes apparent that the character of other things being equal and that of relevant exclusion conditions *cannot* be fully specified. No genuine, universal psychological generalizations – that is to say 'laws' – can be specified. Furthermore, such reason/action generalizations as seem to approximate to law-like status are, if true, *a priori*. Consider

(3) *For any subject x and any action type A: if x believes that A is logically impossible then x cannot sincerely try to A.*

Unlike an empirical causal law, hypothesized on the basis of observed sequences, this principle identifies a relation between elements in a rational order – 'the sphere of reasons'. This comes out in the fact that such principles constrain the application of psychological concepts. If we had good reason to maintain that someone believed that a course of action was logically impossible then we rationally could not describe him or her as sincerely trying to effect it. Anything that supported attributing the belief would *ipso facto* be reason for not attributing the attempt, and *vice versa*.

How then do action explanations work, if not by citing antecedent (efficient) causal factors? Part of my general approach has been to resist reductions, allowing that reality can be, as it seems to be, composed of various distinct sorts of things constituted at different levels. Unsurprisingly, therefore, I see no reason to suppose that the explanation of the intentional behaviour of rational animals conforms to a single pattern. In particular I see no need to subsume every factor that might be adverted to in psychological explanation under a heading termed 'rational causation'. Consider again the scene in which Kirsty is writing a sentence and we ask ourselves why she is doing this. The answer I proposed was that she wants to communicate her ideas, but many other explanations might be offered: she is in a creative mood; she has promised to produce a story; she has abandoned pencil and paper and is experimenting with a word processor; she doesn't have the time to write a whole page, and so on. Notice that these need not compete with one another; they could all be true. Notice also that in many cases the explanation takes the form of a redescription of the actual behaviour, not a move away from it to describe something else to which it is only contingently related – an ontologically independent antecedent cause. To say 'she is writing because she wants to communicate' need not be held to identify some event of wanting to communicate which led to this behaviour; rather it can be viewed as *interpreting* the behaviour as communicative. Here the wish to understand what is going on is satisfied by being told what the agent is doing. No mention of antecedent events is necessary. While one may say 'she is writing because . . .' I have argued that it is a mistake to regard this as necessarily introducing an efficient cause.

In order to act an agent must be able to deliberate, considering the pros and cons of alternative courses. In doing so he or she is not reflecting upon actual events but possible ones. Possible events are always types; the only token events there are are actual ones. So in thinking about what to do one is entertaining general descriptions: 'writing an essay', 'cutting the grass', 'polishing the silver', 'changing the baby', 'phoning a friend', and so on. Unless we could think in terms of types we could not deliberate and without being able to deliberate we could not act. It is also true that when we think about the present and the past we consider events through the mediation of general categories. Even where the object of thought is a particular, the content of the thought will be constructed out of general concepts (whether thoughts are wholly general in content is a matter of dispute). If I think of my wife Hilda I think of someone who is a woman, a mother, a Scot, and so on; and while she is a unique individual these attributes are general and can be multiply instantiated – many individuals are Scottish women, wives and mothers.

Thinking about the future is only ever thinking in general terms and thinking about the present involves bringing individuals under general types. In short, thinking involves universal concepts. This fact creates problems for materialism and for the effort to show that human beings could have developed by physical processes from non-thinking species. Where do concepts come from? Traditionally there have been two main answers to this question: *innatism* and *abstractionism*. According to the first the ability to classify things under general categories is something one is born with. According to the second the mind derives concepts from experience by selectively attending to relevant features and ignoring other aspects of the things in question. In the late 1950s Peter Geach produced a powerful argument against this latter thesis.[13] The suggestion that the concept *square*, say, is acquired by experiencing a variety of square objects and attending to their squareness, while bracketing their other aspects, is absurd because in order to attend selectively to the squareness of square objects you must already have the concept *square*: attending to an instance of a feature F is an exercise of the concept *f*.

Innatism is well placed in this regard since it claims that all normal human beings do have the concept *square* and many more concepts besides. But this quickly gives rise to problems of its own. How many concepts do we have – 1, 10, 100, 1,000, 10,000? how are they related? are we born with the concept *square* and the concept *rectangle* or just the one and, if so, which one? are our innate geometrical concepts Euclidean or non-Euclidean? how could we be born with concepts of things that didn't exist at the time? did cavemen have the concept *telephone* but just never have occasion to use it? how did innate ideas get there? As Jack Smart observes at the outset of his essay there are rarely or never knock-down arguments in philosophy and an innatist can always find something to say; but I am pretty sure that Smart and I agree that to defend this view you have to be willing to make large claims – such as that our ideas were given us by God who implanted the right number, of the right sort, at the right time. In the past this is what many famous innatists maintained. More recently, the fashion has been to rely on evolution, but even those who take a naturalistic materialist point of view and are willing to invoke evolution to explain our existence are generally doubtful that it can offer an explanation of innate ideas.[14]

Where does this leave the issue? We certainly have general concepts but if we were not born with them and we did not acquire them by abstraction how did we come by them? One answer is suggested by the later writings of Wittgenstein when he emphasizes again and again the fact that we are language users whose understanding is shaped by our participation in forms of life that are not of our own making. Wittgenstein never explicitly presents a theory of anything (depending upon one's attitude therein lies his wisdom or his pretension); and in order to develop the possibility that may lie in what he has to say it will be useful to refer back to Aquinas who also has interesting suggestions about the origin of concepts.[15] For Wittgenstein we learn to think as we learn to speak. The ability to structure experience is acquired through the learning of general terms. Alice is enabled to think *cat* by being taught the word 'cat' (or an equivalent). On this account, therefore, the concept is not innate, the child had to be taught it; and nor is it abstracted, she was not able to attend to cats *as cats* prior to being instructed in the use of the concept.

Bringing Aquinas into the picture enables one to see how something of this sort may not just be an alternative to innateness and abstractionism but a *via media*. In order for something like the Wittgensteinian explanation to work it has to be the case that the child has a prior predisposition or potentiality to form concepts under appropriate influences; and it also has to be the case that the influence in question is itself already possessed of the concept. Alice will not pick up the meaning of the term 'cat' unless she has a relevant potentiality, unless the structure of her receptivity is of the right sort. By the same token that potentiality will not be actualized except by an intellect that is already active in using the concept, her older brother James, for example. This vocabulary of 'actuality' and 'potentiality' is drawn from the Aristotelian–Thomistic tradition, as is the less familiar terminology of the mind's 'receptivity' and 'activity'. Aquinas himself speaks of the active and passive intellects as powers of one and the same thinker, which raises a question as to whether he is over-individualistic in his conception of the mind. In any event, here I am forging a link with Wittgenstein's linguistic-communitarian account of the origins of thinking in the individual and that suggests dividing these aspects of the intellect, at least in the first instance, between the teacher and the taught. In these terms one may say that Alice's intellect is receptive to, or potentially informed by, the concept *cat*, while the mind or intellect of James who has already mastered the use of the term is active with or actually informed by this concept. In teaching Alice the word, James imparts the concept and thereby actualizes her potentiality. This picture grants something both to innatism and to abstractionism. On the one hand, in order to explain possession of concepts a native power has to be postulated; but on the other it is allowed that, in a sense, concepts are acquired through experience.

Notice two features of this explanation. First it seems to give rise to a regress, and second and relatedly it instantiates the structure of Aquinas's primary proof of the existence of God. He writes:

> The first and most obvious way is based on change. For certainly some things are changing: this we plainly see. Now anything changing is being changed by something else. This is so because what makes things changeable is unrealized potentiality, but what makes them cause change is their already realized state: causing change brings into being what was previously only able to be, and can only be done by something which already is. For example, the actual heat of fire causes wood, able to be hot, to become actually hot, and so causes change in the wood ... what is changing can't be the very same thing that is causing the same change, can't be changing itself, but must be being changed by something else ... But this can't go on for ever, since then there would be no first cause of the change, and as a result no subsequent causes ... So we are forced eventually to come to a first cause of change not itself being changed by anything, and this is what everyone understands by God (*et hoc omnes intelligunt Deum*).[16]

This is a cosmological proof, that is to say it argues to God-as-Cause from the mere fact of existence – here the existence of change or motion. I shall be returning to this general style of argument in section 6. For the present, though, note that while the coming-to-be of a conceptual power in the mind of a child is certainly a change, and hence qualifies as a starting point for the first way, the particular change in question suggests a more specific proof. To bring this out consider the regress arising within the 'Wittgensteinian–Thomistic' account of concept formation.

Alice possesses a power that parrots lack, for while a bird may pick up a sound and repeat it – quicker and more accurately than the child – no amount of 'instruction' will teach the parrot the meaning of a term. Alice's innate power is in fact a second-order one; it is a power to acquire a (conceptual) power. Another human being – James – already has the first-order power; he uses the term meaningfully and thinks thoughts with the same conceptual content. Through instruction Alice's hitherto unrealized potentiality is made actual through the activity of James. But as Aquinas says, this cannot go on for ever. James's conceptual ability calls for explanation and the same considerations as before lead to the idea of his instruction by an already active thinker/language user, Kirsty, say, whose ability is itself the product of an innate potentiality and an external actualizing cause. The Wittgensteinian proposal that concepts are inculcated through membership of a linguistic community suggests an interesting escape from the dilemma posed by the innatist/abstractionist dispute, but it is not itself ultimately explanatory because for any natural language user it requires us to postulate a prior one. This regress will be halted if there is an actualizing source whose own conceptual power is intrinsic; and that, of course, is precisely what God is traditionally taken to be.

The cosmological argument itself is often described as the argument to a 'Prime Mover'; but the particular adaptation I have been concerned with might better be termed the argument to a 'Prime Thinker' or even, though metaphorically, to a 'Prime Sayer'. Here, one may be reminded of two well-known Hebrew and Christian reflections on 'beginnings' – those of the first chapters of *Genesis* and of the *Gospel of John*:

> Then God said, 'Let us make man in our image, after our likeness . . .' [then] out of the ground the Lord God formed every beast of the field and every bird of the air, and brought them to the man to see what he would call them; and whatever the man called every living creature that was its name. (Genesis 1: 26; 2: 19)

> In the beginning was the Word, and the Word was with God, and the Word was God. He was in the beginning with God; all things were made through him, and without him was not anything made that was made. In him was life, and the life was the light of men. (John 1: 1–4)

This line of argument will provoke various objections. Some of these are general complaints about philosophical theology (e.g. whether invoking God as a self-explanatory cause is consistent, and whether philosophy and scripture belong together) and are best dealt with at a later stage. At this point, however, I want to make explicit the connection between the reflections on conceptual thought and the issues of evolution and emergence.

Wittgenstein was a cautious thinker and held back where his reasoning neared the limits of experience. Consequently I am not sure to what extent he can be said to be a philosophical naturalist. He is reported to have said of himself 'I am not a religious man but I cannot help seeing every problem from a religious point of view'[17] and it is clear that he had respect for religious sensibilities. At the same time, these attitudes can be interpreted in ways compatible with atheism. It is difficult to say, therefore, what his attitude to the problem I have posed might have been. Whatever Wittgenstein's own view about it, however, the language-learning account of concept-formation might seem to escape the regress if it can show how at some earlier point the sequence of concept-conferring exchanges could have arisen. Any such account faces two difficulties: first that arising from the dialectic between innatism and abstractionism, and second a version of that presented earlier in connection with Dennett's homunculi-discharging strategy. If the linguistic view is to be a genuine alternative to the other theories it cannot revert to them in explaining earlier stages in our conceptual history. It cannot say, for example, that Adam's (and Eve's?) concepts were innate though Alice's were acquired. If innatism and abstractionism are incoherent they are not made any more intelligible by being introduced to halt a regress.

This sort of difficulty will be generally acknowledged; what is less likely to be conceded is the second objection, namely that no history of thought or language can be philosophically adequate if it tries to meet the genesis problem by postulating 'fading conceptuality'. Though it is not put in these terms, or indeed very often discussed at all, something of this sort is presumably part of a naturalistic version of Wittgenstein's linguistic theory. On this account the history of concept-formation and use is the history of language; a history that leads back to pre-linguistic activities, back further to pre-mental life, to pre-replicating life and ultimately to pre-animate matter. It is unnecessary for me to elaborate my objection. What needs to be accounted for is a natural transition from the non-conceptual to the conceptual and that is not the same distinction as one between degrees of conceptual complexity. Doubtless Stone Age cave dwellers made fewer and less abstract discriminations than a contemporary physicist, but that is irrelevant; the point is that the ability to make *any* general classifications is a conceptual power.

Let me add a further consideration in this cumulative case against naturalism. Thus far I have cast my objections concerning the nature of thought in terms of the genesis of concepts. However there is an additional difficulty for the materialist or physicalist so far as concerns the relation between concepts and the objects and features that fall under them. Consider again the concept *cat*. Setting aside issues having to do with its non-specificity and possible indeterminacy (e.g.

there are significant differences between species of cats and there may be animals concerning which it is an issue whether they are cats) let us say that the extension of this concept (the things of which it is true), or of the corresponding term 'cat' and its equivalents in other languages, is the set of cats.

Smart discusses the need to allow sets into his otherwise material-ist ontology but I am concerned to argue that in the present case this admission is an insufficient concession to non-materialism. It is nat-ural to think that the concept *cat* designates not only actual cats but future and 'counterfactual' cats. That is to say, one might contemplate and discuss with others the prospects for cats in the environment of Chernobyl 30 years hence, or consider what would have been done with the kittens that Mother Cat might have had had she not been neu-tered. Thus there is a problem with the attempt to give the 'semantic value' of this term, or concept, by reference to actual material objects. Additionally, it is easily imaginable that the members of the set of actual cats fall under another concept, let us say that of being the most-common-four-legged-animals-whose-average-weight-is-W, call this the concept '*maxifourn*'. In this situation the extensions of the concepts *cat* and *maxifourn* are identical: they have all and only the same mem-bers. Nonetheless, it is natural to say that the property of being a cat is not the same as that of being a maxifourn. Little Felix would still be a cat even if, because of population changes, he were no longer a maxifourn; meanwhile in the same situation though Derek the dachs-hund might then be a maxifourn he would thereby not have become a cat.

The point is clear: concepts distinguish objects in virtue of their properties and even where two concepts are co-extensive – have all and only the same instances – the properties they designate may dif-fer. This is so even where the properties in question are not merely co-extensive but necessarily so, i.e. where, unlike the *cat/maxifourn* example, there is no possibility of their extensions diverging. Every triangle is a trilateral and vice versa, and in some sense possession of the one property necessitates possession of the other. Yet triangularity and trilaterality are not the same attribute and it takes geometrical reas-oning to show that these properties are necessarily co-instantiated. This latter possibility raises what for the empiricist is the spectre of *a priori knowledge*, i.e., true, appropriately warranted belief that does not require to be verified in experience – because it could not fail to be.

These are various aspects of a general problem for the naturalist. Our concepts transcend material configurations in space–time. As was observed earlier, to think of an item is always to think of it via some conception. A naturalistic account of experience and thought will need to relate such ways of thinking to the nature of the objects in question and very likely add that the genesis of our concepts derives (in whole or in part) from the causal influence on us or on earlier generations of particular material objects. The trouble with this is brought about by the trilateral/triangular example. To the extent that he can even concede that there are distinct properties the naturalist will want to insist that the causal powers – as he conceives them – of trilaterals and triangulars are identical. Thus he cannot explain the difference between the concepts by invoking causal differences between the members of their extensions (as one might *seem* to be able to account for the difference between the concepts *square* and *circle*). For any naturally individuated object or property there are indefinitely many non-equivalent ways of thinking about it. That is to say, the structure of the conceptual order, which is expressed in judgements and actions, is richer and more abstract than that of the natural order, and the character of this difference makes it difficult to see how the materialist could explain the former as arising out of the latter.

In summary, I have been arguing that there is a good deal of life remaining in 'old style' design arguments. Evolutionary theory, and naturalism more generally, are not equipped to explain three important differences which common sense and philosophically unprejudiced science both recognize: those between the inanimate and the animate; the non-reproductive and the reproductive; and the non-mental and the mental. Assuming a history of development, these differences involve a series of ascents giving rise to explanatory gaps in evolutionary theory. Naturalism in its modern materialist versions has negative and positive aspects. It precludes certain sorts of explanations on the grounds that they are incompatible with physicalism, and it presumes the availability, in principle, of wholly adequate naturalistic accounts of reality. I have been arguing that in its negative aspect it begs the question in its own favour, and that its positive claim is demonstrably false in respect of one or more features of the world.

One reaction to this might be to concede both aspects of the case against naturalism, yet to query whether it advances the cause of theism. Philosophers and others have written disparagingly of 'God of the gaps' apologetics, meaning by this the effort to save religion from the onward march of scientific naturalism by finding phenomena for which science has not provided an explanation. These critics have not been short of targets to aim at. For example, it will not do to assert that scientific materialism fails because it cannot explain visitations by the spirits of the deceased. That would indeed be question-begging (and involves a metaphysical assumption of 'spiritualism' that not all theists would accept). Less obviously it is not an effective strategy to point to gaps in the scientific story where one cannot show that they are non-contingent omissions. The fact that a theory has not explained a phenomenon in no way establishes that it cannot do so. It is partly with this thought in mind that 'God of the gaps' defences have usually been criticized. I hope it is clear, therefore, that I have not been concerned with contingent limitations. At least, I mean to have identified necessary limitations, phenomena that it is not within the power of scientific naturalism to explain, and given reasons why I believe this to be so.

It may still seem, however, that allowing what has been argued no movement has been made towards establishing the existence of a creative deity, as opposed to demonstrating a series of mysteries. The earlier 'gaps' criticism might now be directed against what could be seen as simply labelling these enigmas 'works of God'. Against this charge let me recall relevant features of the previous reflections. Throughout I have been concerned with teleology, that is to say with natures, powers, functions and activities the description and explanation of which make reference to instrumental values and final ends. The reproductive behaviour of fleas and the intellectual studies of philosophers can be engaged in well or badly and lead to good or ill. Whatever other functions and goals it may serve, sex is for reproduction; likewise practical reasoning is for successful action, and philosophical speculation is for the sake of attaining and understanding truth. Descriptions and explanations in terms of purposes cannot be ignored. They can only be rejected in favour of mechanism or attributed to the agency of a designer. I have argued at length that the mechanistic option fails especially in relation to thought and action. What then of sources of design? Often these will be empirical agents. In recent years, for example, there has been much research in genetic engineering, and recall the less 'high-tech' image of the gardener discussed earlier. In both cases organisms are evolved that possess functional features whose existence and character is attributable to human design. But this form of explanation is inadequate in cases where the teleology is that of entities which have emerged independently of human intervention; and it also fails as an explanation of *Homo sapiens* itself – or at least if someone wants to argue that human teleology is due to our having been designed by extraterrestrials then he has an obvious regress on his hands.

From what he says about putting aside 'the "as if" teleology in modern biology' I take it that Smart and I are agreed that purpose in nature cannot be a brute phenomenon and consequently that explanations invoking it cannot be truly basic. If my arguments against mechanistic reductions have been effective then the local (and, if they can be established, any global) purposes we find in nature must be imposed and derive from the agency of a designer whose purposes they are, or whose purposes they serve or realize. Such an explanation will not be complete if the source of design is itself vulnerable to external influence or reliant upon the contingencies of nature. If natural teleology is not basic or eliminable then it is only ultimately explicable by reference to a transcendent Designer, a source of the flea's power to reproduce and of man's ability to speak – *et hoc dicimus Deum*.

Some other objections remain but since these apply to all design arguments and not just those I have developed thus far it will be better to deal with them later. Next, I shall examine the argument from cosmic regularity to extra-cosmic design.

5 'New' Teleology

The comparative brevity of this section is made possible by the fact that Smart gives a clear and detailed discussion of the 'fine tuning' argument. He is right to point out the absurdities of some treatments of the anthropic cosmological principle and I aim to steer a course through these that is parallel to his own. Some discussions reduce it to a trivial tautology that cannot introduce anything worth thinking about; others elevate it to a metaphysical mystery so great that it defies comprehension. Both are mistaken.

If the necessary conditions of our existence did not obtain we would not be; and if the necessary conditions of the necessary conditions of our existence had not obtained then neither we nor many other aspects and elements of the present universe would have been. Any scientific theory that is incompatible with things having been as they had to have been, in order for the universe to be as it is, is thereby refuted. None of this may be very profound and it did not take science to establish it; but it does raise a question: is the obtaining of the necessary conditions in question explicable, and if so how? At this point some writers

career to another lane on the far side of the *via media* and argue
that our existence necessitates the laws of the universe – we made
it be the case that the cosmos is congenial to our existence. This is
not only fallacious reasoning; it betrays a lack of intuitive judgement
that is unsettling when exhibited by intelligent people. If you think
you have an argument to show that the fact of your existence determined the initial conditions of the universe, think again, and again,
and again.

The real interest of the issues introduced by the question of the
conditions necessary for the world to be as it is, complete with beings
able to investigate its structure and to ask this very question, lies in
the fact that those conditions seem to call for some explanation. What
we know about the observable universe and that which we can infer
about what lies over the 'visible' horizon indicates that it is composed
out of a number of types of microphysical entities whose members
exhibit common properties and are subject to a small number of simple
laws. There is nothing obviously inevitable about this fact. It seems
perfectly intelligible to suppose that the universe could have been
spatially and temporally chaotic. There might have been little or no
regularity in the nature of its parts and the flow of events might have
been entirely haphazard. Yet it is not so. Chemistry tells us that there
are elements whose instances share well-defined structural properties
in virtue of which they can and do enter into systematic combinations; and physics tells us that these elements are themselves constructed out of more basic items whose properties are if anything
purer and simpler. A stock of components with regular modes of
combination subject to perfectly general laws is not the only possibility, and it invites speculation as to why there is order rather than
chaos. One might say that if there had been chaos then we would not
exist and the question would not have arisen. In a sense that is true
– no actual inquirers, no actual inquiry; but it leaves untouched the
central theme which is that of the preconditions of the possibility of
order. Cosmic regularity makes our existence possible, the underlying
issue concerns the enabling conditions of this order itself, and that
issue 'arises' even if no one exists to raise it.

Some teleological proofs argue from spatio-temporal regularity alone.
They reason that while events in nature can be explained by reference
to the fundamental particles and the laws under which they operate,
these explanatory factors cannot themselves be accounted for by natural
science. Since scientific explanations presuppose them as first principles, they cannot derive them as conclusions from more general facts

about the universe. Natural explanations having reached their logical limits we are then forced to say that either the orderliness of the universe has no explanation or that it has an 'extra-natural' one.

The latter course cannot plausibly take the form of embedding the facts of nature within the laws and initial conditions of a SuperNature. That would amount to retracting the previous claim that one had specified the ultimate facts of the material universe; and 'nature' would then be regarded as a spatial and/or temporal part of SuperNature. The search for the source of order must reach a dead end if scientific explanation is the only sort there is. However, as I have emphasized in earlier sections, there is more than one kind of 'because'. In particular, explanations sometimes proceed by tracing events to rational agency. These words are on the page before you because I chose them to express my thoughts; I found myself thinking about the issues because I accepted an invitation to exchange views with Jack Smart on atheism and theism; and I did this because it seemed fitting. Such facts explain by citing reasons why something was brought into being and made to be as it is. Similarly, the otherwise inexplicable regularity that surrounds and inhabits us will have an adequate explanation if it derives from the purposes of an agent. *Ex hypothesi*, no natural agent could have made the universe; so if the question which its regularity gave rise to has an answer it can only be one that connects natural order to a supernatural order – *et hoc dicimus Deum*.

This traditional argument pre-dates the physical and cosmological investigations that have produced the evidence of 'fine tuning'. What that evidence involves is well described by Smart, and I take it he agrees that it adds to the strength of the argument to the extent that it makes the existence of an orderly universe even less likely than might have been supposed. The basic laws of nature feature contingent ratios that the laws do not themselves explain, and the fundamental particles whose behaviour they regulate also exhibit apparently contingent numerical properties. If any of these ratios and quantities had been different in the slightest degree then not only we, and our predecessors in the history of life, but orderly matter itself would not have existed. Crudely, the conditions necessary for the development and continued existence of anything like the universe lie within a narrow range bounded on one side by the possibility of 'implosion' and on the other by that of 'explosion'. As before, any explanation of this fact has to look beyond the framework of natural causation and that leads to a conclusion of purposeful agency.

Assuming our common commitment to realism Smart and I would

oppose neo-Kantian relocations of the source of order in the minds of observers. Whether the facts are as fundamental science now depicts them we are not of the view that order is always a *projection* and never a *detection* of something that is there independently of our conception of it. So the debate concerns the possibility of explaining finely-tuned order in non-theistic terms. As in the discussion of organic teleology one is faced with an initial branching, down one limb of which lies another fork. First, then, there is the issue of whether cosmological order can be a basic unaccountable fact. To say that it can is to maintain that functional regularity is independent of any other kind of explanation. If one thinks that this is not a satisfactory conclusion, and it is after all no more than a restatement of that for which an explanation was being sought, then two courses present themselves: explanation by reference to purposeful agency; and explanation by reference to chance.

Smart follows the latter course adopting a version of it that postulates many universes. If there is a vast multiplicity of these differing from one another in respect of their components and modes of interaction, some being highly regular, some less so, some fairly chaotic, some utterly so, then it will be sufficient explanation of the general regularity and particular fine tuning of our universe that is it but one of indefinitely many. Chance alone will explain its existence. Given enough opportunities the realization of order becomes unpuzzling.

Note that the question of whether to conclude to design or chance is not one that scientific observation can decide. We need to reason our way ahead. How reasonable, therefore, is the reduction of order to chance? It is not true to say that because any other outcome might have occurred a particular one requires no explanation. One way of bringing this out is in terms of significant orderings. Suppose someone tears out the pages of this book numbered 1 to 100, thoroughly shuffles them and stacks them in a pile. Assuming relevantly similar causal antecedents any stacking has the same prior probability as any other – 1 in 3,628,800, and under the description 'papers in a pile' no particular arrangement is significant. Suppose, however, that one of these piles has the pages lying in numerical order from page 1 to page 100. As a distribution of paper, and assuming similar operative factors, this stack is no more or less likely than any other; but considered as a significant (numerical) ordering – which it certainly is – it invites an explanation which the others do not. For while the probability of its occurring is as before, the probability of some or other non-significant ordering (i.e. any other than it) is 3,628,799. That is to say, while your chance of stacking them in sequence is 0.00002756 per cent, the chances of doing otherwise are 99.99997244 per cent.

Admittedly it remains possible that the significantly ordered stacking is the result of chance, but that hypothesis is much more implausible than one which invokes a different causal ancestry, hypothesizing that the seemingly random shuffling was in fact a well-controlled manipulation designed to order the pages sequentially. Where an explanation is available that renders an improbable outcome more likely one should prefer it to an explanation that preserves the improbability, and the greater the differential the more one should favour the probabilizing hypothesis. I do not know what the probabilities in question are, but on the assumption that the range of possible universes is very large, if not infinite, the chances of any particular outcome are small and diminish as that outcome moves up the scale of significant ordering. Equivalently, the occurrence of 'harmonious' arrangements is less likely than that of 'discordant' ones. The evidence of fine tuning is precisely of this sort. For example, if it is accurate, it tells us that a tiny percentage of possible universes having structurally equivalent laws to our own, but varying in respect of fundamental ratios and quantities, are life permitting. The fact that one such exists (that it is ours is only relevant to the extent that it allows *us* to contemplate the issue) calls for explanation. The hypothesis that this fact is not the outcome of chance renders it far less unlikely than does the hypothesis that it is. Accordingly, unless other factors exclude the hypothesis of design it is to be preferred over that of chance.

Suppose, however, someone argues that there are infinitely many other universes, ordered either in parallel or in temporal sequence, and hence that it is inevitable that one with the fundamental configuration of ours should exist. To begin with this needs correction. Even if there were an infinity of universes it would not be inevitable that this or any other one should be among them. All one can say is that as the number of universes proceeds towards infinity the probability of a difference between the actual distribution and the probable one diminishes to zero. Taking the earlier example of the pages, if one shuffles and piles them over and over again infinitely many times then the chances of not getting 1 to 100 diminish. However it is not guaranteed that 1 to 100 will eventually result. Infinitely many operations may never yield the significant ordering. Nonetheless they will make its occurrence very much less unlikely than if there were only one operation.

The logic of the many worlds response involves postulating an infinity of actual universes because while this does not determine that the significant one will occur it diminishes its improbability. There is another reason for postulating an infinity rather than just finitely many universes and this is connected with the next argument I shall be considering, *viz*. the cosmological one. For if one envisages an infinity of possibilities, but stipulates that only some (however many) shall be realized, this invites the question of what debars the others, or equivalently of what occasions the occurrence of those that are realized. This then introduces the idea of contingency and of the need of a source of selection from among possibilities. In order to avoid this issue, and to eliminate any element of improbability in the occurrence of this universe, one might suggest that the set of worlds (this included), is the totality of all possible universes; or one might claim that there is and could only be one world – the actual one. In either event since it could not fail to exist no question arises as to the fact of its existence.

Deferring consideration of the cosmological argument, how effective is the many universes response? Unless it claims that all possibilities are or must be actualized it concedes that a finely tuned universe might not have existed and thereby allows scope for a probability argument for design. Rather than try to build on that reduced base, however, the theist may query the coherence of the many universes hypothesis itself. Can it be excluded? The question is ambiguous. If it asks whether there is any argument to show that it is contradictory or otherwise impossible then I suspect that there is not; at any rate I do not have one. However, one might mean less than that, for we often exclude suggestions on the grounds that they are obscure or inadequately supported, and here I think there is a significant weakness in the hypothesis.

To bring this out consider a further ambiguity. What is meant by talking about 'many universes'? In futuristic fantasies, space travellers often journey to other worlds. This way of speaking of far away and hitherto unknown places pre-dates science fiction. The European explorers of the fifteenth and sixteenth centuries sailed from the 'old' world and discovered the 'new', but in saying so no one intends that they left the planet. Similarly one might speak of 'other universes' meaning far distant and currently unobservable regions of the Universe – the one spatio-temporal-causal continuum. Alternatively one might mean, though this is much harder to make sense of, entirely distinct cosmic set-ups, wholly discontinuous with the Universe we inhabit.

If the hypothesis of plural universes invokes the former idea then it is clear enough what is being said, but it should also be evident that it fails to serve the purpose intended. Any evidence we could have for the existence of spatially or temporally distant regions and systems would necessarily be evidence for situations generally like those obtaining in our sector – that is to say situations exhibiting the same finely tuned features whose existence seemed to call for explanation. This is so because all that could lead us to postulate and predict the character of distant universes would be the application of observational-cum-inferential methods to empirical-cum-theoretical data available to us here. So if 'many universes' means 'many local set-ups' within the Universe the hypothesis fails to defuse the power of the new design argument. If on the other hand it is being claimed that there could be many Universes – entirely distinct realities, wholly discontinuous and sharing no common elements – then, while it is uncertain how to interpret this, it is clear that there could be no empirical evidence in support of the hypothesis, and nor could it be derived as a necessary condition of the possible existence and character of the only universe of which we have or could have scientific knowledge. In short the hypothesis appears as entirely *ad hoc*, introduced only to avoid what for the naturalist is an unpalatable conclusion, *viz*., that the general regularities and particular fine tuning are due to the agency of a designer – *et hoc dicimus Deum*.

Some readers will be struck by the parallels between the many universes hypothesis and another theoretical construction, namely the so-called 'Many-Worlds Interpretation' of quantum mechanics. This is a response to a deeply puzzling feature of a major part of fundamental physics. In a quantum-mechanical situation it seems that there are indeterministic transitions between states. The theory tells us that a system will go from A to either B or C but in principle it cannot tell us which one it will go to – the outcome is indeterminate. Among those who find this situation unacceptable some maintain that the uncertainty is only epistemological. There is a fact of the matter involving 'hidden variables' but for one reason or another we do not, or cannot, know what it is. A more radical determinacy-preserving proposal is that the transition is to *both* states: at this point the universe divides into two worlds and so does the observer. In world^1, A goes to B and is observed to do so by John^1; in World^2 A goes to C and this event is recorded by John^2. Two points need to be added: first, this is supposed to be happening all the time, there is endless branching; second, it is in principle impossible to have trans-world access. So while the particular motivation and details of the proposal differ from those of the many universes theory the philosophical position is the same: an unverifiable hypothesis of finitely or infinitely many wholly distinct actual universes is introduced in order to save having to yield up doctrines of modern science: the sufficiency of natural explanation and the determinacy of nature, respectively. Both moves look decidedly *ad hoc*.

The basic components of the material universe and the forces operating upon them exhibit properties of stability and regularity that invite explanation – the more so given the narrow band within which they have to lie in order for there to be embodied cognitive agents able to investigate and reflect upon the conditions of their own existence. Even given these improbable cosmic circumstances the emergence of life, the development of species and the emergence of rational animals all call for explanations that it does not seem to be within the power of natural science to provide. The limitations of science in these respects concern its very nature and the nature of the phenomena in question. Obviously I have been arguing philosophically and if these arguments are correct then their conclusions are immune to empirical refutation. Unsurprisingly, I feel more confident about some phases of my reasoning than about others. For example, notwithstanding what has been argued, I think the obstacles to mechanistic reduction of life to chemistry and physics are fewer than those standing in the way of a naturalistic explanation of mind and all that it implies.

In connection with the last point let me add a further argument, picking up some of what I said in sections 1 and 2 about general metaphysical perspectives. The presuppositions of scientific realism are that there are things the existence and nature of which are independent of our investigations, and that we possess intellectual powers adequate to their identification and description. (This claim allows that not all that exists may be mind-independent and not all that is may be knowable by us). There is nothing inevitable about this; the world might not have been intelligible and we might not have had the kind of intelligence that is shaped to understanding it. The fact that there is a harmony makes it possible for us to have knowledge of some of the most profound features of the empirical order. From astronomy to zoology via chemistry, physics and the rest of the natural sciences, we have discovered an enormous amount about reality (not to mention non-empirical orders of logic, geometry, mathematics, and so on).

This is improbable even granting naturalism, and if my earlier arguments against materialism are right it is entirely inexplicable on that basis. I reasoned that there cannot be an evolutionary account of conceptual powers; but even if there could be, that would not account for our having the kinds of concepts we do, ones that go beyond practical utility and so cannot be explained in terms of adaptive value. One might here appeal to the fact I mentioned earlier, namely that present day biologists do not claim that every significant characteristic is an evolutionary adaptation. That, however, is a move away from the possibility of giving a natural explanation of the harmony of thought and world. It would be within the power of an intelligent creator to effect such a harmony, and indeed there would be something fitting in creating a universe that had within it the power of its own understanding which is what in one sense empirical knowledge involves. I offer this as one interpretation of the Judaeo-Christian-Islamic idea that a human being is made in the image, indeed is an image, of God (*imago Dei*). The hypothesis of theism explains the existence of an orderly universe, of rational animals and of the harmony of thought and world. Scientific materialism explains none of these things.

6   The Cause of Things

A few years ago, in keeping with general developments throughout the British education system, the University of St Andrews decided to introduce a staff appraisal scheme. This was to involve a system of 'progress review' according to which every member of the university would periodically be reviewed by a colleague. A draft was circulated setting out the various arrangements for the introduction of the proposed scheme. It included a section on the role and responsibilities of reviewers, from which I quote:

> The reviews of colleagues who have not been reviewed previously but are to act as reviewers will also have to be arranged . . . so that all reviewers can be reviewed before they review others.

The well-intentioned point was that no staff should act as reviewers who had not themselves already been subject to the review process. Additionally the system was to be self-contained: no one's reviewed status could result from having been reviewed outwith the university. At the time this document appeared I was acting as an occasional cartoonist for the university newsletter and it seemed that this was an opportunity that ought not to be missed. The cartoon reprinted here

CAREER DEVELOPMENT FOR ACADEMIC AND ACADEMIC RELATED STAFF:
Appraisal Scheme – 'The reviews of colleagues who have not been reviewed previously but are to act as reviewers will also have to be arranged . . . so that all reviewers can be reviewed before they review others.'

brings out the problem that had been overseen in the drafting. If no one could conduct a review unless and until he or she had been reviewed, and that could only derive from within the system, then the process could not begin. In the cartoon I highlighted the difficulty by depicting an initial review meeting and placing the faculty members in a circle around a table. One asks another 'Do you have any idea of who goes first?'

The solution subsequently arrived at was to postulate an unreviewed reviewer: more precisely the Principal was 'deemed', for purposes of the scheme, to have been reviewed. The point of this anecdote will be obvious, and the issue it raises is addressed in Aquinas's second way:

> The second way is based on the nature of agent (i.e. efficient) cause (*causae efficientis*). In the observable world causes are found ordered in series: we never observe, nor ever could, something causing itself, for this would mean it preceded itself, and this is not possible. But a series of causes can't go on for ever, for in any such series an earlier member causes an intermediate and the intermediate a last (whether the intermediate be one or many). Now eliminating a cause eliminates its effects, and unless there's a first cause there won't be a last or an intermediate. But if a series of causes goes on for ever it will have no first cause, and so no intermediate causes and no last effect, which is clearly false. So we are forced to postulate some first agent cause, to which everyone gives the name God (*quam omnes Deum nominant*).[18]

Before considering the merit of this it is appropriate to lay out the next of St Thomas's proofs and to return to aspects of the first way. Immediately following the passage just quoted he writes:

> The third way is based on what need not be and on what must be, and runs as follows. Some of the things we come across can be but need not be, for we find them being generated and destroyed, thus sometimes in being and sometimes not. Now everything cannot be like this, for a thing that need not be was once not; and if everything need not be, once upon a time there was nothing. But if that were true there would be nothing even now, because something that does not exist can only begin to exist through something that already exists. If nothing was in being nothing could begin to be, and nothing would be in being now, which is clearly false. Not everything then is the sort that need not be; some things must be, and these may or may not owe this necessity to something else. But just as we proved that a series of agent causes can't go on for ever, so also a series of things which must be and owe this to other things. So we are forced to postulate something which of itself must be, owing this to nothing outside itself, but being the cause that other things must be.

This passage is more intricate than the previous one and is often misunderstood. Both call for detailed interpretation, but here I shall be brief since my purpose is not primarily expository. It is usually said that the third way involves a 'quantifier shift fallacy' – arguing 'if each thing were such that there is a time when it does not exist, then there would be a time when nothing exists'. [($\forall$x) ($\exists$t) (x does not exist at t) therefore ($\exists$t) ($\forall$x) (x does not exist at t)]. This is indeed a fallacy but it is not St Thomas's reasoning. Look carefully at the text.

The proof begins with a distinction between two types of existent, the *contingent* and the *necessary*, between that which is but might not have been, and that which could not possibly not exist. The former type is then shown to be instantiated by reference to things observed to be generated and destroyed. Next comes the supposed fallacy. Aquinas argues as follows:

1 A thing that has come into being did not exist at a prior time.
2 If everything were like this, then there was a time when nothing existed.
3 If that were so there would be nothing now (because contingent things require a cause and if previously there were nothing then what now exists could not have been caused to be).
4 There are contingent things existing now, therefore it is not the case that there was a time when nothing existed, and therefore not everything has come into being, not previously having existed.

The standard criticism is that the passage from (1) to (2) involves the fallacy I mentioned. But the point Aquinas is making only involves time(s) because of his characterization of the contingent in terms of coming into existence, i.e. temporal generation. He is not arguing 'for each there is a time therefore there is a time for all'; but reasoning that if each were of the kind 'temporally generated', i.e. *contingent*, then there never would have been anything: in other words (2) generalizes the point introduced in (1). Temporally generated beings require a pre-existent cause, hence not everything that exists can be of the temporally generated sort. His claim, if it is correct, cannot be met by saying let there be, for each temporally generated being, a parent that is itself a generated being. That leaves the general problem of contingency untouched. So, there must be some non-contingent thing or things. Notice that at this point Aquinas does not attempt to derive the existence of a single ultimate cause. Having concluded that not everything can be contingent, he allows that those which are not may be either dependently or non-dependently necessary. Next, however, he refers us back to the previous argument concerning causal series and concludes that on the basis of parallel reasoning we must postulate an unconditionally necessary first cause.

The core issues in these proofs are those of existential and causal dependency. Such themes place them firmly within the tradition of cosmological speculation as to why there is anything rather than nothing and what the source of the universe might be. Before discussing these matters further let me recall the first of the five ways, which St Thomas describes as 'the most obvious'. As we saw earlier this involves the fact that there are changes and the claim that ultimately these can only result from an unchanging cause of change. The argument involves an analysis of change in terms of the transition from potentiality to actuality and the principle that this can only be brought about by something that is already actual:

> what makes things changeable is unrealized potentiality, but what makes them cause change is their already realized state: causing change brings into being what was previously only able to be, and can only be done by something which already is. For example, the actual heat of fire causes wood, which is able to be hot, to become actually hot, and so causes change in the wood.

The example of wood being heated is offered as an illustration (not a proof) of the analysis of change but it is easily misinterpreted in a way that suggests a rapid rejection of the argument. Generalizing from what Aquinas writes, one might think that his claim involves the principle that anything that comes to acquire some feature comes to acquire it from something that already possesses that feature – as the wood is made hot by the heat of the fire [$(\forall x) (\exists y)$ (if x comes to be F, then y is F and y makes x to be F)]. The problem, then, is that it seems very easy to refute this principle by counter-example. A comedian may cause amusement in his audience without himself being amused; a colourless liquid may stain a surface green, and so on.

As a general principle of interpretation one should be hesitant to ascribe silly mistakes to clever thinkers, so if at first they seem to have made an elementary error one should look more closely. That policy encouraged another interpretation of the supposed quantifier fallacy in the third way and here again it suggests a better reading of Aquinas. Prior to the example he writes 'causing change . . . can only be done by something which already is' and this yields the principle 'anything that comes to acquire some feature comes to acquire it from something that already exists and (by implication) has the power to produce that feature in others [($\forall$x) ($\exists$y) (if x comes to be F then it comes to be so from the agency of y which has an Fness-producing power)]. Being made hot by something that is already hot is an instance of this but so is being amused by someone who is not himself amused.

This clarification deflects one objection but in doing so it raises a question about the character of my argument to the existence of a 'Prime Thinker' (see section 4). This reasoned that the acquisition of concepts by Alice depended upon the activity of prior concept users, Kirsty and James, which in turn led to the postulation of an agent whose conceptual power is underived. What needs to be made clear is that this is not presented as an instance of the general principle which the counter-examples give reason to reject. I described my argument as an adaptation of the first way. Interpreting the latter as I have done here shows that the 'Prime Thinker' argument is a case of it, made special by also invoking the principle that the cause of conceptual activity must itself be conceptually active, or more generally (and slightly less misleadingly) the cause of thinking must itself be a thinking thing.

What gives warrant to the latter principle? First, it is supported by the idea that the induction of conceptual ability is an intentional activity and therefore expressive of purposeful intelligence in which ends are conceived. This is a matter of the form of the cause (i.e. 'acting') and will apply wherever intentional 'making to be' is involved. Second, however, there is a special feature of the case in question which concerns the content of the process. As James teaches Alice the use of the term 'cat', in a context, say, where there are particular cats – Angus and Big Feet – James makes these objects intelligible to Alice. He raises them from the sensible level to the sphere of 'thinkables'. Previously Alice could see Angus and Big Feet but she could not think of them as things of the same sort; that and much else besides is what concept-acquisition brings. Concept-induction is an intentional form of making intelligible. Thus while the earlier principle ($\forall$x) ($\exists$y) (if x comes to be F, then y is F and y makes x to be F) is not unrestrictedly true, I claim it is true where the value of F is 'a thinker'.

Leaving the particularities of the 'Prime Thinker' proof to one side, the first three of the five ways might be abbreviated as follows:

I   (1)   In nature some things are changing.
     (2)   Anything changing is changed by another.
     (3)   This sequence cannot go on for ever.
     (4)   Therefore, there is an unchanging first cause of change.

II (1) In nature causes and effects are found ordered in series.
   (2) If there were no prior cause there would be no series.
   (3) This sequence cannot go on for ever.
   (4) Therefore, there is an uncaused first cause.

III (1) In nature some things are contingent.
    (2) Anything contingent is caused to be by another thing.
    (3) This sequence cannot go on for ever.
    (4) Therefore, there is a necessary first cause of things.

From what little expository analysis I have offered it should be clear that there remains scope for dispute about the correct representation of Aquinas's arguments, but I would ask you to draw back from that and consider the main issues raised by these proofs. As I noted earlier these are the questions of existential and causal dependency. In one way and another St Thomas is saying: 'no God, no world; world, therefore God'. Against this stand two familiar forms of objection: first, that the arguments fail; second, that even if they worked they would not establish the existence of *God*. I will return to the latter issue in the next section. Here I consider the former which itself has two main components: first, the claim that there is nothing incoherent in an infinite series of causes; second, the contention that in any case the idea that things (events, objects or whatever) always require explanation rests on a false assumption, *viz.* the Principle of Sufficient Reason (PSR).

Returning to the progress review scheme and the visual depiction of it, I chose a circular seating arrangement at an initial review to highlight the problem. Suppose, however, that I had arranged the figures in a line receding into the distance, each awaiting review by his predecessor. That would have diminished the effect but would it have diminished the problem? Clearly not if the line were finite, since if the member nearest had been reviewed then given the rubric there would have to be a first reviewer (however that had been effected). Assume, though, that the review scheme was already in existence and had been for as long as the university has existed. St Andrews received its Papal Seal in 1413, so on this assumption those currently reviewing would depend in this respect on predecessors no longer existing – still, there would have to have been a first reviewer (deemed such by Pope Benedict XIII, say). Suppose, however, that the university has always existed (and perhaps always will) with each reviewer having been reviewed by a predecessor and reviewing a successor *ad infinitum*. Given these assumptions can one still argue that there must be a first cause of the series?

Although Aquinas believed, on the basis of scripture, that the natural order had a temporal beginning, he argued, against St Bonaventure (1217–74), that reason alone could not show the impossibility of its having existed from eternity (for ever); but that it could show the necessity of its having been created. In other words, his arguments are intended to establish the ontological not the temporal priority of the first cause. For all that they are concerned, therefore, the university could have existed for ever. Still, I suggest we should feel unhappy about the idea that there could be an infinite causal series – for unless there was a reviewer who had not been reviewed – an originating source of the causal power to review – how could the series exist?

The issue is not dealt with by adverting to mathematical infinities. Suppose we draw a section of the number line and just identify some point as –1, then there is a prior point –2, and its predecessor –3, and so on. That is not in dispute; what is contested is that any such infinite series could be one of intrinsic causal dependence. Here we need to distinguish between a series of items the members of which are, merely as it happens, casually related to one another, and a series whose members are intrinsically ordered as cause and effect. To adopt Aquinas's scholastic terminology, the first is a causal series *per accidens* (coincidentally), the second a causal series *per se* (as such). We can (perhaps) imagine objects, marked off by points in the number line and receding to infinity, among which there are causal relations; but this is not an intrinsic causal series. Contrast this with the situation in which each object is an effect of its predecessor and a cause of its successor: but for object –2, object –1 would not be, and but for object –3, object –2 would not be, etc. Here it is essential to any item's being a cause that it also be an effect; but it is not necessary that they be temporally ordered, for in this case the terms 'predecessor' and 'successor' are not being used in an essentially temporal way. That is what it means to speak of a '*per se* causal series'. Since the existence *qua* cause of any item is derived from the causality of a predecessor there has to be a source of causal power from outwith the series of dependent causes – an ultimate and non-dependent cause.

If like Hume one denies that there is anything more to efficient causation than regular succession then the idea of real ontological dependence involved in the definition of a *per se* causal series cannot be applied. It is an interesting question to what extent those who deny the reality of causation are moved to do so by a concern to block cosmological proofs. Certainly without causal realism (and, I believe, the admission of a variety of causes) none of the arguments I have been concerned with can work. As in the earlier discussions of old and new style teleological proofs, however, I would defend such a realism on anti-reductionist, anti-empiricist grounds independently of advancing a case for theism.

Someone might now reply that while there may be real causes, the proofs assume and require more than this, namely that every event and object in nature is caused. This brings me to the second objection which contends that things may not always require an explanation; which is to say, that the principle of sufficient reason or of adequate explanation is false, or at any rate controversial. Hence it may be that a series of real causal dependencies terminates in a 'brute cause', a natural event that does not derive its existence or efficacy from that of anything else.

Unless the question is to be begged, the fact that a principle is controverted does not establish that it is controversial, in the sense of being open to serious question. So anyone who wants to deny that contingent existence or natural causal efficacy is derived from, and hence explicable by, reference to something else needs to give reasons for rejecting what is a first principle of enquiry: given something that is not self-explanatory look for an explanation. Two such reasons are often presented. The first takes us back to Hume who maintains that it is possible to conceive an object coming into existence without a cause:

> [I]t will be easy for us to conceive any object to be non-existent this moment, and existent the next, without conjoining to it the distinct idea of a cause or productive principle. The separation, therefore, of the idea of a cause from that of a beginning of existence, is plainly possible for the imagination; and consequently the actual separation of these objects is so far possible, that it implies no contradiction or absurdity; and is therefore incapable of being refuted by any reasoning from mere ideas; without which 'tis impossible to demonstrate the necessity of a cause.[19]

This short passage draws heavily on Hume's epistemology and metaphysics, both of which have been important ingredients in the modern philosophical case for atheism. Here, however, I am only concerned with the liberality of the reasoning about what is possible and impossible. Hume takes it to be sufficient to show that things can come into being without a cause that we can 'conceive' this, i.e. imagine it, without contradiction. Hence no argument from our mere ideas can refute the claim that things can begin to exist uncaused. Clearly this implies

the denial of the principle of sufficient reason in even a weak form –
for example, that where something comes to be, including a change,
there is something true to be said that renders it intelligible, answer-
ing to the question 'why?' One response to Hume might pick up his
phrase 'mere ideas' and emphasize the element of 'mereness', con-
ceding that on some interpretation of this it may well be that no
such ideas can serve to refute the denial of the causal dependence of
contingent existence but that nothing of any serious interest follows. Suppose, for example, one were to contrast 'mere ideas' with
'adequate concepts', it being a defining condition of the latter (but not
the former) that they are reality-reflecting and rationally constrained;
then while mere ideas might fail to reveal an impossibility of cause-
less coming to be, thinking with adequate concepts does establish this.
The realist, be he a theist or not, has reason to maintain that there are
adequate concepts more than mere ideas, for otherwise general scepticism and/or anti-realism become inescapable. Of itself this does not
vindicate the principle but it blocks part of an argument from imagination to fact.

Additionally, however, Hume offers no account of how we might
determine the content of conceptions based on images and mere ideas.
Try to test his argument by imagining for yourself something popping
into existence, or changing, uncaused. You are sitting at an empty desk
looking at its surface and all of a sudden a book, or an apple, or a lump
of unidentifiable matter appears before you, or the desk top changes
colour. That is imaginable, but what is neither given nor required by
the scenario is that the objects have come to be without a cause and
that is not at all something one would suppose. Rather one would ask
'Where have they come from?', 'How did they get here?', 'Who or what
made them happen?', and so on. In other words once one moves from
Hume's abstractions to an actual example it becomes clear that this
invites questions in search of explanations by reference to antecedent
causes. In short, to the extent that Hume's remarks lead in any direction it is towards and not away from the principle of sufficient reason.

A different argument to a more restricted conclusion is that based
on aspects of contemporary physics. Earlier I mentioned the Many-
Universe hypothesis in quantum theory which arose as an attempt to
overcome the appearance of indeterminacy. This is one of a number
of such efforts but many theorists prefer to accept that quantum phenomena may be indeterminate. Events such as the decay of a nucleus at
one moment rather than another, the emission of a sub-atomic particle
or its disappearance and reappearance elsewhere, may be such as could

not be predicted even in principle, and hence not such as can be fully explained after the fact by citing antecedent causes.

One response is to suggest that this kind of indeterminacy resides only at the quantum level and that 'ordinary' objects and events, from the falling of an apple to the collision of planets, are deterministic and hence are not at odds with the principle. This is unsatisfactory for two reasons. First, by allowing that there are or may be contexts in which it fails one concedes the point to the objector. Even if it is not false everywhere, the fact that it is or may be false somewhere debars appeal to sufficient reason as excluding brute contingency anywhere. Moreover, it is likely that indeterminacy could be fed into cosmology as a part of the story of the development of the macroscopic world, offering the prospect of causal series leading back to events of sorts that have been granted to be without cause. Second, and more significantly, the response assumes in common with the objector that the principle is equivalent to that of universal causal determinism. This I dispute. To begin with I believe that human actions fall within the scope of the principle, while also believing, unlike Smart, that free action is incompatible with complete determinism and that there is free action. More generally, indeterministic phenomena – including quantum events – call for and are often given explanations.

I shall return to the issue of free action later; however, the general point I am concerned with is that not all causal explanations are deterministic. (Indeed given the causal pluralism sketched earlier neither are they all explanations by reference to efficient causation.) Consider again the examples from fundamental physics. Suppose there is an experimental set-up (designed to reproduce types of events that also occur naturally) in which a radioactive source emits particles. Let us say that the frequency and the behaviour of the emissions exhibit quantum indeterminacy. What this is taken to imply is that if it is asked 'why did this happen just then, and not at another moment?', or 'why did the particle take that course and not another?' there may not be an answer – there may not be 'sufficient reason' in the antecedents for just that occurrence, *ex hypothesi* another would have been compatible with them.

I have no wish to deny the phenomena and save 'sufficiency' by insisting that, after all, there must have been determinacy. Instead I claim that a cause need not be a sufficient condition *in the sense presumed by determinism*. There is a very natural and widely exercised way of thinking according to which a sufficient cause is a 'cause enough' and a sufficient explanation an 'explanation enough'. In these

terms the quantum events do have an explanation. For example, it
may be a property of the experimental set-up that a certain percentage
of emissions follow a given pattern. To observe this is not necessarily to confine oneself to a statistical description. Indeed, I take it that
the point of a realist interpretation is to attribute a natural propensity
to the system. Propensities are explanatory even when they are non-
deterministic. If I say that an event occurred because of a reactive
tendency I have answered the question 'why?' in a way that I have not
if I say it *just* occurred. 'Such things happen' can be an empty response
but it need not be, and will not, where the occurrence is attributed to
well-established causal powers. A *cause* is a factor that makes something to be the case; an *explanation* is an account of why something
is the case in terms of a cause. Where the cause is efficient and deterministic an explanation may be inadequate if it falls short of showing that, in the circumstances, only the event in question could have
occurred; it is certainly incomplete. But an explanation of an event is
not shown to be inadequate or incomplete if it does not cite a deterministic cause.

Given the arguments of this section, I conclude that *per se* efficient
cause series cannot be self-explanatory; that Hume's conceivability
argument in support of brute contingency fails, and that quantum
mechanics presents no counter-example to the principle of sufficient
reason – on the contrary it is a useful reminder of the fact that while
the search for explanations is a guiding principle of science we do not
always require them to be deterministic. The questions of existential
and causal dependency, therefore, are real ones, unanswerable by science but answered by postulating a Prime Cause of the existence of the
universe. The 'old' and 'new' teleological arguments add to this the
hypothesis that the Cause of the world is also a source of regularity
and beneficial order; and the argument from conceptual thought and
action imply that this causal source is minded and a conceptual influence upon human thought (*et hoc dicimus Deum*).

7   God and the World

And *this* we call 'God'? While some philosophers have rejected the
traditional proofs outright, others have been willing to grant something to cosmological and teleological arguments but then query the
theistic interpretation of their conclusions. Among those who reject the

proofs some go so far as to argue that there could be no sound reasoning to the conclusion that there is a God. Others maintain that while it is not absolutely inconceivable that there could be such a proof the facts of the matter allow us to reject them in advance because we know from independent reasoning that there is no God. In this section, then, I want to consider some issues involved in these agnostic and atheistic responses.

Showing That and Showing What

Let me begin by saying something about the way in which, following Aquinas, I see philosophical reflection as leading to the existence of God. Famously, St Paul claims:

> What can be known about God is plain to [men] for God has shown it to them. Ever since the creation of the world his invisible nature, namely his eternal power and deity, has been clearly perceived in the things that have been made. (Romans 1: 19–20)

When people discuss the existence of God they usually have, or think they have, a clear enough idea of the kind of thing the possibility of whose existence they are considering. In Western contexts these ideas are generally informed by one of the great monotheistic religions: *Judaism, Christianity* and *Islam*. In their sacred scriptures and in their historic doctrines these religions purport to say a good deal about God, even though they acknowledge the mystery of divinity and the limitations of human comprehension. It is natural, therefore, that the religiously informed think of the question of God's existence in terms of a certain preconceived Divine identity – as if to say 'we know what God is supposed to be like, the question is whether there is such a thing'.

This doctrinally-informed starting point is *not* that of St Paul and nor is it that of the natural theology practised by Aquinas. When Paul claims that God's invisible nature ('his eternal power and deity') has long been perceptible in the things that have been made, he is not supposing that anyone who might come to recognize this must see in it confirmation of prior religious claims. Rather he is asserting that even those who do not already have an idea of God are in a position to determine that God exists simply by reflecting on the natural order. The point is an important one for understanding both the classical proofs

and that which I introduced earlier which argues from the intentionality of thought and action to a transcendent source of mindedness.

In the *Summa*, Aquinas (following Aristotle) distinguishes two kinds
of causal arguments: first, those in which one reasons from an understanding of the nature of a substance to its effects, thereby explaining
their occurrence as caused by that kind of agency; and second, those
in which the argument is from effects to a cause, itself then characterized simply as that which is their source. Aquinas calls these demon-
strations '*propter quid*' (showing *why*) and '*quia*' (showing *that*)
respectively; and he then goes on to write that 'The truths about God
which St Paul says we can know by our natural powers of reasoning
– that God exists, for example – are not numbered among the articles
of faith, but are presupposed to them' (*Summa Theologiae*, Ia, q. 2, a. 2
ad. 1).

Propter quid arguments are very familiar in the sciences and in
everyday causal reasoning. Suppose you notice a mark etched in the
surface of a piece of furniture and ask how it came about. Someone
then points out that a glass of whisky was previously lying there and
explains that some must have spilt and caused the stain due to the
solvent power of its alcohol. The explanation proceeds from a known
cause to one of its effects showing why the effect exists. By contrast
consider the following case. Some while ago I noticed that the elec-
trical shower at home was running at a much higher temperature than
previously. This was a problem since it had become too hot to use,
and so, although I had no illusion that I could repair it, I did set to
wondering why the temperature had increased. The water was hotter
and the flow was less; and given the way in which electric showers
operate – by running the incoming cold water over an electrically
heated element – these two factors seemed likely to be connected.
This phase of the reasoning was in part a case of inference *propter
quid* (inferring the increased heat from a knowledge of the causal
mechanism). What followed, however, was a demonstration *quia*; for
having reasoned that the temperature increase was due to reduced
water flow and having checked from other outlets that the water press-
ure elsewhere in the house was normal, I inferred that there must be
a partial blockage somewhere in the mechanism or in the pipe leading
to it. I thus concluded 'there is an obstacle'.

Notice that this conclusion carries no more information than
would have been given by my saying 'there is a something, I know not
what, which is such that it is reducing the water flow' – to which,
being Thomistically-minded, I might well have added '*et hoc dicimus*

impedimentum', 'and this we call "a blockage"'. Suppose, further, that this blockage is a small piece of masonry wedged in the inflow pipe. My earlier reasoning demonstrated the existence of this stone fragment not *qua* (as a) piece of masonry but simply as an existing blockage. So we might say that I proved that there is a blockage but did not show anything about its nature; after all being 'a blockage' is an extrinsic characterization, in this case a description of the agent from its effects (a blockage = that which blocks). In the terminology of the mediaevals, which is once again current in philosophy, I have proved the existence of the stone *de re* (the existence of *the thing* which is a stone) but not proved its existence *de dicto* (the existence of the thing under the identifying description '*a stone*').

Thus it is with the causal proofs of the existence of God. They aim to establish the existence of a Transcendent Cause of *being*, *change* and *order* and so on, from its effects in the world. They do not claim to show more than what is implied by this. It is not in general an objection, therefore, to argue that they fail as theistic proofs in not demonstrating the existence of God as-He-is-conceived-of-by-Christian-doctrine, say. Oversimplifying, one might observe that they attempt to prove the *thatness* and not the *whatness* of God. Of course, if I can show that some cause exists, and if it is the case that this cause has the property F, then there is *a* sense in which I have proved the existence of an F. Admittedly, the fact that it is an F may fall outside the scope of my demonstration. Nonetheless, we can see that someone goes wrong if they claim that my conclusion is erroneous inasmuch as what it proves is other than what is the case. If I conclude that there is a blockage, what I infer is the case, even though I have not shown that the blockage is a stone.

Moreover, it is not as if in demonstration *quia* one says nothing about what is shown to exist other than *it* exists. Indeed it is difficult to imagine what an argument of this bare sort might be like – one whose conclusion was simply '*It* exists'. The term 'it' usually serves as a pronoun referring back to some identifying name or description occurring earlier in the dialogue or narrative. At other times, however, it may occur as a pure demonstrative as when one asks in seemingly total ignorance 'What is *it*?' In this latter use one may not be able to provide some other identifying description, though it is arguable that a broad classification is presupposed by the circumstance in which the question is raised, and part of this might be made explicit by asking the speaker about *its* shape, colour, texture, movement, and so on. In the causal proofs there is something analogous to contextual presuppositions, for the conclusion 'and it (or this) we call "God"' is reached by way of considering certain events, states and other existents and asking about their causes. When the trail of dependency reaches a source we can then affirm of it – the originating cause – that it is an agent of this or that sort, the sort in question being specified initially by the observed effects.

Reflection on the character of the effects may also allow us to understand more about the nature of the first cause. For example, if we reason that transitions require an ultimate source of change we may then see that this source cannot itself be subject to change and that its impassibility must go along with perfection and simplicity. If that which initiates change itself underwent modifications then it would fall within the scope of the question 'what causes this change?' and thus would be just another case of that which it was our aim to explain. To this someone might respond that while a first cause of change could certainly not be dependent on any *external* factor, nevertheless it might undergo modifications deriving from some *internal* source. There are, however, at least two (related) reasons for rejecting this. First, it involves conceiving of the agent as composed of parts and this is at odds with the idea of divine simplicity. Second, any 'internal movement' would give rise to the sort of questioning that leads to the conclusion that there must be an uncaused cause of change. Let me expand these points (and the relation between them) starting with the second.

In presenting the *prima via* Aquinas writes that anything undergoing change is being changed by something else (*omne quod movetur ab alio movetur*). We will not really understand this claim and appreciate its force if we think solely in terms of one object mechanically interacting with another – a polisher shining a shoe, for example. Certainly this is a case of change deriving from change; but to see the scope of Aquinas's principle we have to recall his analysis of change in terms of the transition from potentiality to actuality. Prior to being polished, the surface of the shoe is dull but it has the possibility of becoming shiny. In Aristotelian-cum-Thomistic vocabulary it is *actually* dull but *potentially* shiny; or even more 'scholastically' expressed, it is *in act* with respect to dullness and *in potency* with regard to shininess. This situation will persist unless some factor operates to change it. Once that factor comes into play the surface of the shoe is 'moved' from potency to act with respect to shininess; or more familiarly, it becomes shiny. This 'becoming' or realization requires an agent, and that agent cannot itself be wholly potential, it must be active (or, equivalently, 'in act'). So wherever there is a transformation or a transition from one state to another some explanation is called for of what effects this, and once that questioning begins it can only be halted by coming to rest in an unchanging cause of change. The activity of this primary agent cannot then be supposed to derive from either an external or an internal source, for that would be to assume that it is not after all the ultimate origin of change.

This reflection brings out part of what is meant by saying that God is perfect. There is no scope for improvement in God or for any kind of development, since this would be a change involving a transition from potentiality to actuality in respect of some feature, and any such transition would then require some prior actuality to initiate it. Young baby John grows through taking in nutrients. The process of growth depends upon input from his environment and upon internal physiological activity. These factors explain the changes in John but neither is itself wholly self-explanatory. Nothing will constitute an ultimate explanation of change if it is itself subject to change either from without or from within.

Reason brings us to a first cause of change and leads us to see that as such it must be perfect and impassible – both in the literal and general sense of not undergoing modification, and in the narrower sense of not being subject to emotion. This reasoning also bears upon the first of the two points mentioned above, *viz.* the idea of divine simplicity. One reason why the activity of the first cause cannot derive from internal changes is that such an agent can have no moving (i.e. changing) parts; indeed it can have no *parts* at all. Once again it is important to be clear as to the nature of this claim. The doctrine of divine simplicity is not the thesis that God is relatively uncomplicated. Ordinarily when we describe something as 'simple' this is to contrast it in point of degree of complexity with other things. But God is not simple in this sense; rather the relevant contrast is between that which is composite and that which is not. God can have no physical parts or else he would belong to the natural order and hence give rise to the same sorts of questions that initiate the five ways. Equally, he can have no metaphysical parts; that is to say God cannot coherently be thought of as composed of such elements as substance and attribute, or form and matter.

In the case of things in the world there is a distinction to be drawn between features or attributes and that in which they inhere. On the one hand there is greyness, roughness and solidity, and on the other there is the subject of these, namely the stone. These features are of kinds that are or can be instantiated by other things. The stone, however, is a particular or individual and is not repeatable, though there may be others qualitatively indistinguishable from it. Moreover, while the stone may change its colour or become smooth, these sorts of changes in its attributes are different in kind from others, such as its being crushed, which would be equivalent to its destruction. Indeed, we can describe destruction philosophically as 'change in respect of identity-constituting essential properties'.

Similarly, in order to make sense of particular changes, and of change as such, we need to identify a medium of change. There are various candidates for this but in keeping with the Aristotelian–Thomistic orientation of the present discussion let me introduce a metaphysical understanding of the notion of matter. In everyday parlance, when we speak of 'matter' we have in mind more or less solid stuffs like wood, plastic, stone or metal; or possibly the microphysical particles invest-igated by science. Since the Greeks, however, there has been another, philosophical, notion of matter which is correlative to the idea of form. In this sense every natural thing is a metaphysical composite of formal and material aspects. In other words everything is a combination of a set of one or more characteristics (essential and inessential) and, so to speak, an 'occasion' or 'place' of their instantiation. Further, the locus for a set of features or forms involves a series of possibilities. So, for example, the apple on the desk has a range of characteristics some of which can and others of which cannot change without its being destroyed. But these forms – colour, shape, texture, and so on – may be shared by another apple lying in the bowl. In each case there is a (movable) 'place' in the universe that is the location for the instantiation of these forms and which is also the site and range of possibilities of change in respect of them. Matter is the potentiality for the instantia-tion of form and form is the nature or characteristic that is instantiated.

This account explains what it is to be a particular thing and thereby provides a basis for distinguishing between things and for identify-ing and reidentifying them. As kinds of fruit, apples and pears differ with regard to their defining properties or forms. As particular pieces of fruit, two apples may not differ qualitatively, but necessarily they will differ with regard to matter, i.e. each has its own 'site' of instantiation and transformation. And we can conclude by implication that an apple viewed on Friday is one and the same as that seen on Monday if and only if it is the same composite of form and matter (or what may be equivalent, the one and only spatio-temporally continuous organization of certain attributes).

With this analysis in mind we can now say that that which is the cause of things cannot itself be composite and hence must be simple. It cannot be composed of metaphysical parts such as substance and attribute, matter and form, potentiality and actuality, and so on; for in being of necessity unchanging it has no unrealized potentiality, and in necessarily lacking potentiality it has no matter; and in having no matter it has no basis for individuality; and in being devoid of individuality it cannot be a particular substance possessed of essential and accidental attributes. In short, God is necessarily simple. He is not a something or other, a this or that; but nor of course is God nothing. Rather we might say, as does Meister Eckhart in a series of fascinating philosophical reflections, that God is no-thing.[20] Or as Wittgenstein wrote in a quite different context 'It is not a *something* but not a *nothing* either'.[21]

In developing this sort of argument I am following the style and direction of speculation advanced by St Thomas, his scholastic followers and more recent analytical philosophers of religion. This speculation traces to and fro a series of mutual implications between various conditions: impassibility, immateriality, eternity, omnipotence, perfection, simplicity, necessary existence, and so on, drawing out various relations of dependence, sufficiency and equivalence. Before proceeding I want to mention a couple of these conditions and certain ways of thinking about them which are sometimes held to be problematic.

It is often maintained that God is identical with his essence and that the divine attributes are one. Such claims might seem to be at odds with my earlier denials that God is subject to various distinctions, and in a sense that is so. Nonetheless, although they use terminology that is more properly attributable to natural beings these ways of speaking aim to make appropriate points. For example, the claim that God is his essence bears on the metaphysical inseparability, even notionally, of the *thatness* and the *whatness* of God. When thinking about cats, say, we can distinguish between a certain species of animal nature and the (realized) possibility of several individuals possessing that nature. Felix and Felicity are both cats in virtue of participating in, or sharing, a common nature. In the case of God, however, there is no possibility of there being more than one instance of the kind, for individuation is tied to materiality and that is a feature of the spatio-temporal order, which is also the domain of change and contingency. Thus, if there is a God identified initially as a first cause, then *that* he is and *what* he is are one and the same reality. Unlike the case of catness, there is no sense to be attached to the question of whether this kind of 'whatness' (*quiddity*) might be shared by more than one thing.

Similarly, the odd sounding 'identity of the divine attributes' is a conclusion derived from reflection upon the simplicity of God. Just as one aspect of not being composed of parts is that there is no distinction in God between that which has an essence and the essence itself, so another aspect of this transcendent simplicity is that each attribute is co-extensive with every other. One way of trying to understand this is by way of an analogy derived from the philosophy of language. Following Frege (1848–1925), contemporary philosophers distinguish between the *sense* and the *reference* of an expression; between, that is to say, the *thing* that the term denotes, and the *way* the referent is presented by the expression.[22] One consequence of this distinction is that two or more expressions can be referentially or extensionally equivalent though they have different senses.

Aquinas was already familiar with something like this distinction for he uses it to explicate the idea that truth, being and goodness – what he calls 'transcendentals' – are in reality one and the same. What he means, I think, is that there is one reality at issue, but that it can be identified from different perspectives and that the nature of these perspectives determines, in distinctive and different ways, what is seen from them. Each perspective conditions one's view and bestows a certain character on the appearance of that which is seen. Nonetheless what they are perspectives *on* is just one reality. Returning to the thesis of the identity of the divine attributes and connecting it with the earlier discussion of the '*quia*' (effect to cause) character of the Five Ways, we might say that the various features such as impassibility, necessity, mindedness, and so on are attributed from different perspectives, which in this case are provided by the nature of the mundane phenomena with which one starts (change, contingency, human intentionality, etc.), but that the implied simplicity of God reveals to reason that they are ontologically one reality: God *is* necessary existence which *is* impassibility which *is* underived mind which *is* God.

From Creature to Creator

In the introduction to the present section, I mentioned that some who reject the traditional proofs also maintain that there can be no reasoning from the world to God. Various accounts of this impossibility are offered but I shall only address what I take to be the general form of the objection. It is usually attributed to Kant but it certainly pre-dates his writings and is probably as old as systematic arguments for the existence of God. The basic idea is that as a matter of logic we cannot reason from the conditions of the empirical world to the conditions of a transcendent super-empirical reality. Sometimes this is taken to establish a mere limitation deriving from the fact that our concepts are acquired from or are otherwise keyed to the empirical world and so can be presumed to fail of meaning when we try to apply them beyond this. At other times it is argued that any attempt to apply them 'transcendentally' will yield contradictions.

As regards the first of these contentions I would only observe that, as was seen earlier, it rests on a series of controversial assumptions about the source and scope of meaning. First, it may be contested that all our concepts derive from empirical experience; but even if this were granted it is a further question whether this implies any confinement of their scope. Consider the terms 'planet', 'distant' and 'travelled to'. Each might be held to derive ultimately from experience, but it is clear that we can easily construct a complex term 'planet more distant than has been travelled to' and apply it out of the range of our actual and perhaps even our possible experience. This is not a rare linguistic or conceptual phenomenon. We are for ever talking and thinking about entities that we do not and could not experience, for example, unrealized hypothetical situations, unobservable (but presumed to be actual) objects and events, infinitely large domains, and so on. We talk and think about the unrecoverable past and the as yet non-existent future; about the spatially distant and about the non-spatial and abstract realms of mathematics and philosophy.

Of course, someone might want to argue that all of these efforts are in vain, or contend that while some are legitimate nonetheless the particular ways of thinking presumed upon by proofs for the existence of God are unavailable to us. It is difficult to see how anything sensible could be made of the former claim, since it would exclude vast tracts of what we otherwise take to be perfectly sensible, explanatory and truth-detecting forms of thought, including, let it be clearly noted, much and perhaps most fundamental science. So far as the second contention is concerned, it supposes that the concepts deployed in the proofs, or the ways in which they are used, can be separated off from other unproblematic notions or uses. But again it is hard to imagine this being done in any coherent and convincing way. Moreover, the concepts in question, *viz. change, causation, contingency, necessity, purpose, thought, action* and so on, are not specific to natural theology and nor is the manner of their use in the proofs unique to that context.

Consider briefly the following supposedly troublesome examples: *causation, necessity, thought* and *action*. It has often been argued that our only idea of causation is that of the link between efficient causes and their effects, and that this is a form of law-governed relationship between contingent and independent entities. If this were so, then indeed the proofs would be fallacious; for given what the theist claims about God and the dependency of the world on his creative activity, they would involve equivocation in the use of the central terms. For example, 'cause' when predicated of God simply could not mean what it means when predicated of a material object. However, as I have argued above, the core notion of a cause is simply that of a productive factor – that which makes something to be the case – and there is nothing in this idea alone that implies laws, contingency and independence. Of course, if the world is caused to be by that which we call God this relationship is not to be assimilated to the mechanical operation of one object upon another; but why should the theist, or anyone else for that matter, want to circumscribe the idea of causation in this way?

Likewise, there has been an inadequate constraining of possibilities in discussions of necessity and contingency. Happily, since the late 1960s the old idea that the only necessities are linguistic or logical has fallen under suspicion and come to be widely abandoned in favour of the view that there can be existential or *de re* necessities. In chapter 1 Smart raises worries about how the idea of God's existence can be fitted into any of the various categories of necessity he discusses, but I think he gives insufficient attention to the way in which the idea of necessity arises in the argument from contingency. What we are led to is the existence of something which exists eternally, which does not owe its being to anything else and which cannot not exist. One might well ask 'Is there any such thing?'; but this notion of necessary existence is not incoherent, and if I am right then reason will require us to apply it once we begin to ask about how to explain the existence of anything that is contingent, i.e. not necessary in this sense.

Causation and necessity are not obviously person-involving features as are thought and action; and it may be conceded that while the former can be deployed intelligibly in the direction of the transcendent, any such use of the latter must lead to incoherence. As before, my illustration and response will be brief. The upshot of the reasoning from effect to cause in the case of teleological or design proofs, particularly

in their 'old' versions, and of the 'Prime Thinker' argument, is the conclusion that the operation of the world and of human beings within
it depends upon the purposeful agency of a transcendent mind. To
this we could now add the sort of reasoning given above to show
that such a mind is simple, unique, unchanging, and so on. However, precisely this addition may seem to create the sort of problem
that the objector envisaged. For if I wish to say that God is unchanging, this raises the prospect that he is not in time (assuming as many
have done that change and time are correlative); and if I also want to
claim that temporal effects are due to his agency I then seem to have
advanced a contradiction: that God's activity is both inside and outside
of time. Or it may be supposed that even to attribute thought to God
is to ascribe a temporal and complex process incompatible with his
eternity and impassibility.

The issue of divine eternity is an intricately structured one and for
present purposes I am happy to adopt the view that God is timeless
in the sense (whatever exactly that is) of being 'outside' time. How
then can he act in it? It do not think it is an option for the theist to
deny divine agency in the world, not least because I have endorsed the
view that the only way to reason to God's existence is from his (or here
one might better say 'its') effects. But the claim that God produces
effects 'in time' is ambiguous, since the temporal reference may either be
to God's effects or to his agency. So far as mundane action is concerned
both the causing and the being effected are temporal, but once again
this is not something that is implied by the idea of agency as such. To
hold that A caused B is only to maintain that B is due to A, and it is
a further step, therefore, to claim that if B occurred at t then A must
also have occurred at some time t' (presumably prior to or simultaneous with t). Of course, someone may reply that such agency as we are
familiar with, i.e. our own, is temporally situated. That, however, is
beside the point. For what would have to be demonstrated is that if
the effects of an action are temporal then so *must* be the action.

A similar rejoinder is available in response to the claim that thought
involves time and complexity. Human thinking takes time and makes
use of 'separate pieces' – for example as we fashion a chain of reasoning out of initially unconnected symbols. But it is possible to assign
these facts to what are plausibly contingent features of human mental
processes. The defining characteristics of reasoning as contrasted with
mere psychological activity are atemporal features, for example entail-
ment and contradiction. Consider the following elementary *modus ponens*
proof:

> If you are reading this then you must be awake
> You are reading this
> ∴   You must be awake

What makes this a valid piece of logic are certain abstract features
and not any empirical relations between a series of marks on paper.
In acknowledging this fact we see the need to distinguish between the
(logical) content of a proposition or set of propositions and its vehicle
or embodiment. Once that distinction is made, however, it is no longer
obvious that anything that possesses reason must exercise this through
the manipulation of symbols in space and time. Indeed once the se-
paration is allowed it is no longer clear that we must speak of rationality
being 'exercised' as opposed to being timelessly possessed. Likewise,
the idea of thought conjoining and opposing various elements seems
to belong to the sphere of psychology rather than to that of reason *per
se*. Yet it is precisely reason as such, and not an empirical psychology,
that we are led to ascribe to a transcendent cause on the basis of order
observed in nature.

8   God, Good and Evil

Obviously the existence of God could not be proved if there were a
sound argument to show that there is no God. Prime candidates for
such an argument are proofs from evil. The general form of these
proofs is as follows:

(1)   The idea of God is that of an omnibenevolent, omnipotent and
      omniscient being.
(2)   If such a being existed then there would be no evil.
(3)   There is evil.
(4)   Therefore no such being (as God) exists.

Any adequate assessment of this argument requires that one think
a good deal about the precise content of the claims involved and it
would be fair to say that there is no general agreement on what the
theist is or is not committed to in his account of the divine attributes
and of what the nature of evil might be. There are, however, a number
of points to be made.

First, then, it is customary to distinguish between *natural* and *moral* evils, that is to say between bad events, processes and states of affairs the existence of which is a result of the operation of natural causes, and occurrences and situations whose badness results from or consists in the thoughts and actions of intelligent beings. If I am struck by a falling branch and my neck is broken that is a natural evil; if you strike me and break my neck that is a moral one. This contrast may suggest that the evil is the same in each case – a broken neck – and that the difference lies in the varying causes; but that is not quite right. The natural evil is the misfortune (to me) of my neck being broken; the moral evil is the fact that someone should be motivated to harm me. Certainly this fact is bad news for me, but its moral badness attaches to the state of mind of my attacker – the moral evil consists in his malevolence not in my broken neck. In both cases the evil to me is a state of nature (a fractured bone) but in the attack there is the additional evil of a malevolent heart.

Second, when people think of natural evils they mostly have in mind physical and organic damage and defects caused by catastrophic events or diseases: destruction through earthquake, fire and tempest; abnormality, illness and pain, and so on. It is worth adding, however, that as well as inorganic and physiological evils there are psychological and cognitive ones such as pathological depression, and imbecility and ignorance. If it is a bad thing that people are physically sick it is also a bad thing that they should be psychologically ill, and uncomprehending about matters of personal and of general importance. Indeed, one might speak of an atheist 'proof from ignorance' parallel to that from evil, but given that ignorance is itself a bad condition it is better to regard this as a special case of the argument from evil.

Looking at the argument above, a theist might be tempted to resist the conclusion by rejecting premiss (3). There are religious believers who claim that the appearance of evil is an illusion but this is wholly at odds with our experience, and at a deeper level it seems to be self-contradictory. If evil is an illusion then anyone who supposes it is real, as most of us do, is in ignorance; but, as we saw, ignorance is a bad state of affairs. Thus either our impressions of evil are veridical or they are illusory; if they are veridical there is evil and if they are illusory there is evil; *ergo* there is evil. In a moment I shall consider a somewhat different reservation about the reality of evil but it should be clear that any attempt simply to deny that bad things happen is easily refutable.

Another and more promising response to the argument is to query premiss (2). Suppose we agree that whatever the other purported divine attributes, the theistic idea of God is of a being that wills only the good, is almighty and is all knowing. Suppose also that it is accepted that there are natural and moral evils. Does the latter fact imply the non-existence of the theistic God? Some writers seem to have thought so but there is certainly no logical incompatibility between the claim that there is an omnibenevolent, omnipotent and omniscient God and the assertion that there is evil – any more than there is between the claims that there are cats and that there are mice. However, as in the latter case, it might be thought that given the existence of the one thing the other will be excluded. Something about cats – their strong tendency to hunt and kill small animals – is at odds with the existence of mice; likewise, it is supposed, something about God is at odds with the existence of evil. This is the point of premiss (2): to *assert* the incompatibility of God and evil. Why, then, should one accept that assertion? The familiar answer is that a being who is wholly good and has irresistible power and comprehensive knowledge would not let evil occur or would act to overcome it.

Theodicies (Gk. *theos* (god) *dike* (justice)) are attempts to show why (2) is false, or equivalently, how the existence of evil is compatible with that of a just God. However, a fully adequate theodicy has to do more than show the mere compatibility of God and evil: it has to reconcile the two in a religiously significant manner. Accordingly, it must draw upon philosophical *and* theological resources, and in respect of the latter aspect that means invoking particular claims about God. The neo-Thomistic approach I favour does so by conjoining Aristotelian metaphysics and Christian revelation.

Earlier I mentioned a 'reservation' about the reality of evil. It is the thought that evil is not *something* in the world along with other things but a condition of them involving some deficiency or limitation; it is a 'privation'. This can be brought out by reflecting on the fact that like 'good', the term 'bad' is a logically attributive adjective: it requires completion by a substantive term whose meaning provides a criterion of evaluation.[23] If someone says only 'there's a bad one in this box' we are not yet in a position to make sense of his claim, let alone to assess it. Once he has said what the bad thing is, however, one can set about checking this. Suppose it is a pair of scissors; then knowing what scissors are for and what sorts of conditions detract from their effective functioning, one can determine whether this is a bad (i.e. defective) pair. Perhaps the blades are blunt, or the metal is fatigued, or the rivet is loose. In each case the consequence is that the functioning of the scissors is impeded and because of this we can say that it is a 'bad' pair. So it is in general: a heart is bad because the absence of a valve or an accumulation of fat impedes its proper function, an apple is rotten because of the presence of certain bacteria that induce changes in its structure, and so on.

Wherever it is apt to speak of a natural evil there is some further description of the situation which explains what this consists in and shows how it arises because one thing is securing its well-being at the cost of that of another (cats eating mice, bacteria consuming apples), or the proper development and flourishing of a thing is impeded by external or internal factors such as a shortage of a necessary element or a superfluity of it – a plant can suffer from too little water and from too much. Such states of affairs are certainly bad, but the point is that in order to show why this is so one needs to advert to certain goods – the presence of actual goods (the cat satisfying its appetite) or the absence of anticipated ones (the mouse growing to maturity). So part of the answer to the question of how the existence of a good God is compatible with that of evil is that God neither creates nor sustains evil; rather he creates and sustains a system of natural substances and forces whose operation has the effect that the well-being of some is secured at the expense of that of others. Where there is a bad there is a good involving the realization of the powers and liabilities of inter-acting systems.

In general there cannot be a world of living things developing in accord with their inbuilt teleologies – growing, moving, sensing, re-producing and so on – without interactions that are to the detriment of some individuals and species. In creating such a system God brought into being and sustains a domain in which natural values are every-where to be seen as organisms realize their natures. The inevitable cost of this to others is also evident and constitutes what we regard as natural evils.

Here two points of clarification are necessary. First, let me repeat that I am not denying that bad things happen. When bacteria flourish at the expense of an apple, or a cat at the cost of the life of a mouse, that really is bad for the fruit and for the animal. Also, it is generally supposed that some gains and losses are more important than others. On the view I am presenting this is not a matter of subjective prefer-ence for the well-being of one thing over that of another. In the system of interacting organisms there is a hierarchy of substances, since liv-ing things can be ranked according to the character and range of their natural powers. In the traditional Aristotelian scheme this involves the three-fold classification described below.

Organism	Powers
Rational	Intellect – Will – Memory
Sentient	Perception – Appetite – Locomotion
Vegetative	Nutrition – Growth – Generation

Corresponding to each kind of living thing is a set of defining characteristics – vital powers. What makes this a *hierarchy*, rather than a mere list, is that types of organisms higher up the table have all the powers of those lower down but not *vice versa*. Thus, like trees, rabbits take in material from their environment, grow according to species-specific principles of development and reproduce themselves; but they also perceive their environment, have attractions and aversions towards aspects of it and move around within it. Human beings share powers with both vegetative and sentient species but in addition are intellectual beings capable of rational thought and action.

Beings possessed of more and greater powers have open to them higher forms of self-realization. By this very fact, however, they are vulnerable to more and greater losses. In drought a tree may wither and die for want of water, a rabbit may suffer the pain of dehydration, but in addition to undergoing these physical and sensory ordeals a human being may experience despair at the end of her hopes for herself and her children. Those who have more, have more to lose. The death of a human being thus constitutes a greater loss than does that of a rabbit or a tree.

Notice, however, that by virtue of their speculative and practical reason human beings have considerable abilities to avoid and recover from the injurious effects of nature, and more profoundly to discover how nature operates and to direct its operations in ways beneficial to human and other interests. Realizing one's nature as a psychophysical being is a great good, but the general condition of being able to do so includes various dangers and limitations. We can try to reduce these but we cannot wholly eliminate them. Moreover, the hazardous character of organic existence provides occasions to develop our intellectual and moral powers. The inescapable challenge of life is to live well, i.e. intelligently and virtuously. To have created a world in which this is possible is to have made something good, notwithstanding that it is a place of loss. As the tree grows tall towards the light, the grass beneath it withers for want of water, food and sun.

So much for natural good and evil. What of moral virtue and vice? How could a good God create beings capable of the horrors of this and previous centuries and why does he not intervene to halt them? While theists have offered a variety of responses, I believe the pattern of reasoning developed thus far leads towards the conclusion that although God is responsible for everything we do he is not the author of moral evil, and that it is incompatible with the good that he *has* authored in creating rational animals that he should then override their decisions wherever these are morally wrong.

Moral wrong is a deficiency with respect to reason, emotion and will. The virtuous agent discerns his own and others' physical and psychological goods and strives to achieve and preserve them. The vic[e]ious agent by contrast culpably either fails to discern the good or acts to inhibit or destroy it. Once again evil is a privation, not a something added to a life but a lack of what should be there – in this case certain orientations of thought, affection and volition. In making human beings, God creates animals with a rational teleology including the potential for knowledge and right action. Shortly, I will argue that he is also creatively involved in sustaining and realizing these potentialities; however, if *we* are to be thinkers and doers then the role of providence can be no more than an enabling and co-operative one. God cannot do our reasoning and acting for us or else we would not exist. To be a rational agent is to think and act; so to assert one's existence as a self is to claim that there are deeds for which one is responsible. Without God we would not be, but nor would *we* be unless God created us free and responsible, and in making us such he invites us to participate in creation.

Just as in making a world of living things God indirectly causes and continuously permits the obstruction and destruction that results from the flow of life, so in making free agents he is causally responsible for circumstances in which wrongs are done; but in neither case does God directly bring about evil. In the first case he intends the good of organic life with its inevitable ebb and flow, and in the second he empowers beings freely to direct their lives towards moral perfection, but it is logically impossible that he should compel such a movement towards the good. In short, it is wrong to suppose that if there existed an omnibenevolent, omnipotent and omniscient being then there could not be evil, or – contraposing – that the existence of evil implies the non-existence of God. Thus, premiss (2) is false.

What I have offered is a sketch of a theodicy but it is incomplete in various respects. First, there arises a question of the scale of collateral damage. An implicit assumption of my argument has been that the goods of organic and rational life outweigh the harms resulting from them. It is difficult to conceive of how the various values and disvalues might be compared but I would allow that if it could be shown that overall the universe is a bad thing then that would refute the claims of theism. Since I maintain that theism is true, I hold by implication that the universe is overall a good thing. However, one significant aspect of its deficiencies is not within God's power to limit short of destroying the universe, or a part of it. For much that is bad results from or consists in human wrongdoing, and God cannot inhibit this while still maintaining our powers of free agency. He can, and I believe he does, act exceptionally to limit the evil caused by human choices but to do so always and everywhere would involve his removing our freedom, frustrating our agency or reducing us to the level of unreasoning animals. Rather than do that, which would involve a reversal in divine creation, it may be that if human action falls so far short of the good to which it is called then the human story will be brought to an end. There is reason for God to co-operate in our actions so long as more good than evil results, but it would be folly to assume that he will keep us going come what may. Indeed it is required for the justice of providence that he should not. In such circumstances, for God to close the book on human history would not be a reversal of the divine plan but a completion of it – and there is scriptural support (couched in harrowing imagery) for the expectation of this:

> Just as the weeds are gathered and burned with fire, so will it be at the close of the age. The Son of Man will send his angels, and they will gather out of his kingdom all causes of sin and all evildoers, and throw them into the furnace of fire; there men will weep and gnash their teeth. Then the righteous will shine like the sun in the kingdom of their Father. He who has ears, let him hear. (Matthew 13: 40–4)

This passage suggests a partial remedy to a second omission in my treatment thus far, namely the absence of any account of how, if at all, natural and moral evils are addressed by God. So far as the matter of strict compatibility with bare theism is concerned no such issue may arise. It may be enough to show that evil is a privation parasitic upon the good and that the good outweighs the bad. But I remarked that any fully adequate theodicy must have a religious aspect and that this should express the content of a particular theology. Here I must be brief. Christianity teaches that suffering is a route to moral self-realization and that God himself entered into the valley of death. What is to be made of these claims?

It is a fact of human experience that suffering has immense potential for growth. Anyone who has lived through painful illness, emotional distress, anxiety and depression, and other familiar terrors and woes, knows that these give rise to 'spiritual' challenges which, if met, leave one a stronger and wiser person. To put it paradoxically, people are often grateful to have suffered harms. This is not perverse and nor does it imply that the experiences were not really harmful. What it suggests is that it is possible to fashion something good out of evil by accepting it for what it is and by making oneself stronger so as to be able to absorb it, and in the process reorder one's priorities in better accord with the hierarchy of objective values. These are commonplaces of mature human reflection. What Christian theism adds is an account of how heroic victory over evil is possible. How can someone be so gracious in the face of evil as to forgive the murderer of their only child? 'By God's Grace alone is it made possible' – is the Christian answer. An atheist may speak in psychological or evolutionary terms of 'self-preservation' and of 'adaptive utility', but it is difficult to see how he can construct out of these any adequate account of what so forcibly presents itself as a moral or spiritual victory.

To suffer evil, and to a lesser extent to contemplate such suffering, is to be faced with an occasion for moral growth. It is obvious, however, that not all harm elicits gracious and heroic virtue. Where the victim is a rational agent the failure to respond morally *may* be culpable and not a ground for complaint against God. Yet there is much suffering involving natural and moral evils that cannot be an occasion for growth on the part of the victim because he or she is a non-human animal or a sub-rational human. May we not call out to heaven in protest against this? It might be reasonable for a heathen to do so, but the doctrine of the incarnation and crucifixion of Jesus Christ should give the Christian cause for hesitation.[24] This is the most profound religious idea ever entertained by the human mind: that God, the unconditioned cause of being, entered into the precarious condition of his creation. From St Paul to the present day, libraries have been written on this theme. I must rest content with five sentences. (1) Whatever else is to be said about the incarnation of God in Christ this much is true: that by becoming a human animal God rendered himself vulnerable to the harms arising from the divinely ordained activity of bacteria, the uncertainties of being born of a poor young woman in first century Palestine, and the self-interested actions of imperial governors and religious leaders. (2) Sacred history teaches that this was for the sake of re-establishing (for ever) the original covenant between man and God; but it also meant that God moved among the dark shadows of his creation. (3) Justice did not require this of him, since the shadows are a consequence of the light, and hence not something that might have been eliminated in redrafting the cosmic design; yet he did it and in doing so subjected himself to conditions which his beneficial designs made inevitable. (4) God so cares for his creation that he will not have it endure alone the costs of its goodness; whatever it must suffer he will suffer. (5) This is the ultimate demonstration of the justice of God: that he elects to endure whatever losses his creation may sustain.

9   Liberty and Providence

In discussing moral evil I have assumed that we are metaphysically free agents. Jack Smart and others dispute this; as he puts it 'I will not grant the theist the notion of libertarian free will, which seems to me an absurd one'. The presumed absurdity derives from the following dilemma or 'paradox of freedom': either an event is determined or it is random. If a movement is a purposeful action it is not random; hence it is determined. In rejecting determinism the libertarian is left only with randomness but that is the very antithesis of intelligent behaviour. Thus the occurrence of actions is not merely compatible with determinism, it requires it.

This last claim seems to me false in both respects. First, if universal causal determinism is true then we are not free. If it were the case that the movement of my hand as I write is wholly determined as the upshot of a series of events leading backwards from muscle contractions to nerve stimulations to brain events and so on, then I am not freely responsible for it. All that has happened is that the course of world events has passed through my body. The libertarian alternative is that prior to acting it was not determined what would ensue. In the limiting case just the same antecedents might have obtained in conjunction with different consequences. The difference between the outcomes is ascribable to my power of free choice (in scholastic terminology my *liberty of indifference*).

So far as the purported dilemma or paradox is concerned the claim that an event is either *determined* or *random* (in the sense of unconditioned chance) remains an assertion which nowadays lacks even the support apparently once given it by science. Clearly these are *contrary* predicates – something cannot be both determined and random – but it has to be shown that they are *contradictories* – that it is not possible that something may be neither. Physical theory no longer holds that all causation conforms to exceptionless laws, but now regards sequences of events at the microphysical level as conforming to patterns that are precisely instances of non-determined, non-random behaviour. This is because it views them as possessing indeterminate probabilities.

While I do not believe that the liberty of human choice is to be identified with the indeterminacy of quantum systems, there is nevertheless a parallel between on the one hand the notion of objective probabilities rooted in the natures of physical systems, and on the other the idea of behavioural tendencies issuing from habitual rational agency. Physical events and human actions may both admit of a high degree of predictability without either resulting from deterministic causes. In the case of the former, reliable prediction is based on natural propensities, in the case of the latter upon rational inclinations and responses.

As I argued earlier, the relation between an agent's reasons and his actions is not in general a causal one, at least as causation is typically understood. To explain what someone is doing it is not necessary to identify something 'lying behind' his movements – in a more or less literal interpretation of those words. Action is the exercise of rational and appetitive powers. To understand how an agent may act freely on a given occasion one needs to ask how it is possible that a human being should act at all. Stones are moved by external forces but, as the scholastics say, agents are moved 'from within' (*ab intrinseco*). What this means is something very different from the neuropsychological events envisaged by present-day causal theorists. An adequate theory of intentional behaviour needs to combine the idea of non-random indeterminacy with that of intelligent sources of action.

We are rational animals; living things whose principles of organization and functioning are ordered towards a form of life that is responsive to reason. Voluntary action is a capacity of rational agents expressed in intrinsically intelligible behaviour. When a human being acts there need be no event in the agent prior to the action and which is its immediate cause. The only required 'source' is the very agent whose powers are exercised thereby. In a mature human being these powers are possessed continuously even when he or she is not doing anything 'in particular'. Thus most action calls for no explanation, for if one knows that one is dealing with a rational animal then there is no need to say why it is doing things, for animals are active by nature (even sitting quietly and sleeping are activities). Activity is the norm, and most activity is normal, i.e. it is what would be expected of a reasonable human being in familiar circumstances. The first point is a general one true of all agents, rational and otherwise; but the second derives from the fact that if we say a piece of behaviour is an action then we are committed to the claim that in doing it the agent was aiming at some end (even if this was just the performance of an action of that sort). Action differs from mere movement in being purposeful, in aiming to advance an interest of the agent. This thought is what lies behind the scholastic doctrine that all action is performed under the species of the good (*sub specie boni*).

An obvious question to ask is whether the claim is that every action is necessarily directed towards a real good or merely to what is believed by the agent to be a good. Clearly the second interpretation is weaker and may seem to be the more plausible, yet the former deserves further consideration. In the case of non-rational agents it is reasonable, both philosophically and as part of biological science, to maintain that their powers and tendencies are ordered or adapted to objective natural goods. If the general pattern is to be maintained we should then say that the power of rational choice is similarly directed towards states objectively beneficial to the agent. But that claim seems to be refuted by the fact that agents often choose actions that are naturally or morally bad. However, it may be that every end of action is objectively good in some respect relevant to the agent's real interests as a being of a certain sort, but that this goodness is more or less partial.

This possibility returns us to the idea that evil is a privation. I argued that God permits moral evil because of the good of free agency that gives rise to it. There is nothing inevitable about wrongdoing but in creating free agents God creates the possibility of it. What needs to be added is that for the most part he even sustains us in our folly and maintains the sources of suffering. This is because the creative activity of God is continuous and omnipresent; the qualifying phrase 'for the most part' refers to the possibility of special acts or *miracles*.

Deists hold that the universe is a strictly deterministic physical system brought in being by a God who thereafter had nothing further to do with it. This philosophy of divine indifference is hardly an attractive one; it has very little explanatory power and it will not sustain a religion of prayer and worship. According to theism, by contrast, the dependence of the universe upon God is continuing and complete, for he is active in every event – but not at the cost of the agency of his creatures. This doctrine of immanent participation may be comforting but how is it possible? God makes things with their various defining powers and liabilities; he sustains them from moment to moment; he provides opportunities for the realization of these powers and, finally, he concurs in their operation. Nothing happens without God's active presence yet creatures make their own contribution. This account treads a path between two extremes: *quasi-deism* according to which God does no more than create and maintain the existence of basic matter; and *occasionalism* in which he is the sole cause of every event – the appearance of secondary causation (the exercise of powers by creatures) being an illusion resulting from the fact that God acts regularly on the occasion of the co-presence of various things.

The present account also provides a fruitful way of understanding something of the metaphysical nature of miracles. Smart gives a very good assessment of Hume's strictures against the miraculous and I refer the reader back to it. *Contra* Hume, there is no compelling philosophical case for thinking that miracles are logically impossible, whatever other reasons there may be for doubting whether this or that purported event really happened. What I wish to emphasize, however, against a common assumption among theists who claim to believe in the miraculous, is that it is a mistake to think of miracles as interventions from outside creation. The miraculous belongs to the category of the preternatural (L. *praeter* (going beyond) *naturam* (the natural)) but as Aquinas very soberly explains in his chapters on miracles in the *Summa Contra Gentiles* III, God's special actions are additions or subtractions within an order in which he is already active.

Imagine for example that a long and densely packed commuter train starts to accelerate out of control towards the crowded main platform of a central station. The seemingly inevitable collision will result in hundreds of deaths. Now suppose that unaccountably the hitherto jammed brakes take effect and disaster is averted. This might be a fluke but let us suppose that it is in fact a miracle. We could try to think of God's action as arising outside the causal order and thus as in a sense coming from nowhere; but that generates interactionist puzzles and suggests a basically deist God suddenly deciding to make a contribution to a creation to which he is otherwise indifferent. According to the view developed above, however, the miracle consists in God extending his many-part contribution to a process in which he is already involved. The designs of Providence are little known to humankind but it is a comfort nonetheless to know that Providence is always with us.

10   Theism – Philosophical and Religious

Finally, let me offer a brief observation about the relationship between
the conclusions of speculative reason and the deliverances of religion.
As I have explained, I am committed to a version of theism – Roman
Catholicism – that is not light on doctrine. Some readers might imagine, therefore, that I would claim that given time and intellectual
power a thinker could reason from metaphysical first principles to
such theological details as the Trinity, transubstantiation, the dogma
of the Immaculate conception of Mary (that she was born without
stain of original sin) and the doctrine of the Virgin birth. This is not
so. Indeed, as Aquinas (thus far the greatest philosopher-theologian)
was wont to observe, the knowledge of God provided by reason alone
amounts to a form of agnostic theism: a warranted conviction that there
is a God and equally warranted uncertainty as to his nature.

Nonetheless, I maintain that there is also warrant for the wealth
of doctrine taught by the Church. By implication, therefore, I believe
there are other sources of knowledge about God. Some make much of
the potential of personal religious experience but this is fraught with
epistemological uncertainties, and notoriously liable to social and
psychological eccentricity. Without the possibility of a well-attested
general revelation protected for all mankind by an inspired teaching
authority there would be no reason to be optimistic about transcend-
ing the agnostic theism arrived at and defended through philosophical reason. Catholicism holds that this possibility has been realized
through the incarnation of God in Christ and his establishment of a
Church to which has been given, in the office of Peter and his suc-
cessors, the 'extraordinary magisterium' of doctrinal infallibility. The
scale and profundity of these religious claims is unmatched by any philosophical or scientific theory and I cannot even begin to elaborate, let
alone defend, them now. What I wish to urge, however, and I think
Jack Smart would agree with this, is that it is absurd to try to arrive
at an intellectual assessment of these claims, and the evidence for
them, independently of taking a view on such philosophical questions
as the intelligibility of the universe, the existence and character of evil
and the possibility of miracles. The New Testament is a set of texts
admitting of many interpretations, none of which is self-authenticating
though some of which may be inspired as, I believe, is the text itself.
Miracles aside, a reader will not find God in its pages if he is not looking for him there. Unmistakably, however, the texts address a series of

questions – principally 'who is Christ?'; and the reply: 'the way, and the truth and the life' (John 14: 6) is an answer that should elicit from the philosophical theist the response 'and this is what *we* call God', or in the Latin of Aquinas '*et hoc dicimus Deum*'.

Notes

1 See, for example, Smart, 'Realism v. Idealism', in J.J.C. Smart, *Essays Metaphysical and Moral* (Oxford: Blackwell, 1987), and J. Haldane, 'Mind-World Identity Theory and the Anti-Realist Challenge', in J. Haldane and C. Wright (eds), *Reality, Representation and Projection* (New York: Oxford University Press, 1993).

2 All quotations from Hebrew and Christian Scripture are taken from *The Holy Bible, Revised Standard Version Catholic Edition* (London: Catholic Truth Society, 1966).

3 The *Summa Theologiae*, sometimes referred to as the *Summa Theologica*, but generally known as 'the *Summa*' exists in a definitive Latin/English edition published in association with Blackfriars (the Dominican house of study in Oxford) in sixty volumes (London: Eyre & Spottiswoode, 1963–75). A very good, single volume abridgement is Timothy McDermott (ed.), *Summa Theologiae: A Concise Translation* (London: Methuen, 1989). More recently McDermott has produced *Aquinas: Selected Philosophical Writings* (Oxford: Oxford University Press, 1993). As would be expected this includes many of the philosophically most interesting passages from the *Summa*, and I strongly recommend it to anyone who wants to read Aquinas.

4 For essays in this vein see the issue on *Analytical Thomism*, *The Monist*, vol. 81, 1988.

5 A well-known British Christian atheist is the theologian and Anglican priest Don Cupitt. Representative samples of his approach are *Taking Leave of God* (London: SCM Press, 1980) and *The Sea of Faith* (London: BBC Publications, 1984). For a rejoinder on behalf of orthodox Christianity see *The Ocean of Truth* by Brian Hebblethwaite (Cambridge: Cambridge University Press, 1988) a colleague of Cupitt in Cambridge.

6 Anselm's reflections are set out in the *Proslogion* and *Responsio editoris*. Translations of the relevant passages are to be found in S.N. Deane, *Anselm's Basic Writings* (La Salle: Open Court, 1962) and reprinted in A. Plantinga (ed.), *The Ontological Argument* (London: Macmillan, 1968). For an interesting, though difficult, exchange concerning the correct interpretation of Anselm's reasoning see C.J.F. Williams, 'Russelm', and G.E.M. Anscombe, 'Russelm or Anselm', both in *The Philosophical Quarterly*, 43 (1993). In large part the issue between Williams and Anscombe arises in virtue of the insertion by an editor of a comma into Anselm's text.

7 In this connection see the interesting essay by Max Hocutt, 'Aristotle's Four Becauses', *Philosophy*, 49 (1974). For Aristotle himself see *Metaphysics*, Book Δ (V) ch. 2; this is subjected to scholastic commentary by Aquinas in his *Sententia libri Metaphysicorum*, V, lectio 2.

8 This modern translation comes from T. McDermott, *Aquinas: Selected Philosophical Writings*, pp. 201–2.

9 J. Haldane, 'Psychoanalysis, Cognitive Psychology and Self-Consciousness', in P. Clark and C. Wright (eds), *Mind, Psychoanalysis and Science* (Oxford: Blackwell, 1988).

10 D. Dennett, 'Artificial Intelligence and the Strategies of Psychological Intelligence', in J. Miller (ed.), *States of Mind* (London: BBC Publications, 1983); see also Dennett, 'Artificial Intelligence as Philosophy and as Psychology', in Dennett, *Brainstorms* (Brighton: Harvester Press, 1986).

11 K.V. Wilkes, 'Analysing Freud', *The Philosophical Quarterly*, 40 (1990).

12 See P. Churchland and J. Haldane, 'Folk Psychology and the Explanation of Human Behaviour' I and II, in *Proceedings of the Aristotelian Society*, supplementary volume 62 (1988); reprinted in S.M. Christensen and D.R. Turner (eds), *Folk Psychology and the Philosophy of Mind* (New Jersey: Erlbaum, 1993). Our debate is continued in *Proceedings of the Aristotelian Society*, 93 (1993).

13 Peter Geach, *Mental Acts* (London: Routledge & Kegan Paul, 1958).

14 See, for example, D. Dennett, 'A Cure for the Common Code?', ch. 6 in Dennett, *Brainstorms*, and H. Putnam, 'Does Evolution Explain Intentionality?', ch. 2 in Putnam, *Renewing Philosophy* (Cambridge, MA: Harvard University Press, 1992).

15 For further discussion of Aquinas's views see J. Haldane, 'Aquinas on the Intellect', *Philosophy*, 67 (1992).

16 See *Summa Theologiae*, Ia, q. 2, a. 3 as translated by McDermott in *Aquinas: Selected Philosophical Writings*. This translation differs in being less formal than that which appears in Volume 2 of the Blackfriars *Summa* – of which McDermott was also the translator.

17 This comes from notes of a conversation made by M. Drury, a former student of Wittgenstein. See Rush Rhees (ed.), *Recollections of Wittgenstein* (Oxford: Oxford University Press, 1984), p. 79. For a clear and interesting account of how Wittgenstein's philosophical anthropology might bear upon religious questions see Fergus Kerr, *Theology after Wittgenstein* (Oxford: Blackwell, 1986). For further subtleties regarding the place of religion in Wittgenstein's thought see Norman Malcolm, *Wittgenstein: A Religious Point of View*, edited by P. Winch (London: Routledge, 1993).

18 *Summa Theologiae*, Ia, q. 2, a. 3 as translated by McDermott in *Aquinas: Selected Philosophical Writings*.

19 David Hume, *A Treatise of Human Nature*, edited by L.A. Selby-Bigge (Oxford: Clarendon Press, 1965), Book I, section III, pp. 79–80.

20 See Master Eckhart, *Parisian Questions and Prologues*, translated by

Armand Maurer (Toronto: Pontifical Institute of Medieval Studies, 1974), Question 1.

21 Ludwig Wittgenstein, *Philosophical Investigations*, translated by G.E.M. Anscombe (Oxford: Blackwell, 1976), I 304. Wittgenstein is writing about the sensation of pain.

22 See Gottlob Frege, 'On Sense and Reference', in *Translations from the Philosophical Writings of Gottlob Frege*, edited by Peter Geach and Max Black, 3rd edn (Oxford: Blackwell, 1980).

23 This fact about the meaning of 'good' (and 'bad' and other evaluative terms) is invoked by Aristotle in opposition to the view of Plato that goodness is a single, simple property possessed by all good things. He writes: 'Since "good" has as many senses as "being" . . . clearly it cannot be something universally present in all cases and single', *Nicomachean Ethics*, Book I. 6, 1096a23–29, translated by David Ross (Oxford: Oxford University Press, 1925). The definitive modern discussion of this point is the essay 'Good and Evil' by Peter Geach, *Analysis*, 17 (1956), reprinted (and revised) in P. Foot (ed.), *Theories of Ethics* (Oxford: Oxford University Press, 1967).

24 In the lapidary words of the Nicene Creed 'For us men and for our salvation he came down from heaven: by the power of the Holy Spirit he became incarnate from the Virgin Mary, and was made man (*homo factus est*). For our sake he was crucified under Pontius Pilate; he suffered death and was buried (*passus et sepultus est*)'. These words derive from the first and second ecumenical councils of Nicaea (325) and of Constantinople (381), hence it is strictly the 'Niceno-Constantinopolitan Creed' – the common declaration of Christian faith of all the great Churches of both East and West.

3

Reply to Haldane

J.J.C. Smart

1 Methodology

John Haldane's defence of theism is based on a well thought out
and sophisticated metaphysics. In this he is right: theism cannot be
defended without an appropriate metaphysics. I look back with horror
on my unregenerate religious days when I failed to come to terms with
reconciling my church-going on the one hand with my philosophical
and scientific opinions on the other hand. Here my pro-religious
emotions were at war with my intellect and I tried to reconcile the
two in what I came to see later as an evasive manner, and which I am
tempted to think of as partly inspired by neo-Wittgensteinian ideas
even though this is perhaps unfair to Wittgenstein.[1] Wittgenstein himself seems to have had a conflict between his respect for religious
ideas and his inability actually to believe them. Haldane has no weakness of this sort and he is aware of the need to defend theism in the
context of a system of metaphysical ideas. My metaphysics is naturalistic, whereas Haldane holds that naturalism does not do justice to the
real facts. In particular he holds that naturalism cannot deal with the
following important differences: the animate from the non-animate,
the reproductive from the non-reproductive, and the mental from the
non-mental.[2] Also he has problems for naturalism over the individuation of species and over the emergence of consciousness. Perhaps the
matter of consciousness is the most contentious, and I will postpone
saying something about it until later. The question has indeed been
discussed in an earlier 'Great Debates' volume.[3]

Let us consider the important differences mentioned above. In reading Haldane's discussion here the reader may suppose that Haldane is

open to the objection that his apologetic is that of a 'God of the gaps'. Haldane recognizes this danger. To argue for theism on the basis of gaps in scientific explanation is a risky endeavour, since the gaps may be filled in. Thus Newton held that God would have to readjust the motions of the planets from time to time as the perturbations due to their mutual accelerations built up. Later La Place proved the stability of the solar system.[4] E.W. Barnes was a fine mathematician who became a theologically modernist and sceptical bishop. Nevertheless, more than sixty years ago he wrote 'The mystery of life is unsolved, probably insoluble'.[5] If he had known of all the developments in biochemistry and molecular biology that have occurred in more recent times he would no doubt have thought the mystery to have at least been greatly diminished. However Haldane holds that he has *philosophical* arguments for certain of the gaps, and that since the arguments are *a priori* or apodeictic they will not be overturned by developments in biology or other sciences.

What is Haldane's philosophical argument against the emergence of the reproductive from the non-reproductive? But I find it obscure (see pp. 102–6). Why could not a self-replicating molecule come about through the coming together of a number of non-replicating molecules? No doubt this would have been a very rare event but the universe is immensely large and was in existence for a long time before the beginning of life. Of course such small proto-replicators would have to evolve by natural selection into the DNA molecules of present-day life. But I see no impossibility in this. Haldane thinks that self-replicating molecules need pre-existing channels of information (see pp. 102–3) and this produces a circularity or unacceptable regress in the physicalist account. As far as I can tell there is no talk of channels of information in contemporary accounts of self-replicating molecules. They just replicate. Of course they do require a sea of common molecules from which to build up the replicated molecules.

This illustrates an important methodological point. When confronted with some alleged gap in the story of the evolution of life, I do not feel constrained to point to some well tested theory of how the gap was filled. It is enough for me as a naturalistic philosopher if I can point to reasonable speculations as to how it might have been filled. These speculations will have to be informed by well tested theory but they would be speculations none the less. There might be more than one speculation about the origin of life. (For example, the recent discovery of various sorts of organic molecules in interstellar space might or might not be relevant.) If there is only one plausible speculation we are to some extent warranted in believing that this is in fact how things happened. As a philosopher I am happy enough if we can see that the origin of life is not impossible according to physical principles and cosmological knowledge. We do not need a detailed theory of it to prefer a naturalistic explanation (thin and as yet speculative as it may be) to a supernaturalist explanation. It would be nicer for me, as a naturalistic philosopher, to be able to point to a well-agreed hypothesis of the origin of proto-life and its development into bigger self-reproducing molecules which then carry the information to build other structures around them, such as the coating that a virus has, and how there might evolve bigger and more complex structures, namely living cells. Still, the plausibility, in the light of recent knowledge, of how in sketchy outline it *might* have happened is enough for me to prefer the naturalistic hypothesis to a supernaturalist one. A philosopher who *antecedently* finds supernaturalism plausible can reasonably jump the other way. I am not expecting agreement with John Haldane. Sympathetic understanding of one another's position is what I here aim for. Still, we should keep one eye on the scientific literature: a more detailed and acceptable account of how life could have evolved might well be in the offing.

Though Haldane has given a good and sympathetic account of my philosophical methodology, I think that he may possibly have misled the reader in his talk of the physicalist as a *reductionist*. Of course I do not believe that talk of tomatoes, say, can be *translated* into talk of electrons, protons, and other entities postulated in physical theory. For one thing 'tomato' is learned partly ostensively. For another thing the molecules in a tomato are immensely numerous and their arrangement immensely complicated so that we could never give a complete description. Moreover the arrangements in one tomato would not be the same as those in another. In a certain sense 'tomato' is a more abstract word than 'hydrogen atom' is, for example. In calling a thing a tomato we abstract from very many constitutional differences. Also words of ordinary language can be very contextual, linked to anthropic interests. Thus 'tree' is not a word of botanical classification, and if we were small enough a dandelion might count as a tree. I can concede all this without prejudice to my conviction that a tree is just a very complex physical mechanism. My physicalism is an *ontological* one, not a *translational* one.

I can even talk, in a weak sense, of levels of organization. Consider an old-fashioned radio receiver. One can look at it and see thermionic valves, capacitors, inductors, resistors, a transformer and a loudspeaker, all connected together in determinate ways by wires and at one end to an aerial wire. Now consider the components themselves. The thermionic valve (I take the simple case of a triode valve) has an evacuated glass tube which contains a wire, the cathode, heated by an electric current so that electrons are given off and are attracted to a bit of metal called the anode, which is positively charged. In between the anode and the cathode is another bit of metal in the form of a grid, into which is fed a varying charge, the signal, and which causes amplified variations in the flow of electrons from cathode to anode. In fact all the components can be explained in physical terms in this sort of way. Now consider the radio receiver itself. It can do things that a mere jumble of components cannot do. The components have to be connected together in a definite way. We can explain the behaviour of the receiver by physics together with a wiring diagram. Thus in the sense in which we might think of electronics (or part of it) as physics plus wiring diagrams, so the biochemical core of biology can be thought of as physics and chemistry plus natural history.[6] Of course the natural history needn't be about tigers or gum trees: investigating the small structures seen by means of electron microscopes counts for me as natural history. In natural history we have mere generalizations, to which exceptions are the norm, hardly requiring explanation, and relating to things on planet earth, and so cosmically parochial. Thus consider a biochemical investigation of the functioning of a liver. 'Liver' is understood partly ostensively and partly in terms of what it usually does, what it has been selected for.[7]

One can therefore be an ontological physicalist without believing in emergence in any stronger sense than the weak sense that I have just elucidated.[8] Nor need we be able to make detailed predictions from one level to the next to have good scientific and philosophical reasons to see the higher level as not only ontologically a matter of the lower level but as plausibly *explained* by it. Steven Weinberg puts the matter very persuasively in his *Dreams of a Final Theory*.[9] He argues as follows. The quantum theory of the chemical bond can be used in cases of simple atoms and molecules to explain the properties of the chemical bond, and even if this cannot be done in the case of very complicated molecules, this failure can be put down simply to the mathematical intractability of the problem. Because the nature of the chemical bond can be deduced from the quantum theory, this gives us a very good plausible reason for thinking that nature works in this way in mathematically intractable cases. We can still hold, as he says, that 'there are no autonomous principles of chemistry that are simply independent truths, not resting on deeper principles of physics'.[10]

Having said that my reduction is ontological and not translational, I am not sure that I am using 'ontological' in quite the way in which Haldane is (see p. 93). The weight of the average plumber is definable as the sum of the weights of plumbers divided by the number of plumbers. So talk of the average plumber is translatable into talk of the plumbers. However I do not require translation for ontological reduction. I can still say that a tree is nothing over and above a physical mechanism, just as a radio receiver is, even though talk of a tree is not translatable into talk of electrons and protons. If non-translatability implied non-naturalism, non-naturalism would be too easily come by.

I would also suggest that Haldane's term 'explanatory reduction-ism' is not quite what I would mean by the term 'reductionism'. Recall the matter of some chemical reaction. One could explain it by purely chemical considerations involving the chemical bonds of the molecules concerned. Nevertheless the molecules might be rather large and complex and a complete quantum mechanical account of the process could be beyond the fastest computers. We could still feel, as Weinberg suggested, that there is some sort of explanation of the chemical process. We could say that the chemical process is similar to that in the simple case, and that prediction is here defeated only by sheer complexity. Similar situations of course exist with respect to deterministic mechanisms in classical mechanics, as it is demon-strated in chaos theory. Chaotic systems can indeed be deterministic but unpredictable.

On p. 101 Haldane says that if a materialist explanation of life seems incomplete then 'only a non-scientific insistence on reductionism motivates the thesis that [living systems] must be no more than mech-anism even where there could be no deductive explanation of how it is so'. I would reply that if there are plausible ideas about how some-thing could be so, in accordance with naturalistic principles, even though this cannot be deduced in detail, and if there are no plausible alternative naturalistic explanations, then it is reasonable to suppose that things did come about in the hypothesized way. I do not think that scientists regard this sort of reasoning as 'unscientific', even though (often *per impossibile*) detailed predictions or retrodictions would be regarded by them as better. Rejection of appeal to non-natural causes (in any of the senses of 'cause' distinguished by Haldane) is really only an application of Ockham's razor, the principle that entities should not be multiplied beyond necessity. No doubt Haldane holds that the non-naturalistic explanation is simpler, but any appearance of sim-plicity could be deceptive, if the appeal is simply to a God whose ways are beyond our ken. I agree that the argument is not over. Readers of this book must make up their own minds.

2 Representation and Intentionality

On pp. 103ff Haldane sees difficulties for naturalism in the notions of representation and intentionality. Now undoubtedly there are such things as representations. A portrait is a representation of a person, and an irregular blue line on a map is a representation of the twists and turns of a river. Whether there are representations in the brain or mind is a further matter, and quite controversial. For example, if the brain is entirely a connectionist device then there is no place for representations (pictures?) in any obvious sense. Perhaps 'information' is a more useful word than is 'representation', in a rather abstract, information-theoretic use of the term 'information'. It is a familiar thought that DNA codes genetic information, much as instructions in a computer are programmed in. There seems to be nothing very difficult for naturalism in supposing that such capacities for acquiring and storing information about the world in general could have evolved by natural selection. Whether or not the 'homunculus' strategy in neuroscience is the right one I cannot see any philosophical objection to Haldane's quotation from Kathy Wilkes. Detecting horizontals (see p. 104) falls far short of intentional or goal-directed behaviour.

A simple case of goal-directed behaviour is that of a predictor-controlled gun. However the target twists or turns the gun will orient itself so as to have a high probability of hitting the target. If the target had twisted differently the gun would have moved itself differently. Similarly, consider a robot which moves around obstacles in a room, however they are situated, to get to a plug to recharge its batteries. All this is quite mechanistic. Such robots have of course been built. In the case of organisms the mechanisms will have arisen by natural selection. Now the goal-seeking behaviour 'seeking to orient itself to hit the target' or 'moving to recharge batteries' is on any particular occasion a sequence of gun movements or robot movements. However, the interesting thing is that for the behaviour to be intentional there must be something about the gun plus predictor or the robot's inner construction that ensures that if the target had moved differently the gun would have moved differently so as to maximize the chance of hitting the target, and if the furniture had been arranged differently the robot's route to the plug would similarly have been different. In more sophisticated sorts of intentional behaviour, as in the human case of writing an article, say, a lot of pen movements are involved but many alternative sequences of such movements would count as writing the article. I agree that writing an article cannot be defined in terms of a sequence of hand movements and even a particular instance of such writing would be inadequately described as a sequence of hand movements. *Things go on in the mind.* A materialist would not deny this, though he or she would contingently identify the mental occurrences and control mechanisms with brain events and brain states.

There is indeed something philosophically puzzling about intentionality (with a 't'). This is because it is related to intensionality (with an 's'). Intensionality is a matter of context. Consider 'Joe believes that the head of the philosophy department is the dean of the faculty of arts'. Suppose that the head of the philosophy department is in fact the dean of the faculty of arts. We cannot substitute for identicals here and retain the same meaning. To say that Joe believes that the head of the philosophy department is the head of the philosophy department is to ascribe only a trivial belief to Joe. Or again consider 'Joe wants a lawn-mower'. It does not follow that there is a lawn-mower that Joe wants. Any lawn-mower might do. And what about 'Joe wants a unicorn'? There is no unicorn that Joe wants because there are no unicorns. We cannot say that 'wants' signifies a relation between Joe and a unicorn: it is not like 'Joe kicks a football' where there must be both Joe and the football. Contexts such as 'Joe believes that . . .' and 'Joe desires that . . .' are examples of intensional contexts. We can get round the difficulty roughly by saying with Quine 'Joe believes-true S' where S might be the sentence 'The head of the philosophy department is the dean of the faculty of arts'.[11] This sentence is certainly different from the tautologous sentence 'The head of the philosophy department is the head of the philosophy department'. And we could say 'Joe wants-true of himself "possesses a unicorn"'.[12] 'Wants-true of himself' signifies a relation between Joe and a predicate. Sentences and predicates certainly exist. We can of course say this whether or not Joe knows English, and we can talk in this way even of the beliefs and desires of cats. The sentence just serves vaguely to single out a belief or desire, a mental state, and in my opinion a brain state. (If someone prefers to think of beliefs and desires as functional states which are multiply realized by brain states, I can agree without compromising my materialism. Incidentally 'functional' here is more like 'function' in mathematics: it is not a teleological notion.) The development of this sort of approach in a sophisticated way would go beyond the confines of the present book, but the general approach suggests how it can remove some mystery from both intensionality (with an 's') and consequently 'intentionality' (with a 't').[13]

Thus when I use the word 'unicorn' I do not refer to a unicorn because there are no unicorns to be referred to. 'Cat' refers to the set of cats, past, present and future. It does not refer to counterfactual cats because there are no such. I here differ from David Lewis[14] who has a realistic theory of possible worlds other than the actual world. I deal with counterfactuals in a different way, following Quine.[15] 'If it had been the case that p then it would have been the case that q' said by me to you is true relative to me, you and the context if and only if q follows by first order logic from p together with contextually agreed background assumptions. Because counterfactuals have this contextual and relativist character they are to be avoided, where possible, in science and metaphysics. Thus I disagree with Haldane when he speaks of future and counterfactual cats (see p. 118). I believe in future cats (there they are up ahead of us in space–time) but not in counterfactual cats.

3 Consciousness

Consciousness may be thought to provide a particular difficulty for a physicalist philosophy of mind. I concede that there seems to be something mysterious about the fact of consciousness, as if some strange supernatural light was lit up in our minds. I hold that all the properties of immediate experience are 'topic neutral' ones, neutral between materialism and mind–body dualism. These are such things as typical external causes and effects, waxings and wanings, and positions in similarity spaces. This depends on ability to perceive bare similarities and differences between our inner goings on without our being able to say in what respects these similarities consist.[16] My argument here does not rest entirely on the plausibility of physicalism. I can draw on the elusiveness of so called 'raw feels' to which B.A. Farrell drew attention in a fine article 'Experience' nearly half a century ago,[17] as well as the work of the later Wittgenstein, Gilbert Ryle and others, and more recently fine books by Robert Kirk and Austen Clark.[18]

Nevertheless there does seem to be a strong tendency to believe that in consciousness we are aware of radically 'psychical' properties unreconcilable with materialism. David Armstrong has suggested that this tendency can be understood by comparison with what happens in the headless woman illusion.[19] A woman is seated on a brightly lit stage with a black background. She has a black cloth over her head. The audience think that she has no head: they confuse not seeing her head with seeing that she has no head. Similarly we may be aware only of the neutral properties, and not being aware of them as physical we think of them as non-physical.

We are familiar with times at which we go on 'automatic pilot'. Sometimes, cycling to the university, I have realized that I have steered my cycle on the bicycle path, crossed a busy road and avoided traffic, gone round bends, and so on and yet I have no recollection of having done so. In a sense I am conscious: I am not asleep or anaesthetized. I have reacted correctly to stimuli. Still, in the full sense I have not been conscious. I have had experiences, which I hold to be brain processes, but I have not been aware of them. Armstrong has suggested that consciousness of my experiences is a sort of direct monitoring by one part of my brain of other brain processes that constitute sense experiences and the like. This monitoring would certainly have survival value. Armstrong holds that it would be analogous to proprioception. In proprioception we can be directly aware of such things as the positions of our limbs. In the same way we can be directly aware, in what I have called a 'topic neutral' way, of goings on in our brain that constitute sensations and imagings. Consciousness comes out as awareness and monitoring of awareness, and there can presumably be awareness of awareness of awareness, though without finite minds this will not go very far up the possible hierarchy. I like this suggestion of Armstrong's that consciousness is a sort of proprioception, not requiring neuronal receptors external to the brain, but of the brain directly by itself.[20] The suggestion implies that a robot constructed to monitor its own control system would have consciousness as a sort of proprioception; this may not be wholly satisfying, but it is not clear what more is needed or if it is needed, how it should be described.

4 Chicken and Egg

Which came first, the chicken or the egg? I am here indebted to a witty discussion note by Roger Teichmann.[21] Since each chicken is hatched from an egg and every egg is laid by a chicken, it would appear that neither can come first. On the other hand since the durations of the generations of chickens have a lower bound (so the sequence is not like, say, ... $\frac{1}{8}, \frac{1}{4}, \frac{1}{2}$, 1, ...) and because life on earth has not existed for ever, it would appear that there would have to be a first egg or first chicken. The answer of course must be that 'chicken' is a vague term. We get the same appearance of contradiction with any vague term, as is exemplified by the so-called Sorites paradox. If a man with only a few hairs on his head (say 10) is bald, so also is a man with one more hair (say 11). Also if a man with n hairs on his head is bald so is a man with $(n + 1)$ hairs. (One more hair does not make the difference between being bald and being not bald.) So from this we seem to be able to deduce that the hairiest head of hair that you've ever seen is that of a bald man. Much has been written on the Sorites paradox, and as far as I know there is still no agreed solution. The trouble comes from the vagueness of language, as with 'bald'. Similarly 'chicken' is vague. There is no first chicken. Species evolve imperceptibly from earlier species. Unless, of course, some miraculous occurrence singled out a first chicken or a first egg.

We should take 'egg' here in the sense of 'ovum'. (The eggs we eat consist mostly of nutrient for the growing chicken foetus.) Wouldn't there have to be a first ovum? Well, there might have been a first coming together of bits of DNA to form the first prototype of bisexual reproduction, and one of them might be regarded as proto-egg and proto-sperm.

Haldane likes to stress the discontinuities: the reproductive from the non-reproductive, the organic from the non-organic, the conceptual from the non-conceptual.[22] These things arise by sequences of small jumps. Each jump may have a low probability, but evolutionary time is long compared with the time of human affairs. If a jump consisted simultaneously of millions of jumps its probability would be exceedingly low. However, a sequence of millions of small jumps filtered by natural selection can have a much higher probability. There is a problem about how the evolution of a complex organ, such as the eye, might have occurred. The answer lies in the opportunist character of evolution whereby something that gives one sort of advantage at one stage may lead to different advantages at later stages. Haldane might say that small jumps are still jumps. So they are, but the smallest jumps are a matter of chance comings together and chance mutations. But you shouldn't be reading me on this. Read the biologists and make up your own mind whether you think that the naturalist story or the supernaturalist story is the more plausible.

5   Eternity and Sempiternity

In my discussion of the cosmological argument I suggested that the
theist is on stronger ground (though in the end I thought still not on
strong enough ground) if he or she thought of the Deity as an eternal
or atemporal being who causes the existence of the whole space–time
universe in some tenseless sense of 'cause'. So God would not be a
first cause in any temporal sense of 'first'. This would be a plausible
modification of Aquinas's view in his 'third way'. (As he puts it himself Aquinas seems to me to refer unnecessarily to temporal matters.)
So if I can be an 'angel's advocate' (i.e. the contrary of a devil's advocate) Haldane's argument for a first cause in the temporal sense is
unnecessary. The universe might have no first cause because it might
be like this: . . . big bang, big crunch, big bang, big crunch . . . , with an
infinite sequence of big bangs and big crunches in both temporal directions. Or it might be a space–time whose topology is such that it
makes no sense to talk of a beginning in time. Stephen Hawking proposed the latter possibility in a conference at the Vatican. Hawking
seemed to think that his proposal could have been seen as shocking,[23]
but I do not think that it ought to have worried an admirer of Aquinas.
Aquinas can be supposed to have thought of God as imperishable in
the sense of necessarily being unable to be destroyed, and being such
that its being destroyed makes no sense, not being sempiternal, not
even necessarily sempiternal, but outside time like the number 9. Or
perhaps like the whole space–time universe which cannot be said to
change or stay the same. I hold that to say that a signal lamp changes
(tenseless present) is to say that a *later* temporal stage of the lamp
differs (tenseless present) from an earlier temporal stage. The whole
space–time universe obviously cannot change in this way. Presumably God would be something very different from the number 9 and
different from the space–time universe. (At least if we can rule out
pantheism.) Of course God is thought of as everywhere and everywhen,
but this could be interpreted in terms of an atemporal being having
various relations to every point of space–time. I hold that God as the
creator of the universe and hence of space–time itself could not be a
spatio-temporal being (or a spatial or temporal one). Later in his essay
Haldane seems to be in agreement that an adequate conception of God
should be that of an atemporal being.

   After this brief excursion into being an 'angel's advocate' I still have
my bothers about the notion of a necessary being and of whether the

complexity of God's nature (his desires and power to create *ex nihilo*) does not mirror the complexity of the laws of nature themselves. In the latter case Ockham's razor would be a problem for the theist.

Aquinas seems to elucidate necessity by contrast with the contingency of perishable things. His discussion needs a bit of modification if we are to look at things in a space–time way. Consider a thing which did not exist before time t_1 and exists until time t_2 when it perishes, that is, it contains no temporal part later than t_2. (Note that here I am using 'exist', 'contains', etc. as tenseless verbs.) Well, there is no temporal stage later than t_2 and no temporal stage earlier than t_1. But might the temporal stage between t_1 and t_2 have not existed? Or could we say that the t_1 to t_2 stage was necessary though perishable? If there were a suitable sense of 'necessary' (which I am querying) perhaps we could have said this, but no doubt we would not have done so because if there had been a temporal stage later than t_2 it would have been very like the t_1 to t_2 stage, and would therefore have been necessary too. Thus I think that I can agree with Aquinas that the perishable is contingent. I doubt, however, whether everything that is contingent is perishable. What about an instantaneous event for example? Also in my longer essay I raised doubts about the necessity of Platonic entities. Of course Aquinas was talking about *substances*. I do have some trouble with the Aristotelian notion of substance, in so far as metaphysically I like to think of the world as a four-dimensional space–time entity.[24] However, setting this aside, let me raise some doubts about the Aristotelian and Thomist notions of substance which are more properly related to some things which Haldane says in his essay.

I am indeed not clear how far an Aristotelian notion of substance could be made to fit a scientifically oriented view of the world. Is an electron a substance? Consider quantum statistics, in which one distribution of particles is sometimes to be considered as the same state as another. Swapping over two particles makes no difference. This makes such a particle unlike a substance as traditionally conceived. One rough analogy would be a wave. A wave in the sea is not constituted by the water: as the wave goes forward the water under it is not the same. We could swap over two waves of the same form without making any difference to the sea. Indeed, it wouldn't really be a swap, as it would be if we swapped over the actual water under the waves. Again, another analogy might be the idea that what exist are just space–time points and field strengths characteristic of these points. I do not want to press this objection to Aristotelianism and Thomism too hard, because I suspect that someone as familiar with these ways of thought as Haldane is could reconcile talk of substance and attributes, potentiality and actuality with the considerations that I have suggested here.

Haldane points out that what the traditional arguments for the existence of God should be taken as proving is the *thatness* not the *whatness* of God. There must surely be *some* whatness in what is proved. To prove the existence of a something I know not what is hardly to prove the existence of anything. However, it does resonate with the expressions of yearning by some anti-dogmatic church-goers. 'I feel that there must be *something*.' This ties up with a feeling that an atheist can have: a feeling of the evident ultimate mysteriousness of the universe, the fact that it exists at all. This is surely not enough for theism in any sense in which it need be distinguished from atheism. I think that Haldane's and Aquinas's point is that God, as they think he is proved to exist, is something only very abstractly described, for example as simple and the cause of the world. As Haldane points out the proofs are not claimed to prove a thick 'whatness', i.e. God as conceived by some particular religion. But Haldane rightly points out that there must be some 'whatness' in the conclusion. I also agree with Haldane that any worthwhile concept of God must describe God as eternal in the sense of being outside space and time, a changeless cause of change. I would add that changelessness here would be a matter not of staying the same through time but of being like the number 7, say, neither changing nor staying the same. I concede that Haldane gives a subtle and attractive form of the cosmological argument. Nevertheless I am not persuaded, for the usual reasons as adumbrated in chapter 1. I do not see how God's *thatness* and *whatness* can be the same reality. To say this would surely be to treat 'exists' as though it were a predicate.

The arguments that I used against the cosmological argument do not, however, depend on any extreme empiricism or positivism about meaning, which would deny any meaning to talk of the transcendental. Indeed, I think that this ascent to the transcendental can happen in science when meaning is transferred upward through the hypothetico-deductive method, and further through considerations of simplicity when the empirical evidence is indecisive. Hence I do go a long way to agree with the remarks about meaning and the transcendental (see p. 149). My objection to the hypothesis of theism is the unclarity of the notion of necessity that would be required. At the bottom of p. 150 Haldane perhaps rightly objects that I give insufficient attention to the way in which the notion of necessity arises in the argument from contingency. He says that 'what we are led to is the existence of something which exists eternally, which does not owe its being to anything else and which cannot not exist'. The nub is in the last clause. Following Quine, my notion of modality is highly contextual. Except for mere logical necessity, where the background assumptions are null, the notion of 'can' is relative to these background assumptions. 'It cannot be the case that p' can be said when mutually agreed background assumptions imply (by first order logic) that not-p. For example, 'you cannot live without oxygen' can be said because 'you do not live without oxygen' follows from agreed assumptions about human physiology. Perhaps the background assumptions could be assumptions of theological theory, or 'necessary' here be a primitive of that theory. This, however, would make theology question-begging and ready to be sliced off by Ockham's razor.

As I pointed out in chapter 1, the universe could fill the bill of something that does not require anything else for its existence. According to the atheist there is nothing beyond the universe and so it is not dependent on anything else for its existence. If God also exists then God could be necessary in the same sense, but this would not be a good enough sense of 'necessary' for Aquinas or Haldane, since the same question 'Why does it exist?' would recur in relation to God. The universe could also be said in a sense to fill the bill for the other desideratum put forward by Haldane in the quoted passage. If to be eternal is to be outside space–time, the whole space–time universe including space–time itself is at least not itself *in* space–time and so might also merit the epithet 'eternal'. Moreover, in a space–time way of looking at things we do not speak of change or staying the same, except in the sense of temporal parts of objects differing or being similar, and motion is just relative inclination of world lines. Similar remarks could be made about a super-universe if the total universe of everything there is contains many universes as we normally conceive them, as in the speculations of Carter and others that I mentioned in chapter 1. This does not of course constitute a conclusive answer to Haldane. The reader will have to decide for himself or herself whether he or she understands the notion of necessity that Haldane requires. Certainly I yearn for such a notion: it might help us to answer the compelling but apparently unanswerable question 'Why is there anything at all?' But I can't see how I can find such a notion that would strike me as intelligible.

In my main essay I suggested that an adequate concept of God for the theist should be that of an atemporal being, not that of a sempiternal being. I'm not sure that Haldane is right in laying stress on a realistic notion of causation (see pp. 136ff). I am myself suspicious about the use of the notion of causality in fundamental physics and metaphysics. (It is a very useful word for plumbers, instrument mechanics and brain surgeons.) A key element in the notion of causation is that of 'If *A* had not happened then *B* would not have happened'. I take this as meaning that the happening of *B* follows by logic from the happening of *A* together with contextually agreed background assumptions. So the notion of causality is a contextual one. Another element in the notion of causality is a temporal one, but I think that if we *do* have a notion of causality it should not rule out backwards causation. Huw Price has made use of the notion of backwards causation in dealing with the problem of non-locality in quantum mechanics.[25] My own view is that Aquinas's third way (as Haldane states it on p. 131) might be improved by replacing 'cause' and 'caused by' with 'explains' and 'is explained by'. Of course the notion of explanation is contextual too. The main issue between us is over our relative happiness or unhappiness at the notion of a necessary being in any other sense than one (such as that of 'depending on nothing else') which can be sliced away by Ockham's razor. Thus the atheist could say that the universe depends on nothing else.

Haldane raises questions to do with Hume's epistemology. Certainly, I have an inclination to defend something like a regularity view of laws of nature but my motives have nothing to do with a desire to block cosmological proofs. See Haldane's remark on p. 136. I would love to have a cosmological proof if I found it convincing. I do feel the force of the question 'Why is there anything at all?' even though I seem to see that it could have no possible answer.

I worry still about the notion of God's *simplicity*, the assertion of which is an important part of the argument. Can there be a simple cause of a complex world? Perhaps there could be if simplicity is just a matter of the ultimate laws of nature (or for Haldane the attributes of God) hanging together in a nice way, such as is hoped for by those physicists who search for a final theory uniting physics and cosmology. Still, the laws or attributes must be distinct: they cannot follow from one another as a pure matter of logic. Haldane refers to the distinction between sense and reference. Now the words 'is powerful' and 'is good', for example, have different senses *and* different references. So we might say, Platonistically, that the attributes of power and of goodness are different attributes and indeed apply to different sets of objects. Different sense, different reference. However the attributes of infinite power and infinite goodness, according to the theist, apply to one and only one object, namely God. This still, as far as I can see, leaves the attributes distinct: as a matter of logic the possession of one attribute does not imply the possession of any of the others. Indeed theorists who deny the existence of God because of the existence of evil do so by supposing an incompatibility between the conjunction of observed evil with the simultaneous possession of the two attributes of infinite power and infinite goodness.

This leads me to pass a few remarks on Haldane's treatment of this problem of evil. I do not hope to get agreement with him on this matter, any more than on the cogency or otherwise of the Aquinas–Haldane argument for the existence of God. The reader must weigh up the two sides of this 'Great Debate', and make up his or her mind, and ideally do so in the light of further reading.

6 Theism and the Problem of Evil

I do not wish to add a great deal to the treatment of the problem of evil in my main essay, except to take account of certain features special to John Haldane's interesting theodicy in his main essay. He rightly rejects suggestions that evil is an illusion. Even the illusion of evil would be horrible. Still, he has a reservation here. He holds that though evil is not illusory, it is not something positive in the world but is rather a *privation*. It is something that impedes something positive, the proper functioning of a thing. In chapter 1, I questioned the intelligibility, in the light of the theory of evolution, of the notion of the proper function of an organ of an animal or plant. I said that it was often useful for a biologist, who is wondering about hypotheses of biological mechanism, to think in an 'as if' way of purpose since natural selection sees to it that organs are by and large conducive to the survival of the organism. Alternatively, function may be defined in terms of 'what something (e.g. an organ) is selected for' (see p. 188, n. 7). There is no reference to actual purposive design or Aristotelian function.

Dogs do not have as acute vision as we do. A much larger part of the cortex of a dog is devoted to processing the sense of smell than is the case with humans. So perhaps in a way it is part of the function of a dog's vision to be weak: it leaves room in the cortex for the sense of smell that is so important in doggy existence. Still, this is stretching even the biologist's 'as if' notion of a function a bit far.

These remarks are just hints towards a possible appreciation of some of the difficulties in the way of an Aristotelian notion of 'function'. Perhaps in the end they are quibbles which Haldane may be able to accommodate to his notions.

Suppose that you are suffering from a violent toothache. Does this seem like a *privation* of good and not something positively horrible? Perhaps the pain is good as a means – it alerts one to the necessity of not chewing on the tooth. (Before dentists nothing much could indeed be done! So it is not all that easy to state what avoiding or remedial action natural selection has in this case operated to promote.) One might wonder why an omnipotent God could not have fixed the laws of nature and even the course of evolution so that more pleasant signalling systems might have existed.

Mice obviously do not like being eaten by cats. However according to Haldane God does not create this evil. What he did was create an interacting system of cats and mice in which the well-being of the cats is secured at the expense of the mice (see p. 155). 'Where there is a bad there is a good involving the realization of the powers and liabilities of interacting systems', says Haldane. Well, given the laws of nature maximized self-realization could perhaps come about in this way. But could not God have created a universe with different laws, non-metabolizing non-competitive spirits, all engaged in satisfying non-competitive activities such as pure mathematics or the production of poetry? Perhaps Haldane could concede that this might be a good and even better universe than ours (with its cats and mice, etc.) but go on to say that provided the cat and mouse universe is good on balance why not create it also? In the spirit of Leibniz we could say that the more universes the better, so long as none are on balance bad.

If one accepted this, one need not indeed suppose that evil is always a mere privation of good. A positive balance of good and bad would be enough. One's reluctance to accept this is due to the thought that if God is able to create many universes, why not many universes which contain no positive evils? This thought does not undermine Haldane's position if one accepts his view that evil is not something positive but only a privation of good. Now the death of the mouse may be a privation in so far as it consists in the absence of the anticipated future life and growing to maturity of the mouse. But what of the actual terror and painful death throes of the mouse? I find it hard to think of this as consisting of mere privation.

Haldane distinguishes natural and moral evils. Moral evils consist in the thoughts and actions of intelligent beings (see p. 153). They arise from the misuse of free will. Of course from my naturalistic point of view there is a sense in which moral evils are a species of natural evil. Hitler and Goebbels were horrible, but for a naturalist there is nothing puzzling about this. There are more ways for a thing to go wrong than to go right. We inherit atavistic parts of our brains, and the cortex itself can easily get wired up in peculiar ways. For the theist there is a puzzle and Haldane tries to resolve this by reference to freedom of will. Freedom of will, he holds, is a great good but essentially carries with it the possibility of wrongdoing.

In my main essay I defended, near enough, a compatibilist account of free will. Haldane disagrees with this, as I think that he must if he is to deploy the free will defence to account for the possibility of God allowing a universe with moral evil in it. If the compatibilist position is correct we can go on to ask why God did not create a universe in which moral beings were given such strong motives to aim at the right that they would always do so. (They may fail actually to do the right because of non-culpable factual ignorance or mistake, but this would not constitute *moral* evil.) Would we lack free will if we had a passionate and overwhelming desire to do the right? I find it odd to answer this question in the affirmative. Is a person's engaging in symbolic logic the less free the greater is his or her enjoyment of it?

Thus I hold that even if God had planted in us motives which always caused us to aim at the right this would not be in contradiction to our having free will. Let us recall my remarks, in my main essay, about the article by R.E. Hobart. We need to have at least an *approximation* to determinism in the working of our minds (our central nervous systems) for free will to be possible. Otherwise it would be mere chance what we did. I can concede that the compatibilist theory of free will, as in Hobart, does not give us everything that the person in the street wants from the concept of free will, since he or she wants something logically impossible, both to be determined and not determined, but I hold that compatibilism can, properly argued, give us all we should want or need for practical and legal purposes. Haldane proposes to go between the horns of the dilemma.

'When a human being acts', says Haldane, 'there need be no event in the agent prior to the action and which is its immediate cause' (see p. 161). A naturalistically minded philosopher might concede that there might be no simple cause – e.g. the firing of a neuron – but would find it mysterious that the total neural state prior to the action together with its changes under internal or external stimuli should not have to be the cause of the action. The naturalist can even agree with Haldane

that most action calls for no explanation. Explanation is a highly contextual matter. Often the explanation is not called for because it is too
simple and obvious. If a person desires to eat an apple and sees an
apple on the plate it is not mysterious that the apple should be eaten,
and quite compatible with desire and perception being neural states,
processes or events. Furthermore, Haldane is right in saying that causal
explanation is often not needed because we know that we are dealing
with a rational animal. What we call for are not explanatory reasons
but justifying reasons. If you ask me why I make a certain inference
I will perhaps reply by citing the rule of *modus tollens*. But that an
inference falls under the rule in no way implies that it was not caused.
It was caused partly by my neural make-up having been trained to
operate in accordance with the rule of logic.

Nor need the naturalist disagree with Haldane in saying that 'Action
differs from mere movement in being purposeful, in aiming to advance
an interest of the agent' (see p. 162). The naturalist will, however, look
to an elucidation of purpose on the analogy of purposive mechanisms
so familiar in modern engineering. (Recall my remarks about intensionality earlier in this Reply.) Purpose can be an *explanans*, but is
not ultimate. It is also an *explanandum* and Haldane needs to show
that the explanation of purposive activity cannot be a mechanistic one.
This is because I hold to a variant of Ockham's razor, that mysteries
should not be multiplied beyond necessity. Haldane probably will agree
with me here. Perhaps we differ on what we find mysterious. Aristotelian teleology seems mysterious to me, but not to him. This is a question on which the reader will have to make up his or her mind on the
basis of the general attractiveness or otherwise of our respective metaphysical positions. I will, however, mention one thing that must be
avoided. We should not confuse 'reason as cause' with 'reason as justification'. We must distinguish 'reason' as cause, a sense in which a
desire can be a reason, and 'reason' as justification, where asking for
a reason is asking for a logical or moral rule, a missing premiss, or
something like that. Rules and propositions are not causes though our
attitudes to them may be. Haldane is too acute a philosopher to have
fallen into this elementary confusion, but for ensuring clarity in exposition and argument this possibility of confusion needs to be mentioned.

I have found Haldane's notion of voluntary action unclear, and
unnecessary for explaining the facts. Of course Haldane and I may
differ as to what the facts are that need explaining. Haldane says that
human beings are 'moved from within' in a sense different from that in
which neurophysiological events are thought of by neurophysiological

theorists (see p. 161). I am tempted to close the discussion simply by saying that I do not understand Haldane's special 'moved from within'. I do not really like this neo-Wittgensteinian ploy. In my younger days it was possible in certain circles to win an argument by looking at the ceiling and saying in a plonking tone of voice 'I don't understand', where upon the opponent was supposed to feel a fool for having said something meaningless. I have a delightful memory of when a brash young Oxonian tried this on Russell and Russell replied 'I am not responsible for your intellectual deficiencies, young man'. Still, I do have difficulty, whatever the reason, with Haldane's account of free action.

Haldane concludes chapter 2 with an important statement of the need to supplement abstract philosophical theology with the deliverances of revelation. For my part I am sceptical about whether supposed revelation really is revelation. See my remarks in my main essay on the argument from religious experience and on the higher criticism of the New Testament. I am nevertheless impressed by these final pages: if I agreed with Haldane on the abstract theology I might indeed be more disposed to accept the additional claims of revelation. This illustrates the fact that philosophical disputes are not easily settled even between intelligent and intellectually honest participants. Individual theses come to some extent as part of a package deal: metaphysics has a holistic character. Let John Haldane now have the last word!

Notes

1 See two rather horrible articles of mine, 'Metaphysics, Logic and Theology' and 'The Existence of God', in Antony Flew and Alasdair MacIntyre, *New Essays in Philosophical Theology* (London: SCM Press, 1955).

2 See p. 99.

3 D.M. Armstrong and Norman Malcolm, *Consciousness and Causality: A Debate on the Nature of Mind* (Oxford: Basil Blackwell, 1984). Here I am in broad agreement with Armstrong. I think that indeed Haldane would not be in much agreement with Malcolm's approach.

4 Perhaps Newton said this merely to put into theological language his awareness that he had not proved the stability of the solar system. Perhaps when La Place replied to Napoleon, à propos of the existence of God, 'Sire, I have no need of that hypothesis', he may have been alluding only to proof of stability. I am no historian, but it is a nice thought.

5 E.W. Barnes, *Scientific Theory and Religion* (London: Cambridge University Press, 1933), p. 420.

6 For my views on biology (in which I include psychology) see ch. 4 of J.J.C. Smart, *Our Place in the Universe* (Oxford: Basil Blackwell, 1989).

7 Earlier (see section 2, p. 66) I described teleological talk in biology as 'as if' talk. Equally one might, as I have done here, follow Karen Neander, in what ontologically comes to almost the same thing, in describing the function of an object in evolutionary terms, as what it was selected for. See Karen Neander, 'Functions as Selected Effects: The Conceptual Analyst's Defense', *Philosophy of Science*, 58 (1991), 168–84.

8 See also my essay 'Physicalism and Emergence', in J.J.C. Smart, *Essays Metaphysical and Moral* (Oxford: Basil Blackwell, 1989). This essay originally appeared in *Neuroscience*, 6 (1987), 109–13.

9 Steven Weinberg, *Dreams of a Final Theory* (London: Vintage, 1993). See ch. 3, 'Two Cheers for Reductionism'.

10 Ibid., p. 42.

11 See W.V. Quine, *Word and Object* (Cambridge, Mass.: MIT Press, 1960), pp. 212ff.

12 See David Lewis, 'Attitudes *De Dicto* and *De Se*', *Philosophical Review*, 88 (1979), 513–43.

13 I have of course oversimplified. 'Sentence' has to be relativized to a language, or else we should have to talk of classes of intertranslatable sentences, and Quine has pointed out the obscurity or indeterminacy of individuation of a language and of the concept of translation. Folk psychology gives only an approximation to truth, and it is part of the natural history of humans and animals. (An animal does not itself need to have a language to have its beliefs and desires singled out by mentions of *our* sentences.) Thus desires and beliefs are woolly like clouds but nevertheless can be identified with brain states imprecisely described. If and when we make robots that can learn and use a language this part of natural history will be seen to be ontologically reducible to the physical. The reduction already looks a plausible speculation. In metaphysics I try to eschew indexicals, but the sort of indexical in 'true of himself' above is all right. It is not a true indexical and is only a device for cross reference.

14 David Lewis, *On the Plurality of Worlds* (Oxford: Basil Blackwell, 1960) and David Lewis, *Counterfactuals* (Oxford: Basil Blackwell, 1973).

15 W.V. Quine, 'Necessary Truth', in W.V. Quine, *The Ways of Paradox and Other Essays* (New York: Random House, 1966).

16 See my essay 'Materialism' in J.J.C. Smart, *Essays Metaphysical and Moral*.

17 B.A. Farrell, 'Experience', *Mind*, 59 (1950), 170–98.

18 L. Wittgenstein, *Philosophical Investigations* (Oxford: Blackwell, 1953); Gilbert Ryle, *The Concept of Mind* (London: Hutchinson, 1949); Robert Kirk, *Raw Feelings* (Oxford: Clarendon Press, 1994); Austen Clark, *Sensory Qualities* (Oxford: Oxford University Press, 1993).

19 D.M. Armstrong, 'The Headless Woman Illusion and the Defence of Materialism', *Analysis*, 29 (1968–9), 48–9. This article was written in less feminist times: no doubt now it would be a headless person illusion.

20 See D.M. Armstrong, in Armstrong and Malcolm, *Consciousness and Causality*, especially pp. 110–5.

21 Roger Teichmann, 'The Chicken and the Egg', *Mind*, 100 (1991), 371–2.

22 The evolution of the conceptual is partly cultural, depending on the evolution of language. Having the concept of, say, 'electron' is being able to use the word 'electron' in sentences intelligently. It is not an all or nothing matter. J.J. Thomson and P.A.M. Dirac would have said many incompatible things in sentences containing 'electron', but since there was a great core of such sentences that they both asserted we could say roughly that they had the same concept. Some concepts do not consist of linguistic skills but may be skills at geometrical imaginings, or of reading contour lines. 'Concept' is not a simple notion.

23 See Stephen Hawking, *A Brief History of Time* (London: Bantam Press, 1988).

24 See my essay 'Space–Time and Individuals', in *Essays Metaphysical and Moral*.

25 See Huw Price, 'A Neglected Route to Realism about Quantum Mechanics', *Mind*, 103 (1994), 303–20.

4

Reply to Smart

J.J. Haldane

1 Methodology

Jack Smart's challenge to theism is direct and systematic. Again and again he expresses dissatisfaction with claims to the effect that theism is better placed than physicalism to account for aspects and elements of reality with which common experience and scientific investigation have made us familiar. In his 'Reply' he revisits much of the territory covered in chapter 1 and urges the adequacy of naturalistic explanations, or where these are not in sight he commends faith in their existence.

Thus Smart expresses disbelief at my claim that theories of physical interaction are insufficient to explain the origins of life, i.e. of *intrinsically* functionally organized, teleologically ordered activity; and that theories of natural selection are inadequate to account for speciation in general and the emergence of minded animals in particular. He argues that, on the contrary, there is nothing about thought and meaning that places them beyond the realm of matter or renders them opaque to scientific enquiry. As he puts it at one point 'Read the biologists and make up your own mind whether you think the naturalist story or the supernaturalist story is the more plausible' (chapter 3, p. 177).

In responding to the cosmological argument and to my discussion of the being, nature and activity of God, Smart moves from scientific to more purely philosophical assumptions and contends that the version of theism for which I argue is fraught with metaphysical difficulties surrounding the notions of time, necessity, substance, existence, causation and action. Indeed, reading his reply one should notice how technical philosophical claims become increasingly prominent as the text proceeds.

For example, in response to my claim that naturalism cannot account for conceptual thought, Smart seeks to resolve the puzzle of intentionality by appealing to Quine's proposal that reports of mental acts be treated as describing attitudes of thinkers to sentences and predicates. Thus 'Joe wants a unicorn' is to be rendered for philosophical purposes as 'Joe wants-true of himself "possesses a unicorn"' (chapter 3, p. 174). And in reply to my argument that the meaning of a general term such as 'cat' cannot be identified with its extension (the set of things, *cats*, to which it applies) – because, for example, claims about the prospects for cats in the future may be meaningful though they do not concern actually existing animals – Smart contends that 'cat' refers to the *set* of cats, past, present and future. To which he adds 'I believe in future cats (they are up ahead of us in space–time)' (chapter 3, p. 175).

Our difference over the nature of intentional states clearly involves competing philosophical theories and even Smart's last, seemingly straightforward, reply has a complex of abstract metaphysical theses lying behind it. The primary issue between us is not so much about what it is that 'cat' refers to, as about how it is possible for a general term to have 'sense' and thereby to refer *at all*. On my neo-Aristotelian account someone who is competent in the use of the term 'cat', or has the corresponding concept, has intellectual possession of an abstract 'intensional' entity, a formal structure which is also possessed by cats (exemplifying this structure naturally or materially is what makes them to be cats).[1] Informed by the concept one can then raise questions about types of circumstances which do not obtain but in which cats might exist. (Likewise someone who has the concept of a unicorn possesses a thought-structuring principle which gives 'shape' to his or her thoughts notwithstanding that there are no unicorns outside the imagination.) Smart's rejoinder requires that reference be accountable for in general without invoking abstract senses, and that in particular we accept a theory of the material universe as, in effect, a four-dimensional object some temporal parts of which feature stretches of cat.

Here I am not concerned to dispute these ideas, though I regard them as untenable. I only wish to alert readers to the fact that they are thoroughly metaphysical, quite revisionary of ordinary ways of thinking, and far from being obviously true. The same points hold good for Smart's Quinean-inspired discussion of modality, and for his suggestion that the notion of causation is not metaphysically robust and may be eliminable. Similarly his repeated attempts to use Ockham's razor to excise non-physical entities presume a background against which non-naturalist, and more specifically theistic hypotheses stand out as onto-logically extravagant. Notice also that contrary to its being presented in a matter-of-fact, commonsensical fashion, the background in question is a distinctly theoretical one. Readers may have assumed that a physicalist would have nothing to do with abstract entities, but Smart's philosophical physicalism turns out to have its own non-material objects, namely space–time points, numbers and sets. Just how far his views are removed from pre-philosophical thought is made clear when he observes that 'If Quine is right [which Smart takes to be so] we must regard the mathematical objects as physical, and yet they are not material' (chapter 1, p. 10).

Let me repeat that here I am not challenging these opinions, let alone criticizing Smart for holding them. The point is rather to highlight the fact that in making his case for atheism he relies upon a range of controversial *metaphysical* claims. There is no scope, therefore, for his rejecting theism on the grounds that, as contrasted with philosophical atheism, it is committed to strange and extravagant ideas. Ontological commitments are tied to descriptive and explanatory theses; more prosaically, we have to allow the existence of what is implied by our best attempts at understanding. And as Smart notes in his original essay, it is a highly contextual issue whether an explanation is simple or com-plex, economical or extravagant. Our situation as opponents in the debate about atheism and theism, therefore, is that we are in the same sea, if not in the same boat, using broadly similar nautical methods, but drawing different conclusions about the layout of the oceans and about the best direction in which to proceed.

At the outset of his essay Smart affirms the principle that '*an import-ant guide to metaphysical truth is plausibility in the light of total sci-ence*' (chapter 1, p. 6 – my emphasis) and he goes on to explain that he means 'science' to be understood in a very broad way. This quali-fication is necessary if the charge of narrow scientism is to be avoided. Yet his methodological principle may still harbour some unwarranted assumptions about what qualifies as knowledge and understanding. For example, Smart lists as sciences history, archaeology and philology; in other words spheres of investigation of human actions, artefacts and meanings. But if we are concerned with understanding aspects of the personal then it may be that there are no law-like scientific principles to be had, only interpretations the forming of which may rest on non-discursive intuitions and emotional reactions.

This consideration touches on an old issue in philosophy, namely the distinction between explanation by reference to causal regularities, and understanding in terms of comprehended meanings. The German philosopher Dilthey (1833–1911) investigated the ways in which in interpretation one draws upon 'lived experience' (*Erlebnis*) and human 'understanding' (*Verstehen*) in order to describe, evaluate and make one's way through the 'life-world' (*Lebenswelt*).² Abstracting from Dilthey's terminology the basic idea is clear enough. If we are after understanding, then we have to deploy the resources of our humanity; we have to let ourselves see and feel as human animals and not restrict our methods to those of a science which aspires to an ideal of describing the world in an observer-free way. Thus, to the extent that archaeology aims to understand human history and not just to chart the causal impact of those long dead, it requires the archaeologist imaginatively to 'relive' (*nacherleben*) the past by interpreting cultural and personal meanings.

There is an important counterpart to this requirement in semantic theory. Contemporary philosophies of language divide into two broad camps. On the one hand there are those which aim to give the meaning of speech acts either by relating them to their behavioural causes and effects or by calibrating them against the states of the world with which they are correlated. Thus one might hold that the meaning of the uttered sentence 'snow is white' is to be given by the causes and effects of its utterance, or by specifying the conditions under which it would be true (or by combining these two aspects). Though theories of these two sorts differ from one another they have in common the assumption that it is possible to give the content of an utterance by identifying something outside the sphere of meaning – behaviour or states of the world.

Sometimes this attempt is two staged. For example, among those who think that meaning is fixed by causes and effects, some attempt to specify the content of a speech act by reference to the (typical) beliefs and communicative intentions of speakers who use it.³ There are difficulties in identifying the relevant psychological states (for speakers can be dishonest, distracted or confused) but even if this can be done the account is regressive. If we say that the utterance 'snow is white' means snow is white if and only if the speaker believes that snow is white, intends to communicate this to a hearer and has certain expectations about the hearer's powers of understanding, then we still have to say what it is to have beliefs, intentions and expectations with these contents. The naturalist's task is not complete until meaning has been explained in terms of non-semantic(-cum-intentional) causes and effects.

Ingenious as they often are, theories of the sorts mentioned thus far invariably founder on the simple fact that nothing short of understanding its *sense* can amount to grasping the meaning of an utterance. Non-intentional causes and effects underdetermine meaning as do correlated states of affairs. This gap can be demonstrated in various ways, but referring back to my own earlier discussion (chapter 2, p. 118) the point can be made by observing that descriptions outside the sphere of meaning are extensional while those inside it are intensional. The diagram to which someone is causally related who uses the sentence 'that is a triangle' to refer to a figure on the board, is also a trilateral; but the meanings of the sentences 'that is a triangle' and 'that is a trilateral' differ. This difference is one of *sense* not causal influence, extension or truth conditions.

How then should we understand meaning? The question is ambiguous, for it may be read *metaphysically* as asking how meaning is possible; or *epistemologically* as asking how we can know what an utterance means. The metaphysical answer involves acknowledging the existence of intensional entities – concepts and senses – which organize the realms of thought and meaning in a manner analogous to that in which natural forms organize the material world. The concept 'cat' stands to a thought of a cat, as the form *cat* stands to a cat. In each case a structuring principle makes something to be of a certain sort; and the question of how thought can relate us to things is answered by the fact that concepts and forms are isomorphic. More directly and intimately they are two ways of being of one and the same nature. This has an interesting theological implication to which I shall return.

So far as epistemology is concerned the only possibility for a theory of meaning is that of an interpretative one. This brings us to the second broad camp in the philosophy of language. The effort to understand what someone means is an effort to make sense of what they are saying, to construe it in one way or another by assigning a content to it. Practically this is something we do without much, if any, thought about guiding principles; but theoretically it is no easy task to say what the constraints on interpretation are. Donald Davidson, who follows Quine in regarding the theory of meaning as the theory of interpretative translation, has proposed various principles the common core of which is that if we are to understand a speaker we must be able to see him or her as saying things that we might reasonably say were we in his or her circumstances.[4]

Interpretation of the sort in question is making human sense of human words and deeds. In doing this we cannot appeal to behavioural

laws or reduce the task to the application of other causal regularities, like observers on the beach watching the motion of the waves.
Instead we have to enter into the ocean of meanings and values and
find our bearings there. To do so, all we have to rely on is our considered judgement as to what seems plausible, significant or compelling. If Smart is willing to allow cultural studies the status of knowledge
then he will have to countenance meanings and non-scientific modes
of understanding. But once this is conceded there is no longer any
good reason (if there ever was one) not to allow emotional and intuitive responses, as well as scientific enquiry and philosophical reasoning, to inform our opinions about the nature of reality. With this
further broadening in mind let me recommend the following reformu-
lation of the methodological principle: *an important guide to metaphysical truth is plausibility in the light of total understanding.*

2   The Existence of God

How does theism fare given this principle? In my essay (chapter 2)
I offered arguments to the existence of God that fall under two broad
patterns: *teleological* (sections 4 and 5) and *cosmological* (section 6).
Contemporary philosophical theists who find merit in reasoning of the
first sort generally favour arguments from regularity. While presenting
a version of these I have also claimed, in contrast with most philosophers,[5] that the possibility of an old style design argument from the
'directedness' of things is not excluded by the development of evolutionary theory. Here it may be useful to have a 'map' (Figure 4.1) sum-
marizing the various lines of reasoning presented in chapter 2.

These diagrams are intended only as reminders and I shall not
attempt to repeat the details of the arguments they abbreviate. However, a short résumé of part of the argumentation mapped in Figure
4.1A is appropriate. First, I began with the assumption – which Smart
and I share – that science is the systematic study of a largely mind-
independent world. That world contains a plurality of kinds of things
animate and inanimate. The members of these various kinds are united
by sharing qualitatively similar natures. In the case of living things
these natures include principles of organic development and activity.

With regard to the apparent functional or vital attributes, powers
and activities of organisms one must either be a realist or an eliminativist. Realism is the claim that such features are genuinely as they seem
and are possessed by their subjects independently of our conceptions of

Figure 4.1

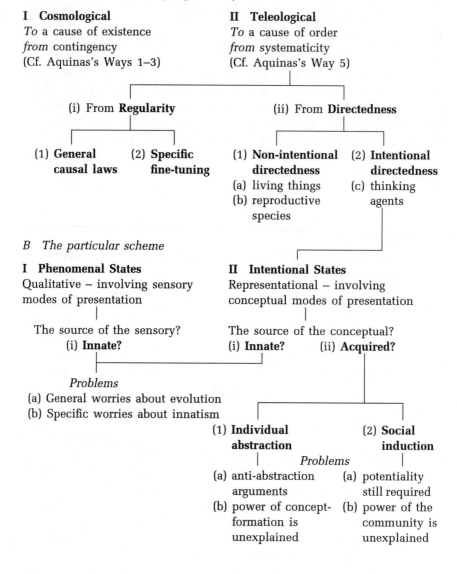

A   The general scheme of arguments from world to God

I   Cosmological
To a cause of existence
from contingency
(Cf. Aquinas's Ways 1–3)

II   Teleological
To a cause of order
from systematicity
(Cf. Aquinas's Way 5)

(i) From **Regularity**

(ii) From **Directedness**

(1) **General**   (2) **Specific**
     causal laws   **fine-tuning**

(1) **Non-intentional**   (2) **Intentional**
     directedness   **directedness**
(a) living things   (c) thinking
(b) reproductive   agents
    species

B   The particular scheme

I   Phenomenal States
Qualitative – involving sensory
modes of presentation

The source of the sensory?
   (i) **Innate?**

II   Intentional States
Representational – involving
conceptual modes of presentation

The source of the conceptual?
(i) **Innate?**   (ii) **Acquired?**

Problems
(a) General worries about evolution
(b) Specific worries about innatism

(1) **Individual**   (2) **Social**
     abstraction   **induction**
        Problems
(a) anti-abstraction   (a) potentiality
   arguments   still required
(b) power of concept-   (b) power of the
   formation is   community is
   unexplained   unexplained

them. For one reason or another eliminativism rejects this, holding instead that what appear to be real biological and teleological attributes of such and such a sort are either reducible to more basic properties which are real, or else are simply shadows cast by the light of human interest. My first argument was to the effect that the natural sciences are realist in their assumptions and that Smart faces a dilemma: either to endorse this view, thereby giving scope for an old style 'directedness' design argument, or else to reject it without scientific warrant in favour of an ideologically driven, mechanistic reductionism. The point of the latter disjunct is that nothing in the study of nature requires that we only allow as real what physics deals with; to suppose otherwise is a prejudice of philosophy not a discovery of science.

In his reply Smart reaffirms his physicalism but denies that it forces him to be a conceptual reductionist; as he writes 'My physicalism is an ontological one, not a translational one' (chapter 3, p. 170). The possibility of such a position is not in dispute; indeed I allowed for it and described an example when discussing the difference between ontological and conceptual or explanatory behaviourism (chapter 2, p. 93). My point was rather that while Smart may allow the non-translatability of teleological descriptions he denies that there is – in reality (*ontologically*) – any teleological behaviour. What he has to say later about levels of organization understood 'in a weak sense' does not alter this fact. On his account a tree is still 'nothing over and above a physical mechanism . . . even though talk of a tree is not translatable into talk of electrons and protons' (chapter 3, p. 172). The reductionism remains, as does my objection that it is unwarranted by empirical observation and theory. On the contrary we should suppose that the irreducibility of explanatorily rich and powerful biological theory is evidence for the reality of biological entities and powers – including teleological ones. This is in no way incompatible with the claim that such entities are composed of electrons and protons; but *composition* is not *identity*. We need to distinguish in living things, as in artworks, between the medium of realization and that which is realized in it, and to acknowledge that both are real.

My next step was to argue that natural 'mechanico-evolutionary processes' are not sufficient to explain the emergence of living things, reproductive species and thinking animals. Smart addresses the transition from the non-reproductive to the reproductive by suggesting that there is no problem for naturalism and that a hypothesis of this sort is to be preferred. Why is naturalism unembarrassed? Because, Smart supposes, there is no difficulty in principle to the natural emergence of replication: 'Why could not a self-replicating molecule come about through the coming together of a number of non-replicating molecules?' (chapter 3, p. 169). Well, first of all self-replication is not sufficient for evolution. The latter requires reproduction involving the coming to be of entities sufficiently like their predecessors to be continuants of their basic nature but sufficiently different to allow for selection, in point of varying degrees of adaptation, to take place. And what reproduction requires is a highly adaptive mechanism of the sort which it has been the goal of evolutionary theory to explain. Given teleology, evolutionary theory has a role; the question is whether it is intelligible to suppose that it could be the whole story.

Second, however, is the fact that there is no satisfactory naturalistic account even of primitive replication. There is nothing unintelligible about the idea which Smart mentions, that life on earth may have begun in consequence of organic molecules having arrived here from interstellar space. The problem with this suggestion, which Smart does not himself endorse, is that it is regressive. In answer to the question of *ultimate* origin Smart offers what is in effect a 'why not?' reply. Why could replicating molecules not just arise from non-replicating ones – be it that this occurrence may have a very low probability? My objection, however, was not to this being more or less likely, but to the very idea that there *could* be a natural explanation of the emergence of replicators from non-replicators. Indeed, this is just the sort of case that illustrates the notion of radical emergence. Some feature F is radically emergent if it is novel in a subject S (i.e. if it is not just a linear combination of instances of the same property type, as the size of a quilt is a linear function of the sizes of its constituent squares), and no naturalistic theory of the components of S can predict or explain F.[6] Thus my claim is that the power of self-replication is novel and not explicable by reference to lower-level entities and properties.

Standard evolutionary explanations posit replication as spontaneously arising some three or four billion years ago in a form more primitive than DNA. Needless to say there is no direct evidence of this, rather it is an assumption of naturalistic theory. The behaviour of DNA itself is acknowledged to be so qualitatively advanced that it is unimaginable that it could just have sprung into being uncreated. So the task is to show how DNA could have arisen from more primitive replication, say RNA, and how that could have resulted from non-replicating systems. Although molecules exhibit dynamic properties they are not normally self-duplicating, so the question remains: how could replication and hereditary variation arise?

Talk of 'proto-replicators' is vulnerable to a version of the dilemma with which I challenged the claim that intentionality arose from proto-representation. Representing or replicating very many features is certainly different from representing or replicating very few, but (*pace* Smart's remarks in his reply, chapter 3, p. 169) it is a difference of the wrong kind so far as the needed explanation is concerned. *Low level is not no level*, and it is the jump from none to some that needs to be effected. I conclude, *a priori*, that this gap is one of kind not quantity. The emergence of reproductive beings is radical and thus by definition not naturalistically explicable. If natural explanations were the only sort available we might despair of understanding. But there is another way of accounting for the emergence of novel entities as when a painter brings together quantities of powder suspended in oil and fashions a likeness of a sitter. Such is the style of explanation I offer of the emergence of life. Like the portrait it is the work of creative intelligence.

I have already touched upon the question of how mindedness introduces a domain distinct from that of physical properties and relations. The character of this difference has an important part to play in the extended argument (schematized in Figure 4.1B) from thought and language to the existence of God as source of conceptual activity. Smart's rejoinder is principally addressed to the premiss concerning intentionality. Since I remain attached to what I argued earlier I suggest that readers compare what each of us has had to say on the matter and draw their own conclusions. I would only add by way of encouragement that the issue of intentionality is of immense interest and importance in its own right.

3   Metaphysical Matters

Thus far, the left-hand side of Figure 4.1A has not been mentioned. The cosmological reasoning set out in section 6 of chapter 2 is really a presentation and defence of Aquinas's first three ways, and primarily of the first and second of them. In passing, let me strongly urge those who have not already done so to read the relevant article of the *Summa* (*S. T.*, Ia, q. 2, a. 3). The whole thing only runs to three pages! There cannot be many such short sections of text that have deserved or received so much study.

In his reply, Smart observes that it is not necessary in arguing for a first cause to assume that it is temporally prior. I agree and said as much, noting that Aquinas's proofs are intended 'to establish the ontological not the temporal priority of the first cause' (chapter 2, p. 136). What then followed, in order to show that there could not be an infinite series of causes, is not essentially tied to temporality. Smart introduces a reason to suggest that it had better not be, namely that the theistic conception of God should not locate him in time. As I suggested, however, the question of God's relation to time, especially as that bears upon the issue of divine agency, is complicated by the fact that there is a sense in which an 'activity' may be dated and timed though its source cannot be. If x caused y at t, we can say that x's agency was effective at t without being committed to the claim that at t, x began to do something. Thus one *might* wish to argue that a series of causes and effects could not regress infinitely in time, while yet denying that its originating source – effective in a temporally first event – was itself temporally located.

Smart remains worried about other metaphysical and theological ideas deployed in my presentation. There is not the space to elaborate on these matters here, but again I would ask readers to go back and try to judge the adequacy of what I wrote in the light of Smart's criticisms. For the most part he is generous in allowing that what I claim is defensible, and only contends that better – non-theistic – options are available. But on one topic he is clearly quite unsympathetic, or at any rate bemused. This is the issue of free action.

It is a common experience that there are certain philosophical issues where differences of view are accompanied by perplexity as to how one's opponents imagine that what they maintain is or even could be satisfactory. One such issue is weakness of will; another is consequentialism in ethics; a third is free will and determinism. Smart recognizes that part of my defence against the argument to atheism from evil rests on the claim that were God to act continuously so as to prohibit or limit the evil caused by human choices he would remove our freedom and thereby inhibit the realization of our natures as rational agents. Setting aside the question of the value of rational self-realization, Smart has a more immediate objection to my defence, namely that it presupposes an incoherent notion of free action as action that is uncaused. Once again readers will have to make a judgement from preceding pages but it may be helpful if I address Smart's puzzlement about the idea that human action issues from a source 'within' the agent.

Recall that I rejected the view favoured by Smart, and championed by Davidson,[7] that action is behaviour caused by antecedent mental states – 'reasons'. There are two broad categories of considerations against the identification of reasons with causes: the first is that nothing about the rational explanation of action requires this identification; the second is that the nature of action explanation prohibits it. Smart has the latter concern in mind when he writes that we must distinguish 'reason' as cause and 'reason' as justification. He thinks it would be a mistake to pass from the fact that justifying reasons are normative propositions (e.g. the truth of 'it is wrong to lie' is a 'reason' not to lie) to the conclusion that they cannot be causes, for what is cited in explanation of behaviour is not the truth of the proposition but the agent's belief in or endorsement of it. I agree this would be a faulty inference but it does not feature in my anti-causalist view of reasons. My argument as presented above (chapter 2, pp. 109ff) has to do with the difficulty of conceiving of the relation between beliefs, desires and other mental attitudes and actions as being a causal one.

It was in response to the question of how the connection between them should be understood, if not causally, that I introduced the scholastic phrase 'moved from within'.[8] This troubles Smart because the only relevant 'inside' from his point of view is that defined in relation to the skull. It may help if I explain that the origin of this phrase lies in a contrast marked in Aristotelian thinking about the movements of objects, between those whose behaviour is to be explained in terms of forces acting upon them, and those which are originating sources of movement in their own right. This is not the distinction between mere behaviour and rational action since there may be internal principles of non-rational agency. Rather it relates to the issue of whether some behaviour is expressive of the nature of the thing in question or is an effect imposed upon it.

Among the things there are, are natural substances, that is, unified subjects of predication. Such substances have characteristic powers of action and reaction; and sometimes their names and descriptions indicate these powers. Thus if we hear that something is an 'acid' we know that in certain sorts of circumstances (which we may not be able to specify) it will exert a corrosive effect. Similarly if we know that something is an 'animal' then we know that it has organic powers, typically ones of metabolism, growth and reproduction. In explaining an occurrence by mentioning its agent we are adverting to the operation of such powers as providing a full and adequate account. It is a mistake, I believe, to assume that if a substance is cited as the cause of an event the latter *must*, as a matter of logic or metaphysics, be due to some other event or events having taken place literally *inside* the agent. What it is to be an agent is to be possessed of certain powers with natural tendencies to exercise them in appropriate circumstances. Certainly, if such power is actualized one may well look for a prior event that was the occasion for this, but in doing so it will generally be more appropriate to look to the surrounding environment than to the substance itself, for the operation of the power will usually be in response to an external event.

In the case of intelligent agents the relevant power may be termed 'rational willing'; though in describing it as such it is important not to think in terms of a mechanism the parts of which are brought into operation as one element exerts an influence on the next. Instead one should think of a structural description that relates aspects of agency (reason and action) to one another without assuming that these are distinct items. To emphasize what was said earlier, voluntary action expresses the nature of a being *qua* rational animal. It is in that person-related sense that action proceeds 'from within'; though, of course, there are also physically necessary conditions of human activity including *internal* physiological ones. The distinction to keep in view, however, is that between agency and its causal preconditions. To revert to an earlier example, the latter stand to the former somewhat as canvas and paint stand to a portrait; and just as an interest in character looks to the depicted face of the sitter and not to the chemical bonding of the pigment, so an interest in action looks to the agent and not to his or her neurophysiology.

4   Reason, Faith and Revelation

In conclusion I wish to turn from the issue of theism as an explanatory cosmological hypothesis to evaluate less directly philosophical reasons for religious belief. Earlier I made a case for revising Smart's methodological principle as follows: *an important guide to metaphysical truth is plausibility in the light of total understanding*. It is appropriate, therefore, to consider other aspects of understanding. Religious faith typically encompasses a number of attitudes and objects, such as belief in the existence of a God or gods; a commitment to the content of general and specific revelations; and respect for and trust in the divine governance of the world.

Thus far my thinking has largely been directed to the issue of justifying belief in a God of the philosophers. Often religious believers contrast such a being, thought of as a metaphysical postulate, with a living personal God. Certainly one cannot induce incarnation or wring the blood of redemption out of a 'Cause of causes', but it is a mistake nonetheless to sever the links between reason, revelation and spiritual reflection. Each has a part to play in coming to know and understand the truth about God. In the Prologue to John's Gospel, it is written

> In the beginning was the Word, and the Word was with God, and the Word was God . . . all things were made through him . . . In him was life, and the life was the light of men. The light shines in the darkness, and the darkness has not overcome it . . . The true light that enlightens every man was coming into the world . . . And the Word was made flesh and dwelt among us, full of grace and truth . . . And from his fullness have we all received grace upon grace . . . (John 1: 1–14)

In the space of these few lines the evangelist informs the Greeks and the Greek-speaking Jews of Alexandria that what the philosophers have long sought after – the *logos*, or true account of the nature of things – has been with God from eternity and is that through which all things were made; and that this very same creative principle (for some Jews the 'Wisdom of God') came into the world in the person of Jesus to be its teacher and saviour.[9] Thus the *logos* of philosophy and the *Messiah* of Judaism are identified: Christ (the 'anointed one') *is* the way, the truth and the life. To separate the philosophical theology from the historical claim would diminish each; the text is at once metaphysical and religious, a synthesis of reason, testimony and faith.

Consider also the following verses from a eucharistic hymn attributed to St Thomas Aquinas and translated from the Latin by the Jesuit poet Gerard Manley Hopkins. It begins in contemplation of the consecrated host. According to Catholic teaching that which was a wafer of unleavened bread becomes, in the offertory of the mass, the body of Christ.

> Godhead here in hiding whom I do adore,
> Masked by these bare shadows, shape and nothing more,
> See, Lord, at thy service low lies here a heart
> Lost, all lost in wonder at the God thou art.
>
> Seeing, touching, tasting are in thee deceived;
> How says trusty hearing? That shall be believed;
> What God's Son has told me, take for truth I do;
> Truth himself speaks truly, or there's nothing true.[10]

Various features unite these two texts. First, what is believed of the consecrated host rests upon the words of scripture, both in the narratives of the Last Supper and in statements ascribed to Jesus such as those given in a later chapter of John: 'Truly, truly I say to you, he who believes has eternal life. I am the living bread which came down from heaven; if any one eats of this bread, he will live for ever; and the bread which I shall give for the life of the world is my flesh' (John 6: 47–51). Second, both are testimonies of personal and ecclesial belief: John and Aquinas write as individuals in union with religious communities defined by a common history in faith. Third, recognizing the limitations of the literal, they both use analogical and metaphorical language: the Word is life and is a truth-giving light; the Godhead is masked by shadow but its reality is disclosed by the word of God which is itself truth. Fourth, each writer invokes interpretations that link the empirical and the transcendental: what the 'eye' of faith sees is not just a function of light hitting the retina, but equally what is believed originates in various ways and remains answerable to experience.

Some religious believers take pride and comfort in the idea that their faith owes nothing to reason, historical testimony or doctrinal authority. It is, for them, just a matter of a personal relationship with God. Perhaps they feel that in this way they incur no unpayable debts. Such an attitude is certainly unphilosophical; but it is also alien to the central traditions of Western and Eastern Christianity (and indeed to those of Judaism and Islam). Moreover, it invites the sort of naturalistic, socio-psychological explanation of religious claims proposed by Smart in his discussion of religious experience and the testimony of scripture.

The three monotheistic faiths are all religions 'of the book' – the Hebrew bible, supplemented by later sacred writings. But no value (or sense) can be attached to the idea of discerning and trusting the word of scripture unless one is able to specify which writings and interpretations are to be accepted and which rejected. Every faith of the book presupposes some sort of canon of authentic and authoritative scripture; and one need only ask the question of how such a canon came to be determined, ratified and transmitted and how it would be defended against rivals, to realize the ineliminable role of reason and general understanding. In one of his fine essays G.K. Chesterton says of philosophy that it is 'merely thought that has been thought out' and adds that 'man has no alternative, except between being influenced by thought that has been thought out and being influenced by thought that has not been thought out'.[11] Holy Scripture and the Creeds it inspired is religious

experience that has been thought out; nothing less would be worth trans-
mitting across the centuries.

This leads me to comment briefly on Smart's discussion of the evidential worth of the New Testament. His central point is a reapplication
of epistemological holism, i.e. of the idea that what one makes of some
piece of purported evidence depends on how one understands and
evaluates other claims. On this we agree. Also, I accept the value of
New Testament criticism and have no wish to insulate scripture from
it.[12] On the contrary, Christianity is a historical religion; by itself
philosophy tells us little about the nature of the Creator and his purpose
in creation; and most of what I and others believe about God rests
heavily on the Creeds and on the New Testament – both of which
have their origins in events that are reported as having occurred in
first-century Palestine.

Our disagreement is not whether the scholarly study of scripture is
appropriate but whether it supports or undermines the claims of Christianity. Smart makes some general comments about the character of the
Gospels and illustrates the possibility of naturalistic explanations by
drawing on the thesis (advanced by S.G.F. Brandon and others) that
Jesus was a revolutionary Zealot put to death for threatening insur-
rection against the governing Roman authorities.

Let me reply in order, beginning with some broad points about
scriptural scholarship. First, the New Testament is the main, and by
and large the only, source for the events it purports to describe. There
are some places where external evidence is available but apart from
helping us with very general features of the period extra-scriptural
sources contribute little. This fact, however, is neither surprising nor
problematic. Most of what is described in the Gospels, Epistles and
Acts of the Apostles concerns events that only the followers of Jesus
would have been witness to or had an interest in. That said, the combination of internal and external evidence for the life and teachings
of Jesus is very much better than for most figures in antiquity. For
example, he merits several lines in the only remaining history of
Judaism in first-century Palestine, *viz.* Josephus' *Antiquities of the Jews.*[13]
Also, while it is clearly the case that the Gospels are composite works
put together in stages from sayings and episodes this technique is not
of itself unreliable. Far from diminishing the evidential value of scripture it encourages the idea that certain events were so securely fixed
in the minds of Christ's followers and so compelling to hearers that
they survived in oral form until the passage of time and the growth of
Christianity made it necessary to commit them to paper. Something of

the flavour of these circumstances is conveyed by the very matter-of-fact opening of Luke's Gospel:

> Inasmuch as many have undertaken to compile a narrative of the things which have been accomplished among us, just as they were delivered to us by those who from the beginning were eyewitnesses and ministers of the word, it seemed good to me also, having followed all things closely, for some time past, to write an orderly account for you, most excellent Theophilus, that you may know the truth concerning the things of which you have been informed. (Luke 1: 1–4)

The task of dating the earliest Christian documents is problematic. Given that they probably evolved from anecdotes and aphorisms into comprehensive texts, there is a theoretical question as to what to count as an early version of a Gospel; and given the circumstances of the early Christians it is not to be expected that anything from the first century will be found. Nonetheless, there is a widespread consensus among theist, agnostic and atheist scholars that Paul's Epistles were written in the 50s and 60s of the first century and that the Gospels, in more or less the form in which we have them today, were composed between 70 (Mark) and 90 (John) AD. Smart remarks that the earliest Gospel is dated 'many years after the crucifixion', but the thing to be struck by is how *close* these dates are to the life and death of Jesus. Paul was writing 'Rejoice always, pray constantly, give thanks in all circumstances, for this is the will of God in Christ Jesus for you' (Thessalonians 1: 16–18) at a date more or less equal in distance from the crucifixion as was the Second World War from the Great War. As you read this, think what memorable events occurred 20 to 30 years previously and then consider whether writing about them now would significantly diminish the value of your record. In fact, time and hindsight tend to improve the quality of historical writing and then as now there were plenty of people around to take issue with and correct the account of events. Additionally, the authors of the gospels were not state propagandists or spokesmen for some powerful social group; and nor were they writing for posterity. On the contrary it is fairly clear, even in the later Gospels, that they expected the second coming of Christ sooner rather than later. Indeed it was reflection arising from disappointment on this score that led to the development of a theology of the 'Kingdom of God' and an adequate eschatology (an account of the 'Four Last Things': death, judgement, heaven and hell).

So far as the content of the Gospels is concerned it is necessary to distinguish between a narrative core common to all four gospels, and editorial elaborations and variations. Discerning this difference is not simply an empirical task since one has to make judgements of relative importance. The most common words in this book are probably articles and prepositions but a thematic analysis would not get far on the basis of a word- or even a phrase-count. Here is where some of the critical methods mentioned by Smart have proven helpful though each has its rather strict limits. *Source criticism* tries to identify the early short texts brought together in the composition of a gospel; *form criticism* looks for the main compositional elements, e.g. sayings and narratives; while *redaction criticism* is mindful of the subsequent unity achieved in a gospel and so attends to the purposes and influence of its writer. A more recent trend influenced by modern literary theories emphasizes *reader-response* and regards scriptural texts as being designed less as sources of information and more as occasions for interaction and personal formation.

These matters are genuinely fascinating, but the question to ask from the viewpoint of a debate about atheism and theism is what exactly they show about the evidential value of the New Testament. The answer, I believe, is not a great deal; at any rate not much that is likely to make a difference to the case for or against atheism. The trend of recent scholarship supports a more or less face-value reading of the Gospels. What I mean by this is that there is evidently an ancient common narrative core which reflects the beliefs of the contemporary followers of Jesus.[14] This assumes the existence of a theistic God and a covenant between him and the Jews his chosen people. It relates in turn the birth of Jesus, the teaching of John the Baptist that the Messiah was at hand, the development of Christ's mission through gathering disciples and preaching the priority of the Kingdom of God; his extensive use of parable and his miraculous deeds; his entry into Jerusalem prior to Passover (around the year 30 AD), the disturbance with the money-changers in the Temple, the last supper, his arrest and appearance before the Jewish high priest and his conviction for blasphemy in describing himself as 'Messiah' and 'Son of God', his transfer to Pilate who had him crucified for claiming to be 'king of the Jews'; Christ's death on the cross, his burial, then subsequent appearance to various followers individually and collectively, and his final departure 'into heaven'.

In suggesting that this common core may be taken as it stands I am not claiming that it is intrinsically plausible, let alone that it is self-authenticating. The point is rather that whatever one wants to make of it *there are no good scholarly reasons* for doubting that this is what was pieced together within the lifetime of people who could and may have known Jesus, and that this is what they sincerely believed. Whether one accepts it oneself is another matter, but if one does not that is no good basis on which to doubt that the gospel writers meant what they wrote. Arguments to the contrary tend to import historical speculations less plausible than the narrative, or to make philosophical assumptions about what could or could not happen and then reconstruct the text as deceitful or poetic.

Brandon's account is of the former sort. It argues that since blasphemy was an offence for a Jewish court, Jesus' trial at the hands of Pilate could not have been for that but only for sedition. Consequently, he must either have been, or been perceived to have been, an agitator against the authority of the state. In short, Jesus was a revolutionary (perhaps even a 'Zealot') not a claimant to the title 'Son of God'. Such limited plausibility as this account may possess depends on not taking scripture seriously but assuming that it is foolish or knavish. Smart quotes Brandon's observation that one of the disciples is called 'Simon Zelotes' and the implication that if Simon were a Zealot so too might be his master. Well, to begin with the use of the term '*zelotes*' to identify a member of a revolutionary party only begins after the uprising of 66–70 and even then this was not its only meaning. Admittedly Luke probably comes after this date, but why suppose that in an account of 40 years earlier he would choose to use an expression that did not then have a revolutionary connotation? This interpretation is particularly contentious given that '*zelotes*' (or in the Aramaic '*cananaean*') had a definite *theological* meaning, identifying a person as particularly zealous on behalf of the 'law', even to the extent of enforcing it personally. Whatever its virtue or vice, this is a religious not a political disposition.

As regards the trial by Pilate, there is an entirely adequate explanation given in scripture. Jesus was seen, and saw himself, in the role of prophet. Accordingly his words and deeds were viewed as symbolic of the demands of God. In his visit to the Temple Jesus threw over the tables of the money-changers, and on leaving intimated that the Temple itself would be destroyed: 'There will not be left here one stone upon another, that will not be thrown down' (Mark 13: 2). Incidentally, since the Temple was largely destroyed by fire in 70 AD, had Mark been writing after that date it is likely that he would have harmonized the prophecy to the known facts. That he did not do so provides some reason to regard the text as faithfully reporting the (gist of the) actual words of Jesus.

If you imagine someone turning up at your house and saying, in tones of anger and without reference to some natural disaster, that within a short time it will be destroyed, it is easy to see how Christ's prophecy could be perceived as *both* predictive and threatening. In the circumstances of an impending Passover, when there would have been at least a quarter of a million Jews in Jerusalem, such a remark, in conjunction with Messianic associations, would be sufficient to worry both Jewish and Roman authorities. The high priest had responsibility for maintaining civil order but if he wanted to be assured of Christ's death he needed a civil charge. There would be no shortage of 'witnesses' willing to provide evidence of a threat to the state; and as we know from other sources, such as Philo of Alexandria,[15] Pilate was certainly no stickler for justice. Given Jesus' evident religious challenge and the prospect of trouble arising from the Temple episode, it is unsurprising that as high priest Caiaphas was willing to see him condemned to death. But possibly not being in a position to effect this directly he arranged or allowed for false testimony sufficient to have Pilate do the deed. Such, in effect, is the story of scripture. It squares much better with what else we know than does Brandon's Zealot thesis, for had Jesus really been seen as the leader of a political group intent on fomenting revolution it is very likely that Pilate would have had several of Christ's followers executed also.

Brandon's challenge is of an empirical sort that has become familiar in scriptural studies. Another and now more common critical response to the Gospels is to deny, on *a priori* philosophical grounds, that what they report as having happened could have happened. While not denying the legitimacy – in the abstract – of this strategy, I observe that hitherto it has been operated in ways that are quite unconvincing. So, for example, critics who believe that miracles are impossible then dismiss reports of them as confused, mendacious or symbolic. Certainly, if miracles *are* impossible then any claim to the effect that they have occurred is idle – or worse. But as Smart notes, it is hard to come up with an argument to show that there is something incoherent in the very idea of the miraculous. I conclude, therefore, that the suggestion that New Testament scripture reports the Incarnation of the Son of God, the second person of the Trinity, is not something that can be ruled out on grounds of scriptural criticism. What is wearisome, therefore, is that it is often sceptically disposed biblical scholars rather than philosophers who tend to make question-begging metaphysical assumptions as to what could and what could not be true. Such are the ironies of life.

5   A Religious Conclusion

My themes have been the reasonableness of belief in a creative Divinity and the merit of the claims of Christianity to provide answers to questions about the nature of God and his purposes in creating us. At one point Jack Smart remarks that the history of the universe suggests a very roundabout route to the creation of thinking things. I suppose the idea is that an efficient Deity would just create such beings, and that this not having been done a *reductio ad absurdum* on the assumption of creation is in the offing.

I fear that Smart may have been encouraged in his thinking about this issue by world-bound theologians. My reply is simple: do not underestimate the extent of the Divine economy or its glory. Why suppose that God did not also create thinking things straight off? Given the assumption of a creator God I find it entirely plausible that we are not alone as rational beings; and scripture and the writings of the saints offer evidence for the existence of angels – pure spiritual beings, not the androgynous chorus line of popular culture.

Furthermore, I conceive an expansive and multi-layered creation in which *we* enter in only at a certain stage in the movement of the universe back towards God. Earlier I sketched an account of how the harmony of cognition between thought and thing might be explained. When I think of a cat, the organizing principle which makes it to be what it is also structures my mental activity. There is a formal identity of thought and object. Another way of describing this is to say that a nature has come to be in another mode – intellectually. Generalizing, my suggestion is that creation is purposely dynamic. God has so ordained things that by stages the world comes to understand itself. The process of historical development leads from materially embodied natures to their assimilation into thought as *Homo sapiens* appears on the scene. In us the world of cats and dogs, water and gold, comes to be again cognitively. And as that happens we more adequately realize our status as beings created in the image of God, for it is in God that all natures exist 'eminently'. Aquinas relates this communication of form to the idea of truth defined, following Isaac Israeli (855–955), as the conformity of mind and thing.

> The intellect receives from things, so it is in some way changed by them and measured by them. Hence it is clear that the things of nature, from which our intellect receives knowledge, measure our intellect . . . But

they are in turn measured by the divine intellect, in which there is
everything that is created, as everything that is made by a craftsman is
in his intellect. So the divine intellect measures, and is not measured by
anything: natural things measure and are measured; while our intellect
is measured by, and does not measure the things of nature ... So the
things of nature stand between two intellects and are said to be true
according to their match with either.[16]

These are somewhat intellectualist considerations and I would not
want to end without mentioning the spiritual (not spiritualist) dimension of religion. It is sometimes said that Christianity is a way of life.
No doubt on some understanding this is true; but often those who say
it have in mind an exclusively practical, doctrine-free conception of
the issue. Set against this modern and secularized notion is the ideal
of human life as a religiously informed journey to God; one involving
a continuing struggle to get and then to stay on course towards an
eternal destiny. Often, when people pray for God to be active on their
behalves they have it in mind that He may favour them with a preternatural intervention, a miraculous ordering of nature bestowing success, removing illness or otherwise improving their lot. But what we
should seek continuously and earnestly is supernatural assistance,
help to lift us up from would-be independence to an order of blessed-
ness. It is only that intervention which imparts grace and draws us
closer to God.

It has been the repeated experience of the great spiritual figures
such as St Augustine (354–430), St Catherine of Siena (1347–80), St
Teresa of Avila (1515–82) and St Jean Vianney, Curé d'Ars (1786–
1859) that contemplating (in the light of reason, experience and authoritative doctrine) this idea of life as a journey induces an unshakeable
sense of divine purpose and of personal responsibility to answer the
call to sanctity.[17] Smart expresses some sympathy for the metaphysical
wonder that there should be something rather than nothing. What is
at issue here, however, is a different wonder, namely that the eternal
God who continuously wills the universe in being should be close by,
and accessible to, each and every one of us. The hope this offers is expressed by Cardinal Newman in eloquent but humble words that are
now more often sung than said.

> Lead, kindly Light, amid th'encircling gloom,
>   Lead thou me on;
> The night is dark, and I am far from home,
>   Lead thou me on.

> Keep Thou my feet; I do not ask to see
> The distant scene; one step enough for me.[18]

One step enough. Yet the ambition of philosophy has traditionally been to comprehend the whole. How then are faith and thought
related? If there is any merit in the arguments I have presented, there
is reason to believe that we are part of a created order and that our
role in it involves achieving understanding. By means of thought we
come to mirror the structure of reality and thereby reflect in small and
imperfect images something of the grandeur of God. But to realize our
potential as images of the Divine we also need to engage and direct
the will, the imagination and the passions. God is active in sustaining
creation and we need to find how our actions can be aligned with his
purpose. To help us in that we have been given a revelation and a
Divinely instituted and protected community of faith: Holy Scripture
and Holy Church – so I believe. All the same, the route to salvation
is not so clear that only those who wilfully ignore it lose their way,
and to take it involves sacrificing the little we seem to have secured
by our own efforts. Even Christ entered in a plea to be excused before
saying 'not my will, but thine, be done' (Luke 22: 42). So though it
may be plausible in the light of total understanding to suppose that
there is a transcendent order, and though we may hope one day to see
the distant scene, for now we need much grace to take each step
towards it.[19]

Notes

1 For further discussion of these issues see my essays 'Mind–World Identity Theory and the Anti-Realist Challenge', in J. Haldane and C. Wright
   (eds), *Reality, Representation and Projection* (New York: Oxford University Press, 1994), and 'Forms of Thought', in L. Hahn (ed.), *The Philosophy of Roderick Chisholm, Library of Living Philosophers Volume XXV*
   (Chicago: Open Court, forthcoming).

2 See 'The Construction of the Historical World in the Human Studies', in
   H.P. Rickman (ed.), *Dilthey, Selected Writings* (Cambridge: Cambridge University Press, 1976).

3 The *locus classicus* for this approach is Paul Grice's essay 'Meaning',
   Philosophical Review, 66 (1957). The theory of meaning has been one of
   the most productive fields of analytical philosophy since the 1960s. There
   are many anthologies, surveys and introductory texts. Readers might begin

with R.M. Martin, *The Meaning of Language* (Cambridge MA: MIT Press, 1987) and for authoritative treatments of individual issues see the essays in B. Hale and C. Wright (eds), *A Companion to the Philosophy of Language* (Oxford: Blackwell, 1996).

4 For Davidson's own writings see the essays in the third section of *Inquiries into Truth and Interpretation* (Oxford: Clarendon Press, 1982). Davidson has developed his views in subsequent articles. For an overview see Simon Evnine, *Donald Davidson* (Cambridge: Polity Press, 1991). Further development of a broadly Davidsonian approach but taken in more hermeneutical and Aristotelian directions is offered by John McDowell in *Mind and World* (Cambridge, MA: Harvard University Press, 1994).

5 But not all: see B. Davies, *An Introduction to the Philosophy of Religion* (Oxford: Oxford University Press, 1993), ch. 6; P. Geach, *Providence and Evil* (Cambridge: Cambridge University Press, 1977), ch. 4; and A. Kenny, 'The Argument from Design', in *Reason and Religion: Essays in Philosophical Theology* (Oxford: Blackwell, 1987). Each of these authors raises doubts about the adequacy of evolutionary explanations of beneficial teleology. My discussion in chapter 2 of the problem of accounting for speciation derives from remarks contained in Geach's *Providence and Evil* (pp. 75–7); I believe these are also the inspiration for the arguments discussed by Davies and Kenny.

6 For a recent discussion of emergence see R. Spencer-Smith, 'Reductionism and Emergent Properties', *Proceedings of the Aristotelian Society*, 95 (1995). I reply to this in J. Haldane, 'The Mystery of Emergence', *Proceedings of the Aristotelian Society*, 96 (1996).

7 See the essays in D. Davidson, *Essays on Actions and Events* (Oxford: Clarendon Press, 1982), starting with 'Actions, Reasons and Causes' which remains the best statement of Davidson's view.

8 For a fuller discussion of these matters see J. Haldane, 'Some Metaphysical Presuppositions of Agency', *Heythrop Journal*, 35 (1994). My discussion here and in chapter 2 is drawn from this essay.

9 For a short but very informative treatment of the interplay between Greek philosophy and Christianity see A.H. Armstrong and R.A. Markus, *Christian Faith and Greek Philosophy* (London: Darton, Longman & Todd, 1964). A somewhat longer and more advanced study is Christopher Read, *Philosophy in Christian Antiquity* (Cambridge: Cambridge University Press, 1994).

10 W.H. Gardner and N.H. MacKenzie, *The Poems of Gerard Manley Hopkins* (Oxford: Oxford University Press, 1970).

11 'The Revival of Philosophy – Why?', in G.K. Chesterton, *The Common Man* (London: Sheed & Ward, 1950).

12 It is, for me, a matter of some regret that Catholic scholarship in this area has not been as extensive or as good as it ought to have been. Happily, though, the days of neglect are past; see, for example, the splendid *Jerome Biblical Commentary* (London: Geoffrey Chapman, 1990).

13 This work, written *c.*90 AD, was later transcribed by Christians who 'enhanced' the description of Jesus. However, the reliable core of the passage in question tells us that Jesus was a wise man who taught those who accept the truth with gladness and who won over many Jews and Greeks; that on the accusation of Jewish leaders he was crucified by Pilate; but that he still had followers up to the time of Josephus' writing. See *Flavius Josephus, Complete Works*, translated by William Whiston (London, Glasgow: Pickering & Inglis, 1981).

14 See, for example, the assessment arrived at by E.P. Sanders in his book *The Historical Figure of Jesus* (London: Allen Lane, 1993). Sanders is one of the leading New Testament scholars.

15 In a letter to the Emperor Caligula (*Embassy to Gaius*, 302) Philo complains of Pilate's many injustices, and Josephus tells us that he was eventually removed from the office of Prefect of Judaea because of his over-zealous attitude to execution.

16 *De Veritate*, q. 1, a. 2. as translated in C. Martin (ed.), *The Philosophy of Thomas Aquinas: Introductory Readings* (London: Routledge, 1988).

17 Doctrinally informed and disciplined spirituality, as contrasted with untethered 'new age mysticism', is currently a somewhat neglected aspect of religion. A classic manual of spiritual development is Adolphe Tanquerey, *The Spiritual Life: A Treatise on Ascetical and Mystical Theology*, 2nd edn (Tournai: Society of St John the Evangelist, 1951). For writings of the great spiritual figures of theism (Christian, Islamic and Jewish) see the volumes of *The Classics of Western Spirituality: A Library of the Great Spiritual Masters*, edited by Richard J. Payne (London: SPCK, 1978–).

18 Cardinal Newman, 'Lead, Kindly Light', in *The Spirit of Cardinal Newman* (London: Burns & Oates, 1914).

19 I am grateful to Ernest Sosa the editor of the 'Great Debates Series', and to Steve Smith of Blackwell Publishers, for the invitation to co-author this book; and I thank Smart for the lively and generous style of his contribution. Family and other circumstances delayed delivery of my typescript and I am indebted to all three gentlemen, but especially Jack Smart, for their gracious patience.

Afterword

J.J.C. Smart and J.J. Haldane

In our debate we argue on opposite sides of the issue of atheism and theism. For a philosophical debate to be of any value, however, there must be a fair basis of philosophical agreement notwithstanding the differences that are there at the outset or those that may develop later. Neither of us would find it as easy to have a profitable exchange with (say) a French deconstructionist or a dogmatically unargumentative and obscure Whiteheadian.[1]

One important point of agreement between us is in some aspects of philosophical methodology. As has been emphasized, we are both metaphysical realists: that is, we both believe in a real world independent of our human concerns and categories. Our realism is not that of neo-pragmatists such as Hilary Putnam who speak of 'realism with a human face'. Notwithstanding that we acknowledge the concerns and philosophical ingenuity lying behind such a view we both believe in the existence of a reality independent of thought and language and in the possibility of discovering something of the structure of the world as it is in itself. Elsewhere Smart has written of 'realism with a cosmic face'[2] and Haldane of 'humanism with a realist face';[3] each in his own way taking issue with Putnam's position, though in Haldane's case paying attention to the concern to find a place for the human 'life-world' in the metaphysical scheme of things.

Putnam's rejection of metaphysical realism is not so extreme as that of some contemporary analytical philosophers. For example, Michael Dummett (who, like Haldane, is a Roman Catholic) and Crispin Wright have at times advanced an account of meaning and understanding according to which we can attach no sense to claims involving unrestricted spatial or temporal generalizations, descriptions of the distant past and conjectures about the mental states of others.[4] In contrast we both wish to say that there is such a fact of the matter as (to revert to a theme in our earlier exchange) whether Jesus lost consciousness on the cross before he died, even though we could never know it one way or the other.

Putnam's anti-realism has always been more moderate and further from verificationism than that associated with Dummett and Wright. His concern has been to oppose the view which he describes as 'metaphysical realism' and which he takes to consist principally in the claim that there is a privileged account of reality independent of observer's interests, a true theory of it as it is in itself apart from any representational scheme. Instead, Putnam insists that the evident fact of conceptual relativity – that all thought is structured by principles of classification – must be accommodated; but that this can be achieved in a manner that allows us to hold on to the common sense idea that there is (usually) a fact of the matter as to whether what we say of the world is true or false. This combination of conceptual relativity and facticity yields 'internal realism' (or the more recently coined 'realism with a human face') according to which *within* physics, natural history, etc., one may be a realist. For example, one may meaningfully and truthfully assert the real existence of electrons, or the occurrence of past events for which no evidence remains. Yet it remains an error to suppose that physics or natural history are maps of the pre-existing, mind-independent geography of reality. There is no such thing as *the* way the world is, only the way it is relative to one or another system of description, explanation *and* evaluation.

Independently of this present work we have both been intrigued by, and have written about, Putnam's evolving attitude to the question of metaphysical realism. This is in part because we have thought he is mistaken, and in part because like others we have found him to be one of the best proponents of anti-realist thought and thus a helpful critic of realism. Yet while we seem to agree in broad outline on the form of a general response to one important element in Putnam's anti-realist challenge, we differ significantly in how we think realism itself should accommodate certain of his critical points. Since this difference relates to our earlier disagreements about reductionism, which in turn are related to the prospects of an 'old style' teleological argument, it may be worth commenting on it briefly.

First our agreement. Realism is an ontological thesis and not, as Putnam and others have often painted it, an epistemological one: it concerns existence not knowledge or conceptualization. Consequently, no theory of representation or justification by itself implies the denial of realism. What may or may not be conceived or recognized is one thing, what exists is another. Put simply, metaphysical realism maintains that the way(s) things are is logically independent of our way(s) of thinking about them. Unsurprisingly, realists usually aim to add an account of representation or intentionality to the metaphysical thesis, but to do so is a matter of *addition* and any inadequacies in such accounts do not imperil ontological realism itself.

The deployment of this fact in reply to Putnam and others needs to be adapted according to variations in the way in which epistemological assumptions feature in their critiques of realism, but we are agreed on it as a general point of response. Where we differ is over the issue of plurality as that enters Putnam's argument from conceptual relativity. One way of reading the relativity claim is as another instance of epistemological seepage into ontology. And if it is understood as the argument that since all thought is conceptually structured therefore all we ever think of are conceptual structures, it is easily dismissed. First, because it does not follow from the fact that we think *with* concepts that concepts are what we think *of*;[5] second, because even if that did follow it would not impugn the mind-independence of reality but only provide a basis for scepticism.

However, there is another way of regarding Putnam's insistence on conceptual relativity and that is as the shadow cast upon epistemology by the metaphysical claim that reality is radically pluralistic and hence not such as to be adequately characterized by one style of description, in particular that of basic physical theory. Conceptual relativity is thus the claim that there is no single correct scheme for describing reality precisely *because* reality itself is not 'monomorphic' or reducible to a single level of nature. Smart writes:

> Putnam wants 'realism' with a human face, but I want to see the world *sub specie aeternitatis* (realism with a cosmic face?), by which I mean that we should eschew indexical expressions in our description of reality, and also eschew such concepts as that of colour, which are defined in terms of a normal human percipient ... I can agree with Putnam that causation and other concepts in ordinary life are highly contextual and dependent on particular human interests. I can relegate them to what Quine calls 'second grade discourse', not suitable for metaphysics but highly convenient for our ordinary human practical activities and social intercourse.[6]

Putnam's easily predictable response to this is that no good case can be made for relegating intentional, evaluative and other non-scientific characterizations to the realm of 'second grade discourse'. However, in order to deny truth-bearing priority to physical theory over psychological or moral description he thinks it is necessary to diversify 'reality' by relativizing the 'real' to a plurality of ways of thinking. Like Putnam, Haldane wishes to insist upon the ontological reality of the biological, the psychological and so on – as well as the physical – but to do so while remaining a metaphysical realist. That is, he regards these domains as 'populated' in various ways and to various extents independently of our conception of them: biological and psychological properties are there to be discovered and described and are not functions of our modes of description. As he writes elsewhere:

> Of course the identification and re-identification of substances is conception-dependent but it does *not* follow from this that there is any general relationship of ontological determination between our conceiving of things as being of such and such a sort and their having that nature . . . The metaphysical realist of Aristotelian-Thomistic persuasion is not concerned to deny that one can adopt a variety of ontologies, or that there is a variety of categories of things. Equally he or she should resist such phrases as that the world 'forces us to think of it in a single integrated way'. That is both literally false and liable on interpretation to induce scientific reductionism. There are many 'things' and 'ways of being'. Nonetheless, among these some [those with objective principles of unity] are more substantial than others.[7]

So we end on an interesting combination of alliances and oppositions. Smart and Haldane are in agreement in defending metaphysical realism against the challenges of Putnam and other anti-realists. Yet Haldane and Putnam dispute what they see as the scientistic orientation of Smart's metaphysical world-view. Finally, however, Putnam and Smart may be as one in questioning the combination which Haldane favours of realism and ontological (not just conceptual) pluralism. It would be fascinating to pursue these issues further but to do so would be to embark on another 'great debate in philosophy': *realism and anti-realism*.

Notes

1   Though Smart wishes to put in a good word for Whitehead's Lowell Lectures published as *Science and the Modern World* (New York: Macmillan, 1925).

2 See J.J.C. Smart, 'A Form of Metaphysical Realism', *The Philosophical Quarterly*, 45 (1995), and J.J.C. Smart, *Our Place in the Universe* (Oxford: Blackwell, 1989), ch. 8.

3 See J.J. Haldane, 'Humanism with a Realist Face', *Philosophical Books*, 35 (1994), and J.J. Haldane, 'On Coming Home to (Metaphysical) Realism', *Philosophy*, 71 (1996).

4 See, for example, the essays in Part I, 'The Negative Programme', of Crispin Wright, *Realism, Meaning & Truth* (Oxford: Blackwell, 1987).

5 As Aquinas writes,'we must say that species [ideas] stand in relation to the intellect as that *by which it thinks* or has understanding (*id quo intelligit*) and not that *which is thought of* (*id quod intelligitur*)', *Summa Theologiae*, Ia, q. 85, a. 2.

6 See Smart, 'A Form of Metaphysical Realism', pp. 305–6.

7 See Haldane, 'On Coming Home to (Metaphysical) Realism', pp. 287–96.

Bibliography

This bibliography overlaps at a few points with the references in the text and notes. Its purpose is to offer a guide to basic works and suggestions for further reading to those who may wish to pursue issues discussed in the essays and replies. It is relatively selective and should not be treated as in any way exhaustive.

Introductions to the Philosophy of Religion

Because of its perennial fascination philosophy of religion is well provided with introductory texts. In some of these the authors pursue their own atheist or theist inclinations, but in all cases a range of perspectives is presented. For a clearly written account combining contemporary analytical philosophy of religion with reference to historical figures see Brian Davies OP, *An Introduction to the Philosophy of Religion*, 2nd edition (Oxford: Oxford University Press, 1993). Davies, who like Aquinas is a Dominican, offers a more extended treatment of much the same material in *Thinking About God* (London: Geoffrey Chapman, 1985). Other well-balanced presentations of all the main points in the case for and against the existence of God are given by J.C.A. Gaskin in *The Quest for Eternity* (Harmondsworth: Penguin Books, 1984) and William L. Rowe in *Philosophy of Religion: An Introduction* (Belmont, CA: Wadsworth, 1978). Particularly useful for the complete beginner is C. Stephen Evans, *Philosophy of Religion: Thinking about Faith* (Downers Grove, IL: InterVarsity Press, 1985). Richard L. Purtill, *Thinking About Religion: A Philosophical Introduction to Religion* (Englewood Cliffs, NJ: Prentice-Hall, 1978), carries his discussion beyond the usual agenda of issues to consider such matters as scripture, eastern religion and mysticism. Perhaps the most comprehensive introductory text is Michael Peterson, William Hasker, Bruce Reichenbach and David Basinger, *Reason & Religious Belief: An Introduction to the Philosophy of Religion* (New York: Oxford University Press, 1991).

Historical Writings

Readers not already familiar with the names and writings of the main historical authors might begin with an anthology of selections such as Patrick Sherry (ed.), *Philosophers of Religion: A Historical Reader* (London: Geoffrey Chapman, 1987), or John Hick (ed.), *Classical and Contemporary Readings in the Philosophy of Religion*, 2nd edition (Englewood Cliffs, NJ: Prentice-Hall, 1970). Other anthologies gather writings by different authors on the same theme or argument. Two main examples of this approach are John Hick (ed.), *The Existence of God* (New York: Macmillan, 1972) and Alvin Plantinga (ed.), *The Ontological Argument: From St Anselm to Contemporary Philosophers* (London: Macmillan, 1968).

As regards individual works, no one should neglect the writings of Aquinas and Hume referred to in the text. Aquinas's *Summa Theologiae* is published in a sixty volume Latin/English edition (London: Eyre & Spottiswoode, 1963–75). The 'five ways' appear in the *Prima Pars* (Ia, q. 2, a. 2) and are extracted in various places. The best single source for this and other relevant writings is Timothy McDermott (ed.), *Aquinas: Selected Philosophical Writings* (Oxford: Oxford University Press, 1993). A good general introduction to Aquinas is Brian Davies OP, *The Thought of Thomas Aquinas* (Oxford: Clarendon Press, 1993). See also Anthony Kenny, *The Five Ways* (London: Routledge, 1969) which is critical of Aquinas's proofs, and Joseph Owens, *St Thomas Aquinas on the Existence of God: Collected Papers*, (ed. John R. Catan) (Albany: State University of New York Press, 1980) which is supportive of them.

For Hume's pre-Darwinian critique of the teleological ('design') argument see Norman Kemp Smith (ed.), *Dialogues Concerning Natural Religion* (Edinburgh: Nelson, 1947), and for the famous essay 'Of Miracles' see L.A. Selby-Bigge and P.H. Nidditch (eds), *Enquiries Concerning Human Understanding and Concerning the Principles of Morals* (Oxford: Clarendon Press, 1978), *First Enquiry*, section 10. The standard work on Hume's views on religion is J.C.A. Gaskin, *Hume's Philosophy of Religion* (London: Macmillan, 1978).

Additional sources of historical and contemporary material are the following anthologies: Baruch A. Brody (ed.), *Readings in Philosophy of Religion* (Englewood Cliffs, NJ: Prentice-Hall, 1974); Louis P. Pojman (ed.), *Philosophy of Religion: An Anthology* (Belmont, CA: Wadsworth, 1987); and Keith E. Yandell (ed.), *God, Man, and Religion: Readings in the Philosophy of Religion* (New York: McGraw-Hill, 1973). Of these, that edited by Pojman is the most comprehensive and up-to-date.

Presentations of Atheism

Among contemporary philosophers one of the most prominent advocates of atheism is A.G.N. Flew. His clear and vigorous style is well displayed in the following works: *God and Philosophy* (London: Hutchinson, 1976) and *The Presumption of Atheism and other Essays* (New York: Harper & Row, 1976). Two powerful critiques of theism are presented by J.L. Mackie, *The Miracle of Theism* (Oxford: Clarendon Press, 1982) and C.B. Martin, *Religious Belief* (Ithaca, NY: Cornell University Press, 1959). See also Kai Nielsen, *Philosophy and Atheism* (Buffalo: Prometheus Books, 1985) and Michael Martin, *Atheism: A Philosophical Justification* (Philadelphia: Temple University Press, 1990).

Presentations of Theism

Mackie's approach is shaped by his concern to refute the arguments *for* theism advanced by Richard Swinburne in *The Existence of God* (Oxford: Clarendon Press, 1979) (who replies to Mackie in Appendix A of the revised edition, 1990). In a series of works, Swinburne has produced the most thorough and powerful defence of Christian theism since the Middle Ages. Additional to *The Existence of God* the works to date are *The Coherence of Theism* (Oxford: Clarendon Press, 1977, revised edition 1993), *Faith and Reason* (Oxford: Clarendon Press, 1981), *Responsibility and Atonement* (Oxford: Clarendon Press, 1989), *Revelation: From Metaphor to Analogy* (Oxford: Clarendon Press, 1992) and *The Christian God* (Oxford: Clarendon Press, 1994). In general, Swinburne's approach follows 'modern' – Cartesian and post-Cartesian – philosophy rather than the Aristotelian-cum-Thomistic tradition favoured by Haldane.

While the 'moderns' are in the majority among philosophical theists in the analytical world, neo-Aristotelianism is not without representation; see David Braine, *The Reality of Time and the Existence of God* (Oxford: Clarendon Press, 1988), William Charlton, *Philosophy and Christian Belief* (London: Sheed & Ward, 1988) and Barry Miller, *From Existence to God* (London: Routledge, 1992). The distinctive approach of John Leslie in *Value and Existence* (Oxford: Basil Blackwell, 1979) and *Universes* (London: Routledge, 1989) bears some relation to ancient neo-Platonic tradition, as do the arguments advanced by Stephen R.L. Clark in *The Mysteries of Religion* (Oxford: Basil Blackwell, 1986). For a sophisticated presentation of the more traditional style of ontological argument see Alvin Plantinga, *God, Freedom and Evil* (New York: Harper and Row, 1974).

Particular Themes and Issues

The content and coherence of theistic conceptions of God have been the subject of much recent philosophical theology in the analytical tradition. A useful anthology is Thomas V. Morris (ed.), *The Concept of God* (Oxford: Oxford University Press, 1987). Morris discusses these issues on his own account in *Our Idea of God* (Notre Dame: University of Notre Dame Press, 1991). Another sophisticated treatment, defensive of theism, is that presented in Gerard J. Hughes SJ, *The Nature of God* (London: Routledge, 1995). See also Anthony Kenny, *The God of the Philosophers* (Oxford: Clarendon Press, 1979) who reaches a somewhat agnostic conclusion. Kenny is a fine writer, clear and economical, and two other works of his can be recommended, *viz.*, *Reason and Religion: Essays in Philosophical Theology* (Oxford: Blackwell, 1987), and *What is Faith? Essays in the Philosophy of Religion* (Oxford: Oxford University Press, 1992). For recent philosophical thinking about the the nature of Christian theism see the essays in Godfrey Vesey (ed.), *The Philosophy in Christianity* (Cambridge: Cambridge University Press, 1989) and Michael D. Beaty (ed.), *Christian Theism and the Problems of Philosophy* (Notre Dame: University of Notre Dame Press, 1990).

The problem of evil has been widely discussed and there are chapters on it in the various introductions mentioned above. For a collection of important contemporary essays see M.M. and R.M. Adams (eds), *The Problem of Evil* (Oxford: Oxford University Press, 1990). The atheistic potential of the problem is explored in H.J. McCloskey, *God and Evil* (The Hague: Martinus Nijhoff, 1974); while a vigorous defence of traditional Christian theism in the face of evil is presented in P.T. Geach, *Providence and Evil* (Cambridge: Cambridge University Press, 1977).

The 'free will response' to the problem posed by moral evil raises a number of questions about action, freedom and determinism. For an indication of current approaches to these issues see the essays in Gary Watson (ed.), *Free Will* (Oxford: Oxford University Press, 1982). The topic of freedom and determinism is itself the subject of a volume in the 'Great Debates in Philosophy' series, *viz.* Antony Flew and Godfrey Vesey, *Agency and Necessity* (Oxford: Blackwell, 1987). The nature of free action is related to challenges to theism in Alvin Plantinga, *God, Freedom and Evil* (London: Allen and Unwin, 1975) and Robert Young, *Freedom, Responsibility and God* (London: Macmillan, 1975).

The issue of the bearing of contemporary science upon the question of theism has been the subject of a number of studies. See A.R. Peacocke, *Creation and the World of Science* (Oxford: Clarendon Press, 1979) and Peacocke (ed.), *The Sciences and Theology in the Twentieth Century* (London: Oriel Press, 1981); John Leslie (ed.), *Physical Cosmology and Philosophy* (New York: Macmillan, 1989); and John Polkinghorne, *Reason and Reality: The Relationship between Science and Theology* (London: SPCK, 1991). The need or possibility of an explanation of the physical cosmos is the subject of a short article by Derek Parfit entitled 'The Puzzle of Reality: Why Does the Universe Exist?', *Times Literary Supplement*, No. 4657, 3 July 1992.

Not all philosophers take the view of the present authors that theism involves metaphysical theses concerning the nature of reality. Famously, some of those influenced by Wittgenstein seem to regard religion as a social practice that is not in the business of making ontological claims. The best known proponent of something like this view is D.Z. Phillips. He has authored many works including *The Concept of Prayer* (London: Routledge, 1968), *Death and Immortality* (London: Macmillan, 1970) and *Faith after Foundationalism* (London: Routledge, 1988). At first sight a somewhat similar 'fideistic' approach seems to be taken by Fergus Kerr OP, in *Theology After Wittgenstein* (Oxford: Blackwell, 1986) but in fact most of what Kerr writes is compatible with traditional Thomistic theism.

A fideistic approach is sometimes argued for on the basis of religious pluralism. For comparisons between the various world religions see Ninian Smart, *A Dialogue of Religions* (London: SCM Press, 1960) and *The Religious Experience of Mankind*, 2nd edition (New York: Scribners, 1976). One rather striking form of pluralism is that arising from the idea that there might be several divine incarnations, including extra-terrestrial ones. For discussion of this possibility see John Hick, *The Metaphor of God Incarnate* (London: SCM Press, 1993).

The issue of the status of scripture, in particular that of the New Testament, has traditionally been the preserve of biblical scholars but there is growing interest among theistically inclined philosophers in the epistemology and methodology of scriptural study. A general, non-philosophical introduction to the issues is provided by Christopher Tuckett, *Reading the New Testament* (London: SPCK, 1987). On the subject of the reliability of the Gospels see Peter Vardy and Mary Mills, *The Puzzle of the Gospels* (London: Fount, 1995) which is very introductory, and E.P. Sanders, *The Historical Figure of Jesus* (London: Penguin Books, 1995) which is sophisticated but very clear and readable. Philosophers and biblical scholars come together, though not harmoniously, in Eleonore Stump and Thomas P. Flint (eds), *Hermes and Athena: Biblical Exegesis and Philosophical Theology* (Notre Dame: University of Notre Dame Press, 1993).

In their essays and replies the present authors draw upon a range of philosophical claims lying outwith philosophy of religion as such. The main areas within which these lie are metaphysics and philosophy of mind. Smart has set out and defended his general philosophical views in *Our Place in the Universe* (Oxford: Blackwell, 1989) and both he and Haldane are represented by essays advocating physicalist and anti-physicalist positions, respectively, in Richard Warner and Tadeusz Szubka (eds), *The Mind–Body Problem: A Guide to the Current Debate* (Oxford: Blackwell, 1994). Apart from their differences regarding the truth of theism, they are united in holding to some version of metaphysical realism but opposed over the question of philosophical naturalism. For recent essays on these two central issues in contemporary philosophy see J. Haldane and Crispin Wright (eds), *Reality, Representation and Projection* (New York: Oxford, 1993) and Stephen Wagner and Richard Warner (eds), *Naturalism: A Critical Appraisal* (Notre Dame: University of Notre Dame Press, 1993).

Index

abstractionism, 113, 115, 117
action aimed to good, 162
action caused by desire?, 69–70
actions versus movements, 108, 110, 162, 185
afterlife, 52–3, 87–9
agency, 107, 109, 186–7, 201–2
  not explained by cause, 109–12, 123, 161, 162, 185
  requires deliberation, 112
  rational, 112, 156–7, 161–2, 186, 201–2
  time of, 49, 151–2, 200
  writing as instance of, 107–10, 112, 174
agent moved from within, 161, 185–7, 200–2
altruism favoured by evolution, 14, 34–5, 66
analogical predication, 31
angels, 27, 69–71, 76, 88, 210
Anglicanism, 30, 53
Anselm, St, 36, 95
anthropic principle, 16–23, 121–2
  bad arguments for, 18–20
anthropocentrism, 27, 30–1, 50, 73, 170–1, 197, 217
anti-realism, 85–6, 215–16, 218
apostles, 65, 164, 205–8
Aquinas, 31, 39–41, 46–7, 52, 87, 89, 98, 114–15, 131–6,
141–2, 144, 147–8, 163–5, 178–83, 199–200, 203–4, 210
First Way, 115, 133–4, 144, 199
Second Way, 131, 135, 199
Third Way, 39, 131–3, 135, 178, 182, 199
Fifth Way, 98
argument, from contingency, 35–47, 95
  from religious experience, 48–52
  propter quid, 142
  quia, 142–4, 148
  to best explanation, 24, 29, 33, 39, 44, 84, 91, 180
  to design, 21–5, 30, 77, 95–6, 98–9, 120–9, 141, 195, 197
Aristotelianism, 99, 101, 110, 114, 144, 154–5, 179, 184, 186, 201, 218
Aristotle, 47, 95, 142
Armstrong, D., 46, 175–6
'as if' talk, 14, 29–31, 49, 66, 94, 121, 183, 197
atheism a priori, 141, 209
atheism simpler than theism, 56–7, 76–7, 172, 190–2
atheist theologians, 4, 9, 16, 30, 78, 87, 90, 210–11
Augustine, St, 211
Austin, J.L., 70
Austin, M.C., 18

axiarchic principle, 15, 28–35, 47
  existence of, 33, 47
axiarchism, difficulties for, 30–5

Barnes, E.W., 169
Barnes, J., 36, 38
basic entities, 93, 96–7, 100–1, 106,
  108–9, 112, 118, 122–3, 171–2,
  195, 197
Baur, F., 61
beginning of existence, 40, 137–8
behaviour, 112
'behaviour', meaning of term, 110
behaviourism, 93–4
beliefs, and desires, 70, 93, 107–9,
  111–12, 174, 201
  coherence of, 10, 57–63, 77,
  205
beneficial order, 140
Bentham, J., 27
Berkeley, G., 29
big bang theory, 22, 39, 178
Bigelow, J., 46
biology (*see also* sciences other
  than physics), 11, 13–14, 24,
  97–8, 100–1, 105–6, 171, 177,
  183, 197
black holes, 40, 47
Boethius, 47
Bolingbroke, Lord, 8
Bonaventure, St, 136
Boolos, G., 45
Bradley, F.H., 15, 61–2, 64
brain as computer, 44, 69, 173
brainwashing, 52–5
Brandon, S.G.F., 64–5, 205, 208–9
brute fact, 124, 137–40
Burgess, J., 45
Butler, Bishop, 94

Caiaphas, 209
Campbell, C.A., 15
Cantor, G., 72
Carter, B., 18, 20–3, 36, 42, 75, 77,
  181
Catherine of Siena, St, 211

causal realism, 136–7, 181–2, 191,
  217
causal series, intrinsic, 136–7
causation, 19, 95, 150
  backwards, 182
cause and explanation, 140
cause, efficient, 95–6, 110, 112,
  136, 140, 150
  final, 100, 110
  formal, 134
  must be actual, 26, 115, 133–4,
  144–5
  self-explanatory, 116
  varieties of, 95–7, 100, 110, 112,
  123, 139, 172
chance, 14, 20, 74–5, 77, 92,
  105–6, 123–5, 160, 177, 185
change, cause of, 115, 133–4
chaos theory, 172
chaos, why not?, 122–6
Chesterton, G.K., 204
chicken and egg problem, 176–7
Christianity, 3–4, 27, 31, 60, 72,
  75–6, 87, 90, 158–9, 164,
  205–6, 210–11
'Christianity', vagueness of term, 30
Church, authoritative, 89, 164, 204,
  211–12
Churchland, P., 107, 111
Clark, A., 175
Clement of Alexandria, 3
co-extensive concepts, 118–19, 194
Coady, C.A.J., 62
common sense, 7, 39, 84–5, 107,
  119, 191–2, 216
concept-forming ability, 114
concepts and extensions, 118–19,
  148, 191
  and natures, 93, 119, 194, 210–11
  derived from experience, 149, 150
  distinct from sets, 117–18
  not explainable by evolution,
  128–9
  origin of, 113–17, 128–9, 134,
  149, 191, 210
  possession of, 191

conditions of enquiry, 91–2
conditions of possibility, 1–2
conditions, necessary and sufficient, 19, 139
consciousness, 175–6
  a problem for materialism, 175
  in robots, 176
  value of, 29
constants of nature, 16–17, 20, 22, 26, 28, 32, 123, 128
contingent being, 39, 126, 131–3, 135, 137–8, 140, 150, 179–81
Copleston, F., 39, 41
cosmological argument, 24, 38–41, 115–16, 129–40, 178, 180, 199
counterfactuals, 118, 149, 175, 191
'creationist' science, 56, 106
Creed, Apostles', 87

Davidson, D., 194, 200–1
Davies, P., 7, 9, 16, 77
Dawkins, R., 14
deism, 8, 162–3
deliberation, 112–13
Dennett, D., 103–4, 117
Descartes, R., 27, 36
descriptions, theory of, 36–7
design, appearance of, 13, 23–8, 30
designer, need of, 13–14
desire, higher order, 69–70
  strength of, 69–71, 185
'determined' and 'chance' not contradictories, 160–1
determinism, 69–71, 109, 139, 160, 162, 185
  distinct from predictability, 161, 171–2
  incompatible with freedom, 160
Dilthey, W., 193
doctrine, authoritative, 89, 164, 204, 211
doomsday sects, 65
dualism, 109, 175
Dummett, M., 215–16

earth, age of, 10–11
Eckhart, Meister, 147
Einstein, A., 16
electronics, 171
elementary particles, 12
eliminativism, 107–8
emergence, 109, 116, 171, 198–9
empirical and transcendental, 180
eternal being acting on world, 47
eternity and sempiternity, 46–7, 136, 151, 178–81, 200
ethical attitudes, 34
ethical terms, meaning of, 29, 33–4
ethics, non–cognitivism, 34
  objectivism, 32–4
  sociobiological view of, 35
evil, 27, 29, 32–3
  as illusion, 153, 183
  as privation, 154–5, 157–8, 162, 183–4
  as soul-making, 158–9
  not directly created by God, 155, 157
  balance of, 72, 157–8, 184
  God's response to, 158
  implied by good, 71–2, 155
  incompatibility with God, 154
  natural and moral, 66, 68–71, 153, 157, 162, 184–5
  nature of, 152
  no surprise to atheist, 66
  problem of, 66–73, 152–60, 183
'evil' an attributive term, 154–5
evils of non-rational, 159
evolution of eye, 12–13, 177
evolution, Darwinian theory of, 11, 13, 24, 25, 76, 88, 97, 99–102, 105–6, 116, 119–20, 129, 169–70, 176–7, 183, 195, 198
  opportunistic, 24, 75, 177
evolutionary theory, what it can't explain, 119
existence as perfection, 37–8
  as predicate, 36–8
  of numbers, 46, 178
  of propositions, 47

of universals, 47
tenseless, 37
'experience', meaning of, 48, 51
explaining away, 49–50, 56–60,
    62–5, 68, 84, 208–9
explanation, 2, 19, 182, 186
  as redescription, 112
  not causal, 39, 186, 200–2
  complete, 12
  need for, 1
  qualities of good one, 20
  regressive, 3, 25, 36, 103, 115–17,
    120–1, 123, 198
  simplicity in, 29
  ultimate, 2–3
  varieties of, 39, 95–7, 112, 123
extraterrestrial intelligence,
    probability of, 7, 73–6
extraterrestrials, 16–17, 27, 74,
    120–1

faith, 55–6, 89–90, 92, 202–4, 212
Fall, the, 68
family resemblance concepts, 8, 30
Farrell, B., 175
Feinberg, G., 12
Festinger, L., 65
fiction, 44–5
fictionalism in mathematics, 44–5
fideism, *see* voluntarism
Field, H., 44–5
Findlay, J.N., 77
fine structure constant, 17
fine tuning, 13, 16–18, 20–3, 26,
    28, 30, 33, 77, 95, 98, 121,
    123–9
firing squad analogy, 21–2, 75
first cause, 87, 92, 95–6, 115–16,
    124, 131, 133, 135–6, 140,
    143–7, 200
  not temporal, 40, 46–7, 132, 136,
    178, 200
first moment, 39–40, 46–7
First Reviewer analogy, 129–31,
    135–6
Flew, A., 24, 53, 58

'folk psychology', 107, 111
form and matter, 97, 99–101,
    146–7, 191, 194, 197, 210
forms of life, 114
Forrest, P., 46
free agency, 157–8, 160–3, 200
  implies possible moral evil, 162
free will, 139, 200
  and compatibilism, 69–71, 160,
    185
  as doing what we want, 69–71,
    185
  defence, 68–71, 185
  not indeterminacy, 69
  common sense idea of, 70–1
  libertarian, 68–70, 109, 160, 185,
    200
Frege, G., 43, 148

Galilei, G., 73
Geach, P., 113
Genesis, book of, 116
genetics, 12–13, 24
geology, 10–11
goal-seeking robots, 173–4, 186
God, as creator, 48, 69–72, 95, 120,
    123, 150, 157–8, 160, 162–3,
    178–9, 184–5, 203, 205, 210–11
  as designer, 24, 48
  as ethical principle, *see*
    axiarchism,
  as finite 'big brother', 48, 67
  as 'God of gaps', 11, 119–20, 169
  as necessary being, 36–8
  as sustaining, 155, 162–3, 211–12
  existence of identical with
    essence, 147–8
  existence of knowable by reason,
    4–5, 52, 87, 89, 141–2, 148,
    164
  existence of not logically
    necessary, 38
  impassibility of, 144–5
  nature of not knowable by reason,
    141–4, 164, 180, 203, 205
  omnipotence of, 67, 69, 71–3

perfection of, 145
simplicity of, 24–6, 32, 144–5,
    148, 151, 179, 182
agency of, 47, 49, 57, 150–2, 163,
    180, 200, 211
mysterious ways of, 72
needs designer?, 25
preconceived idea of, 141–2
presence of sensed, 49, 51
properties of, 3, 36, 53, 66–8, 88,
    135, 140, 143–5, 147–8, 151–2,
    154, 157, 178–83, 190, 203
properties of, identical, 148,
    182–3
'God' as a name, 36–8
Gospels, history of, 63, 205–9
    John, 116, 165, 203–4, 206
    Luke, 63–4, 206, 208, 212
    Mark, 61, 63–4, 206, 208
    Matthew, 63, 158
grace, 47, 159, 211–12
'Graphico', imaginary artist, 86
Gribbin, J., 9
Guth, A.H., 22

Haldane, J.B.S., 18
Hartle, J., 40
Hawking, S., 16, 25, 40, 178
Haydn, J., 9
Hazen, A., 45
headless woman illusion, 176
heaven, 52–3
Heidegger, M., 35
hell, 27, 52–3
Heraclitus, 3
Herodotus, 61
Hick, J., 76
Hindu philosophy, 15, 73
historical methods, 60–5, 205–9
Hobart, R.E., 69, 185
Holsten, C., 61
homuncular regress, 103–4, 117,
    173
Hopkins, G.M., 203
Hoyle, F., 17, 25
Hubble, E., 73

Hughes, G.E., 77
human agency, 157
human life, goal of, 156, 210–12
humanity, mechanist view of, 12
humanity, nature of, 106, 120,
    156–7, 161–2
Hume, David, 24–5, 51, 55, 58–9,
    61–2, 85, 136–8, 140, 163, 182

identity, 107–8, 146–7
identity theory of mind, 107–8
identity versus composition, 97, 197
illusion, 15
image of God, 116, 128–9, 212
in act/in potency, 144–5
Incarnation, 75–6, 159–60, 164–5,
    207, 209
    elsewhere, 27–8, 75–6
indeterminacy, 40, 70, 127, 138–40,
    161
    of translation, 188
infinities, 72, 126, 136
innatism, 113–15, 117
intellect, passive and active, 114,
    210–11
intelligible, making, 134
intensionality, 38, 174–5, 191, 194
    as attitudes to sentences, 38, 174,
    191
intentionality, 103–4, 107–8, 110,
    112, 134, 173–5, 191, 199, 217
Israeli, Isaac, 210–11

James, W., 48, 52–6
Jerusalem, destruction of, 64, 208–9
Jesus, life of, 63–5, 73, 88,
    205–9
    nature of, 61–2, 87, 95, 159, 165,
    203–4, 206–8
    resurrection of, 62–3, 65, 88–9,
    207
Joan of Arc, 50
Josephus, 205, 214

Kant, I., 1–3, 70–1, 88, 149
Kelvin, Lord, 9–11

Kirk, R., 175
Kneale, W. and M., 47
knowledge *a priori*, 118
knowledge of world, 91
knowledge, non-scientific, 7
Kuhn, T., 6, 12

La Place, P., 74, 169
laws of nature, 13, 22–3, 40–1,
    55–60, 67, 77, 91, 101, 122–3,
    125, 150, 161, 179, 182, 184
Leibniz, G., 184
Leslie, J., 8, 15, 21, 25, 28–35, 47,
    75
Lewis, C.S., 76
Lewis, D., 42, 45, 175
liberty of indifference, 160
life, emergence of, 99–101, 106, 128
  nature of, 100
  origin of, 11, 13, 17–19, 26,
    74–5, 100, 117, 169–70, 190,
    197–8
Linde, A., 22–3
logic, higher order, 81
logos, 203–4
Löwenheim–Skolem theorem, 42

Mackie, J., 7
maladaptation, 12, 14, 66, 76, 101,
    185
many universes hypothesis, 18,
    20–3, 28, 36, 42, 75, 77, 124–8,
    181, 184
  merely *ad hoc*, 127–8
Mascall, E.L., 76
materialism, 9–10, 90–1, 100–1,
    106–9, 113, 117–20, 129, 172,
    174–5, 192
  possible flaws in, 91, 113
mathematical necessity, 45
mathematical propositions empty,
    42–3
matter (*see also* form), 9–10, 12, 96,
    146
Maxwell, J. Clark, 9
meaning as interpretation, 194–5

meaning, analogical, 204
  causal theories of, 193–4
mechanism, 13–14, 97–101, 105–7,
    120–1, 173, 186, 197
mental states identified by
    sentences, 174
mental terms, 94
metaphysical realism, 4–6, 85–7,
    90–1, 124, 138, 140, 168,
    215–18
methodology, 4, 6–7, 12, 76, 88–90,
    104, 106, 140, 168–73, 190–5,
    215
mind, and matter, 106–12
  distinct category, 109
  disembodied, 29, 31, 69, 210
  identical with brain states, 29,
    107–9, 174–6, 185–6, 201
  origin of, 106, 113, 116–17,
    119–21, 128–9, 134, 197, 199
  powers of, 114–16, 161–2
  value of, 27, 29–31
mind-dependent classification, 86
miracles, 50–1, 56–60, 162–4, 209,
    211
  as contradictions, 57, 163
  as significant, 57, 59
  not intervention, 163
  evidence for, 57–60
  explaining away, 58
  purpose of, 57
modality, 41–2
Moore, G.E., 32
moral improvement, 48
moral perfection cannot be
    guaranteed, 157, 200
mutations, 101

Napoleon, 62
natural selection, 11–14, 24–5, 66,
    68, 92, 94, 99, 101–2, 173, 177,
    183, 190, 198
naturalism as preconception, 12,
    49–51, 56, 58, 60, 63–4, 91,
    93–4, 104, 119, 168–70, 172,
    185–7, 190, 192, 197

natures of things, 85–6, 91–4, 97, 100, 117, 119, 128, 147, 194–5, 203, 210
necessary being, 36, 38–9, 41–7, 77, 131–3, 135, 147–8, 150, 178–82
necessary conditions of existence, 121–2
necessary truth, 33
necessity, 77, 180–1, 191
  and possibility, 150
  understood as contextual, 41–2
  logical, 38, 41, 67, 181
neurons, operation of, 10, 44, 48–50, 65, 69, 173, 176, 185–6, 202
Newman, Cardinal, 211–12
Newton, I., 169
Nineham, D., 61
non-Christian theism/religions, 50, 52, 60, 73, 141, 204
non-human animals, 27
non-natural properties, 32
non-physical perception, 32–3, 44, 46, 48–9, 56, 204
non-scientific knowing, 84, 195
normality, assumptions of, 58–9, 62, 105, 162
numbers, existence of, 10, 41–6, 192
  relations between, 28
numinous, evolutionary explanation of, 49–50

occasionalism, 163
Ockham's razor, 20, 26, 172, 179, 181–2, 186, 191
ontological argument, 24, 36–8, 95–6
open texture, 59
order, beneficial, 98, 101
organisms not designed, 24–5
organisms, functions of and in, 14, 94, 97–9, 101, 105, 120, 171, 173, 183–4, 186, 195, 197, 201
  Aristotelian hierarchy of, 155–6

pain, 27, 184
Paley, W., 13–14, 28, 61
pantheism, 15–16
Parmenides, 47
Pascal, B., 51, 53, 55
Pascal's Wager, 48, 51–6, 72
Paul, St, 50, 56, 65–6, 89, 141–2, 159, 206
  conversion of, 50, 56
Peano's axioms, 42
Penrose, R., 44
perception, causal theory of, 119
phenomenalism, 29, 84–5
Philo of Alexandria, 209
philosophical questions, 1–3, 6
philosophy, purpose of, 1–2, 50, 204–5
  style of, 85, 190–1
physicalism, 10, 97, 109, 170, 175, 192, 197
  ideological, 92–4, 109, 136, 172, 197
physics, the only guide to reality, 46, 90, 92, 94, 97, 100, 108–9, 171, 192, 197
  new, 9–11, 13
Planck's constant, 40
planet formation, 73–5
Plato, 29–31, 47
Platonism, 43–6, 63, 179, 182
plausibility, 7, 12, 31, 49–50, 60, 64–5, 77, 84, 106, 172, 192, 195, 202
polytheism, 3, 8, 46
Pontius Pilate, 64, 207–9
possibility, actualized, 114, 126, 144
  as conceivability, 137–8, 140
  as contextual, 59
possible worlds, 42, 175
potentiality and actuality, 114–16, 133–4, 144–5, 147
powers, 155–6, 161, 163, 201–2
pragmatism, 54–5, 215
  confused, 48
prayer, 9, 30, 47, 88–9, 162, 211
Pre-Socratics, 2–3, 5

Price, H., 182
Prime Sayer, 116
Prime Thinker argument, 114–15,
    116, 119, 134, 151
Principle of Sufficient Reason, 135,
    137–40
Prior, A.N., 54
probabilistic inference, 7
probability of beliefs, 48
proof *de re* and *de dicto*, 143
propensity, 140, 161–2, 186, 201–2
properties and sets, 45–6
proposition, necessary existence of,
    33
  necessary truth, 33
proprioception, 176
providence, 71, 158, 163
psychocentrism, 27
psychological laws, 111
punishment as deterrence, 69–70
purpose, 77, 94, 98–9, 101,
    120–1, 123–4, 134, 151, 161–2,
    186
Putnam, H., 215–18

Quakers, 30
qualitative/quantitative shift, 102–4,
    117, 169, 173, 177, 199
quantification, 37–8
  plural, 45
quantifier shift, 132–3
quantum mechanics, 9–10, 12–13,
    40, 44–5, 60, 69–70, 138–40,
    161, 171–2, 179, 182
  many worlds interpretation,
    127–8, 138
questions, unanswerable, 35–6
Quine, W.V., 10, 21, 41, 43–6, 61,
    174–5, 181, 191–2, 194, 217

randomness, 21–3, 25–6
rational inclinations, 161
raw feels, 175–6
real existence of objects (*see also*
    basic entities), 84–6, 91–2, 94
real things intelligible, 92

reality, 148
  independent of mind, 5, 85, 195,
    215–18
reason-explanations not causal,
    110–12, 161
reasons, as justification, 70–1, 186,
    201
  and causes, 70, 109, 123, 161,
    186, 200–2
  for acting, 107
  not antecedent events, 112
  relations between, 111
receptivity and activity, 114
reductionism, 13, 90, 95, 97,
    99–101, 103, 106, 108–9, 112,
    121, 170, 195, 197
  explanatory, 92–4, 171
  ontological, 92–4, 97–8, 170–2,
    216, 218
  translatory, 170, 172
regularity, explanation of, 122–8,
    140
Reid, T., 85
relativism, 6–7, 12, 85–6
  conceptual, 216–18
relativity, theory of, 13, 46–7, 59,
    62
religion, and philosophy, 87–8, 164,
    168, 204, 211–12
  as dispensable, 55
  as morally improving, 51
  as useful, 48, 50–4
  as way of life, 48, 87–9, 202,
    210–12
  absence of as useful, 54
  personal, 87, 89, 204
religions without God, 30
religious anti-realism, 90
  community, 89, 164
  experience, 7, 48–52, 56, 164
  experience as evidence, 48–9, 51
  experience dependent on culture,
    50
  life as evidence, 51
replication, 14, 99–100, 119–21,
    169–70, 176–7, 197–9

origin of, 102–3, 105, 169–70, 198
power of, 102–3, 105–6
representation, 103–4, 107, 173–5, 199, 217
  as information, 173
  origin of, 103–4
revelation, 63, 154, 164, 187, 202–3, 211–12
Riecken, H., 65
Roman Catholicism, 4–5, 52–3, 87, 164, 203
Ross, W.D., 32
Russell, B., 27, 36–7, 39, 43, 52, 187
Ryle, G., 175

scepticism impractical, 55–6
Schachter, S., 65
science, and religion in conflict, 7, 9–15, 55–6, 90–4, 168
  independent of man, 16
  not parochial, 21
  versus understanding, 192–5, 202
  assumptions of, 1, 91–2, 94, 109, 122, 195
  justifying, 55–6, 106
  limitations of, 101, 119–20, 123–4, 128–9, 168–9, 198
  motive for, 92
  purpose of, 50
  subjects of, 96–7
sciences other than physics, 2, 12, 34–5, 96–8, 100–1, 106, 119, 121, 128, 169, 171, 192, 195, 197, 218
  dispensable, 171
scientific knowledge, 6–7, 149
scientific realism, 12, 84, 128
scientism, 7, 192
scripture, 4, 73, 88–9, 141, 160, 164, 187, 203–4, 211–12
  canon of, 204–8
  criticism of, 60–6, 207–9
self-realization and loss, 156, 184
self-realization, moral, 158–9

semantics, 193–5
sense and reference, 148, 182
series, without beginning, 178
  cause of, 39, 131, 133–7, 139, 200
  intrinsic causal, 136–7
set theory, 10, 43, 45
  mysterious, 45
  significant ordering, 124–5
simplicity, 20, 28, 30–1, 35, 44–5, 49, 145, 172, 180, 182–3, 192
  opposed to composite, 145–8, 151
sin, 68, 76
Singer, P., 35
Smith, N. Kemp, 23
sociobiology, 34, 36
Socrates, 62
solar system, 74–5
something rather than nothing, why?, 35, 40, 133, 181–2, 211
Sorites paradox, 176
soul, Aristotelian kinds of, 99–100, 156
  Cartesian, 9, 31
space, dimensions of, 18–20, 191
space–time, 10, 40–1, 44, 46–7, 91, 108, 118, 178–9, 181, 191–2
  as a whole, no change in, 178, 181
  no absolute axes, 46–7
species, origin of, 102, 105–6, 128, 177, 190
Spinoza, 15, 21
spiritual challenge, 159
spiritualism, 120
spirituality, 8–9
  consistent with metaphysics, 88–9
Strauss, D., 61
structuralism, 45
substances and attributes, 145–7, 179, 201
Swinburne, R., 106
symmetry, 20–2, 31–2

Taylor, S.R., 74–5
Teichmann, R., 176–7

teleological argument, 13
  new, 23, 28, 77
teleology, not needed by science, 94
  new, 13–14, 121–9
  old, 98–121
Teresa of Avila, St, 211
testimony, 56, 58–60, 62, 89, 203–5
Thales of Miletus, 3, 12
thatness and whatness, 95, 141–5,
  147–8, 180
theism, and mathematics, 41–6
  as scientific theory, 67
  emotionally attractive, 77–8
  agnostic, 164
  definition of, 3–5, 8
  historical forms of, 72–5
  metaphysical, 76–7
theodicy, 67, 154, 157–8, 160, 183
theory change, 6, 8, 59, 62
thinking, implies concepts, 112–13,
  119
  learnt in saying, 114, 116–17
  not identical with its
    embodiment, 152, 217
Thomism, 89–90, 110, 114–15, 142,
  144, 146, 154, 179, 218
topic-neutrality, 175–6
transcendent reality, 4
transcendent, no argument to,
  148–52
transcendentals, 148
Trinity, 75–6, 87–8, 164, 209
truth as confirmation, 86
Tryon, E.P., 40
Tunguska incident, 59

uncertainty principle, 40
understanding, 210–12

universals, realism about, 46
universe, as necessary being, 181–2
  awe at, 11, 14–16, 23, 28, 35–6,
    49–50, 77, 180, 211
  best possible, 33–4, 69, 71–2, 184
  complexity of, 15, 25–6, 29, 35,
    182
  expansion of, 22, 47
  external cause of, 24, 39–40
  purpose of, 77
  remarkably large, 27, 72–5
  self-understanding, 128, 210
  unnecessarily complicated?, 27,
    30, 184, 210
  existence of as a whole, 39–41,
    46–7

vague terms, 177
vanity as motive for religion, 27
Vatican Council, First, 52
Vianney, St J., 211
virtue and vice, 157
vitalism, 99–101
voluntarism, 87–9
voluntary action, 161

Waissmann, F., 59
Weinberg, S., 171–2
Whateley, Archbishop, 62
Whitehead, A., 43
Whitrow, J.G., 18–19
Wiggins, D., 34
Wilkes, K., 104, 173
Wittgenstein, 8, 30, 35, 42, 77,
  114–17, 147, 168, 175
Wright, C.J.G., 215–16

Zealots, 64–5, 88, 205, 208